HYMNBOOK FOR
Christian Worship

HYMNBOOK FOR
Christian Worship

THE BETHANY PRESS · ST. LOUIS
THE JUDSON PRESS · VALLEY FORGE

Library of Congress Catalog Card Number 69-14339

MANUFACTURED IN THE UNITED STATES OF AMERICA

Preface

CHRISTIANITY has been a singing religion since the day the Apostle Paul admonished the churches to praise God with psalms, hymns, and spiritual songs. Indeed, Christianity has its roots in a singing tradition. In the Psalms we read, "O sing to the Lord a new song," and through the ages men have done so.

Recently science and technology have ushered in a new age with new problems and challenges to the human spirit. To meet the spiritual needs of modern man, the church has moved toward a deeper theological understanding of the biblical faith and its implications for ecumenicity, education, and social involvement of the Christian community. These far-reaching developments have had important effects upon worship and hymnody.

During the eight years of preparation the Hymnbook Committee has endeavored to produce a hymnal which will retain a great body of Christendom's loftiest hymns, while introducing new texts or adjusting old ones in a manner consistent and helpful to contemporary man. The work of the Committee was facilitated by the appearance of several new and excellent hymnals in the Protestant tradition. All major hymnals, new and old, were examined for materials, as were sources for hymns not yet appearing in any hymnal. The most notable of such sources is the Hymn Society of America, whose material was generously made available to the Committee.

Particular attention was directed toward including a number of hymns which are generally common to all, a "classic" hymnody without which no hymnal can be reckoned complete. Increasing concern was given, among other categories, to securing worthy hymns for the city church, the marriage service, and the Lord's Supper.

The selection of tunes for the *Hymnbook* followed the same general procedure. Although some tunes and texts are wedded by common use, the Committee was mindful that a weak tune can emasculate a strong text, and the possibility of including superior tunes was continually kept in mind. Sources of tunes run the gamut. Included are plainsong melodies, chorales, contemporary and early American tunes, tunes from the Genevan Psalter, and from many nationalities. Every effort has been made to insure ease of congregational singing, including lowering many keys and rendering the makeup of the book as readable as possible.

The presence of several church musicians on the Committee encouraged careful attention to the section devoted to service music. Many choir directors select the bulk of choral responses, and material other than anthems, from the hymnal itself; hence, a large amount was included. No experienced musician would need an admonition, however, to search through the body of hymns as well for choral introits or prayer responses, as much suitable material is contained therein.

It is believed that the proportionately large selection of worship materials will commend itself to pastors and laymen alike. Although the emphasis naturally is on biblical selections, both historic and contemporary material is included. Passages which lend themselves have been arranged for responsive readings, but they may be read in unison.

Extensive effort was made to enter each acknowledgment accurately. Inadvertent omissions will be corrected in subsequent editions.

Members of the Hymnbook Committee were Merrill L. Cadwell, Lloyd V. Channels, John T. Clough, Kenneth L. Cober, Wilbur H. Cramblet, Karl Croel, David M. Evans, Martha Faw, Mary Beth Fulton, Eugene P. Hazlewood, C. Adrian Heaton, Richard Hoiland, Christine Kallstrom, David M. Kellermeyer, Robert E. Keighton, Thomas B. McDormand, Margaret Crain McNeil, W. John Minter, Harold W. Richardson, Victor F. Scalise, Lawrence P. Schreiber, Gentry A. Shelton, John E. Skoglund, Marvin E. Smith, Dorothy Sellers Smotherman, George Oliver Taylor, Edward L. Thompson, Dorothy S. Tolley, Jet E. Turner, Arthur N. Wake, Orville W. Wake, Keith Watkins, David V. Williams, Ellwood S. Wolf, Darrell K. Wolfe, and Robert Young.

This *Hymnbook* is offered to the churches in the name of the Father, the Son, and the Holy Spirit, in the hope that its use will lead congregations into closer communion with God, and into a more vital Christian fellowship one with another.

Charles Huddleston Heaton
Editor

John Paul Pack
Chairman, Christian Church
(Disciples of Christ)

Edward Hughes Pruden
Chairman, American Baptist Convention

Contents

Hymns

Indexes

Hymns

Joyful, Joyful, We Adore Thee

Henry van Dyke, 1852-1933

HYMN TO JOY 8.7.8.7.D.
Arr. from Ludwig van Beethoven, 1770-1827

Words reprinted with the permission of Charles Scribner's Sons from *The Poems of Henry van Dyke* (Charles Scribner's Sons).

All Things Bright and Beautiful

Cecil F. Alexander, 1818-1895

ROYAL OAK 7.6.7.6. with Refrain
Traditional English Melody
Adapt. Martin Shaw, 1875-1958

All things bright and beau-ti - ful, All crea-tures great and small,

All things wise and won - der - ful, The Lord God made them all. *Fine*

1 Each lit - tle flower that o - pens, Each lit - tle bird that sings,
2 The pur - ple - head - ed moun - tain, The riv - er run - ning by,
3 The cold wind in the win - ter, The pleas-ant sum-mer sun,

D.C.
He made their glow-ing col - ors, He made their tin - y wings.
The sun - set, and the morn - ing That bright-ens up the sky.
The ripe fruits in the gar - den, He made them ev - ery one.
D.C.
Music used by permission of J. Curwen & Sons Ltd.
Let Us with a Gladsome Mind
3
Based on Psalm 136
John Milton, 1608-1674, alt.
INNOCENTS 7.7.7.7.
The Parish Choir, 1850
1 Let us with a glad - some mind Praise the Lord, for he is kind;
2 He, with all com - mand - ing might, Filled the new - made world with light;
3 All things liv - ing he doth feed; His full hand sup - plies their need;
4 Let us with a glad - some mind Praise the Lord, for he is kind;
For his mer - cies aye en - dure, Ev - er faith - ful, ev - er sure. A - men.

4 We Sing the Mighty Power of God

Isaac Watts, 1674-1748, alt.

ELLACOMBE C.M.D.
Gesangbuch, Wirtemberg, 1784

This Is My Father's World 5

Maltbie D. Babcock, 1858-1901, alt.

TERRA BEATA S.M.D.
Traditional English Melody
Adapt. Franklin L. Sheppard, 1852-1930

1 This is my Fa-ther's world; And to my lis-tening ears, All
2 This is my Fa-ther's world; The birds their car - ols raise, The
3 This is my Fa-ther's world; Oh, let me ne'er for - get That

na - ture sings, and round me rings The mu - sic of the spheres.
morn - ing light, the lil - y white, De - clare their Mak - er's praise.
though the wrong seems oft so strong, God is the rul - er yet.

This is my Fa-ther's world; I rest me in the thought Of
This is my Fa-ther's world; He shines in all that's fair; In the
This is my Fa-ther's world; Why should my heart be sad? The

rocks and trees, of skies and seas, His hand the won - ders wrought.
rus - tling grass I hear him pass; He speaks to me ev-ery-where.
Lord is King; let the heav-ens ring. God reigns; let earth be glad.

6 The Spacious Firmament on High

Joseph Addison, 1672-1719

CREATION L.M.D.
Franz Joseph Haydn, 1732-1809

HIS WORKS IN CREATION

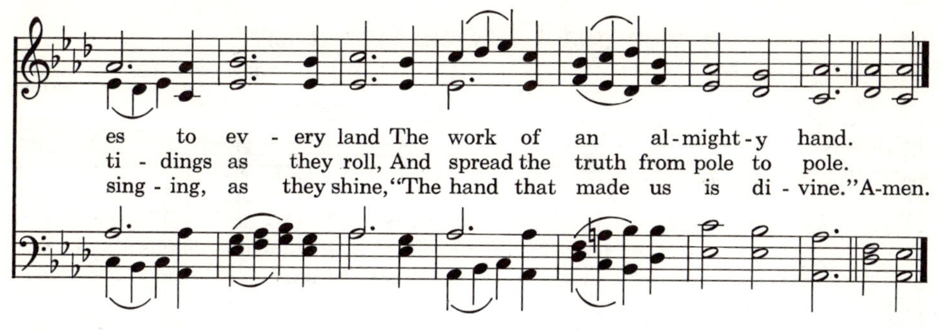

For the Beauty of the Earth

7

Folliott S. Pierpoint, 1835-1917, alt.

DIX 7.7.7.7.7.7.
Abridged from a chorale by
Conrad Kocher, 1786-1872

1 For the beau - ty of the earth, For the glo - ry of the skies,
2 For the beau - ty of each hour Of the day and of the night,
3 For the joy of ear and eye, For the heart and mind's de - light,
4 For the joy of hu - man love, Broth - er, sis - ter, par - ent, child,
5 For thy Church that ev - er - more Lift - eth ho - ly hands a - bove,

For the love which from our birth O - ver and a - round us lies,
Hill and vale, and tree and flower, Sun and moon, and stars of light,
For the mys - tic har - mo - ny Link - ing sense to sound and sight,
Friends on earth, and friends a - bove, For all gen - tle thoughts and mild,
Of - fering up on ev - ery shore Her pure sa - cri - fice of love,

Lord of all, to thee we raise This our hymn of grate - ful praise. A-men.

Words by permission of the Estate of the late F. S. Pierpoint and Oxford University Press.

8 Men and Children Everywhere

John J. Moment, 1875-1959

ROCK OF AGES 7.7.7.7.5.7.4.7.
Ancient Hebrew Melody

1 Men and chil-dren ev-ery-where, With sweet mu-sic fill the air!
2 Morn-ing, eve-ning, bless his name, Skies with crim-son clouds a-flame,
3 Storm and flood and o-cean's roar, Break-ers crash-ing on the shore,

Na-tions, come, your voic-es raise To the Lord in hymns of praise!
Rain-bow arch, his cove-nant sign, Count-less stars by night that shine!
Wa-ter-falls that nev-er sleep, Tower-ing moun-tain, can-yon deep,

Join the an-gel song, All the worlds to him be-long!
Through his far do-main, Love is King where he doth reign!
Tell ye forth his might, Lord of life and truth and right!

HIS WORKS IN CREATION

O God, Thy Great Creation

9

Edward E. Chipman, 1901-

MUNICH 7.6.7.6.D.
Adapt. from *Gesangbuch,* Meiningen, 1693
Harm. adapt. from Felix Mendelssohn, 1809-1847

My Shepherd Will Supply My Need

Psalm 23
Para. Isaac Watts, 1674-1748

RESIGNATION C.M.D.
Southern Harmony, 1855

I Sought the Lord, and Afterward I Knew 11

Unknown
The Pilgrim Hymnal, 1904

PEACE 10.10.10.6.
The Revivalist, 1869
Adapt. George Brandon, 1924-

In unison

1 I sought the Lord, and af - ter - ward I knew He moved my
2 Thou didst reach forth thy hand and mine en - fold; I walked and
3 I find, I walk, I love, but O the whole Of love is

soul to seek him, seek - ing me; It was not I that
sank not on the storm-vexed sea; 'Twas not so much that
but my an - swer, Lord, to thee! For thou wert long be -

found, O Sav - ior true; No, I was found of thee.
I on thee took hold As thou, dear Lord, on me.
fore - hand with my soul; Al - ways thou lov - edst me. A-men.

12 Immortal Love, Forever Full

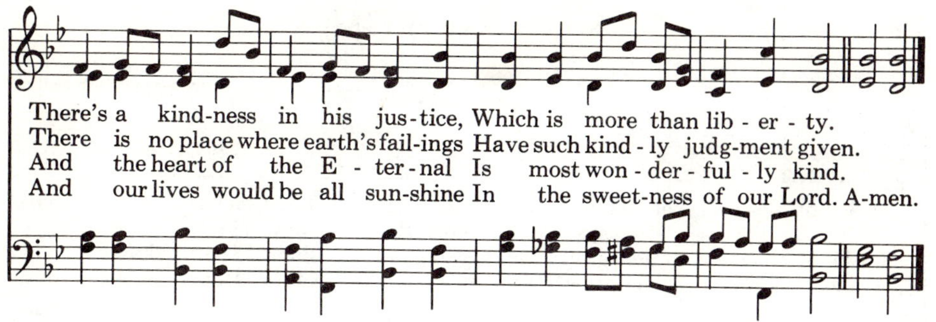

Great Is Thy Faithfulness 14

Thomas O. Chisholm, 1866-1960

FAITHFULNESS 11.10.11.10.
William M. Runyan, 1870-1957

1 Great is thy faith - ful-ness, O God my Fa - ther, There is no
2 Sum - mer and win - ter, and spring-time and har - vest, Sun, moon and
3 Par - don for sin and a peace that en - dur - eth, Thy own dear
4 Great is thy faith - ful-ness, O God my Fa - ther, Morn - ing by

shad - ow of turn-ing with thee; Thou chang-est not, thy com - pas-sions, they
stars in their cours-es a - bove, Join with all na - ture in man - i - fold
pres - ence to cheer and to guide; Strength for to - day and bright hope for to -
morn - ing new mer - cies I see. All I have need - ed thy hand hath pro -

fail not; As thou hast been thou for - ev - er wilt be.
wit - ness To thy great faith - ful-ness, mer - cy and love.
mor - row, Bless - ings all mine, with ten thou-sand be - side!
vid - ed; Great is thy faith - ful - ness, Lord, un - to me! A-men.

15 *Strong Son of God*

Alfred Tennyson, 1809-1892

DEO GRACIAS L.M.
The Agincourt Song, 15th century
Arr. for *The Hymnal,* 1933

O Love of God, How Strong and True

HIS LOVE

17 O Love That Wilt Not Let Me Go

O God Whose Love Compels Us

Daniel B. Merrick, Jr., 1926-

ROCKPORT 7.6.7.6.D.
T. Tertius Noble, 1867-1953

19 O Father Above Us

Percy Dearmer, 1867-1936

MADDERMARKET 11.11.11.9.
Martin Shaw, 1875-1958

1 O Fa - ther a - bove us, our fa - ther in might, All live by thy love, as the flowers in the light; Our fa - ther and moth-er and mak - er art thou. For - ward! For-ward ev - er, for - ward now!

2 In thee move the in - fi - nite stars on their rounds, The plan - ets, the sun, and the moon in their bounds, As they kin - dle and glit - ter and spar - kle and glow: On - ward! On-ward ev - er, on - ward go!

3 O Fa - ther in heav - en, our fa - ther on earth, Thou mak - est new life in each seed and each birth; The in - ven - tor, de - sign - er and ar - tist art thou. For - ward! For-ward ev - er, for - ward now!

4 We praise thee, O Fa - ther of in - fi - nite might, We thank thee for life and for love and for light, We pray thee thy treas-ure on all to be - stow: On - ward! On-ward ev - er, on - ward go!

All My Hope on God Is Founded

Joachim Neander, 1650-1680
Paraphrase by Robert Bridges, 1844-1930

NEANDER 8.7.8.7.6.7.
From Chorale *Unser Herrscher*,
by Joachim Neander, 1650-1680

21 Unto the Hills Around Do I Lift Up

God of Our Fathers, Whose Almighty Hand

23

Based on Psalm 90
Isaac Watts, 1674-1748

ST. ANNE C.M.
William Croft, 1678-1727

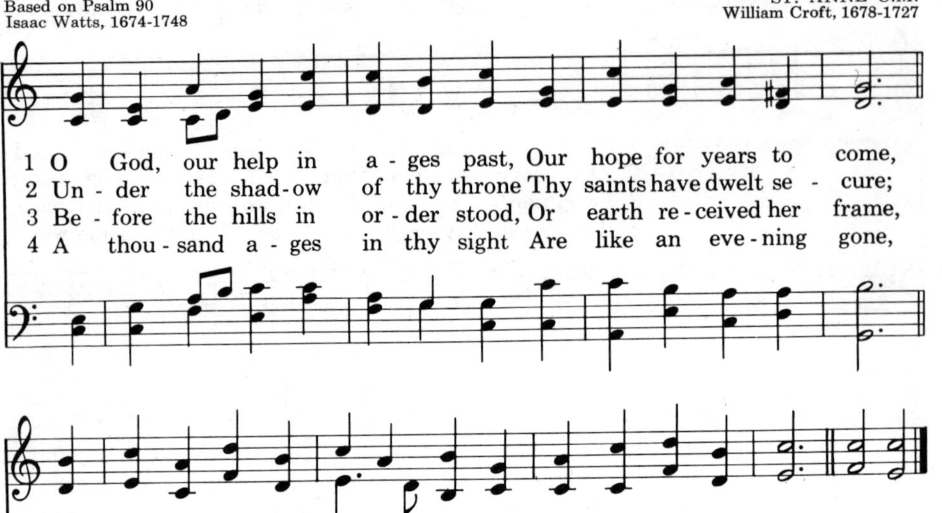

5 Time, like an ever-rolling stream,
Bears all its sons away;
They fly, forgotten, as a dream
Dies at the opening day.

6 O God, our help in ages past,
Our hope for years to come,
Be thou our guard while troubles last,
And our eternal home.

24

Latin: *Matutinus altiora*
Tr. O. B. C. alt.

INNOCENTS 7.7.7.7.
The Parish Choir, 1850

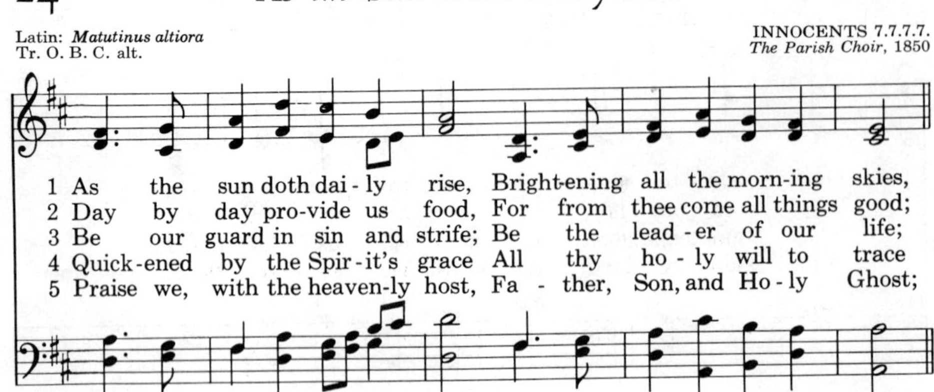

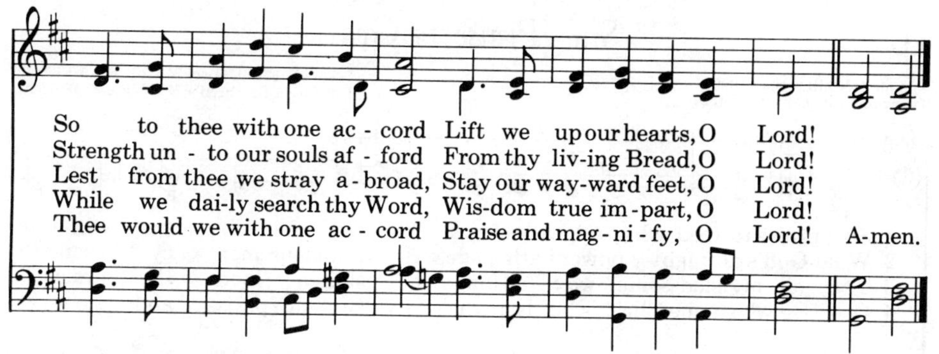

Through All the Changing Scenes 25

Based on Psalm 34
New Version, 1696

CONSOLATION C.M.
John Wyeth's *Repository of Sacred Music, Part Second*, 1813

1 Through all the chang-ing scenes of life, In trou-ble and in joy,
2 Oh mag - ni - fy the Lord with me, With me ex - alt his name;
3 Oh make but tri - al of his love; Ex - per - ience will de - cide,
4 Fear him, ye saints, and you will then Have noth-ing else to fear;

The prais - es of my God shall still My heart and tongue em - ploy.
When in dis-tress to him I called, He to my res - cue came.
How blest are they, and on - ly they, Who in his truth con - fide.
Make you his ser - vice your de-light, He'll make your wants his care. A-men.

26 Sing Praise to God

Johann J. Schütz, 1640-1690
Tr. Frances E. Cox, 1812-1897

MIT FREUDEN ZART 8.7.8.7.8.8.7.
Bohemian Brethren's *Kirchengesänge*, 1566

Golden Breaks the Dawn

T. C. Chao, 1888-
Tr. Frank W. Price, 1895-

LE P'ING 5.5.5.5.D.
Chinese Folk Melody
Adapt. Hu Te-ngai c. 1900
Arr. Paul E. Koch, 1929-

HIS PROVIDENCE

28 God of Our Life, Through All the Circling Years

Hugh T. Kerr, 1872-1950, alt.

SANDON 10.4.10.4.10.10.
Charles H. Purday, 1799-1885

1 God of our life, through all the cir - cling years, We trust in thee;
2 God of the past, our times are in thy hand; With us a - bide.
3 God of the com - ing years, through paths un-known We fol - low thee;

In all the past, through all our hopes and fears, Thy hand we see.
Lead us by faith to hope's true prom-ised land; Be thou our guide.
When we are strong, Lord, leave us not a - lone; Our ref - uge be.

With each new day, when morn - ing lifts the veil,
With thee to bless, the dark - ness shines as light,
Be thou for us in life our dai - ly bread,

We own thy mer - cies, Lord, which nev - er fail.
And faith's fair vi - sion chan - ges in - to sight.
Our heart's true home when all our years have sped. A-men.

God Moves in a Mysterious Way

31

A Mighty Fortress

HIS ABIDING PRESENCE

Come, My Soul, Thou Must Be Waking

Seele, du musst munter werden
Friedrich von Canitz, 1654-1699
Tr. Henry J. Buckoll, 1803- 1871, alt.

RICHTER 8.4.7.8.4.7.
J. A. Freylinghausen's
Geistreiches Gesang-Buch, 1704

33 God the Omnipotent

Sts. 1,2: Henry F. Chorley, 1808-1872, alt.
St. 3: John Ellerton, 1826-1893, alt.

RUSSIAN HYMN 11.10.11.9.
Alexis Lvov, 1799-1870

1 God the om - nip - o - tent! King, who or - dain - est
Thun - der thy clar - ion, the light - ning thy sword,
Show forth thy pit - y on high where thou reign - est;
Give to us peace in our time, O Lord.

2 God the all mer - ci - ful! Earth hath for - sak - en
Thy ways all ho - ly, and slight - ed thy word;
Bid not thy wrath in its ter - rors a - wak - en:
Give to us peace in our time, O Lord.

3 God the all right - eous One! Man hath de - fied thee;
Yet to e - ter - ni - ty stand - eth thy word;
False - hood and wrong shall not tar - ry be - side thee:
Give to us peace in our time, O Lord. A - men.

God Hath Spoken

34

George Wallace Briggs, 1875-1959

HYMN TO JOY 8.7.8.7.D.
Arr. from Ludwig van Beethoven, 1770-1827

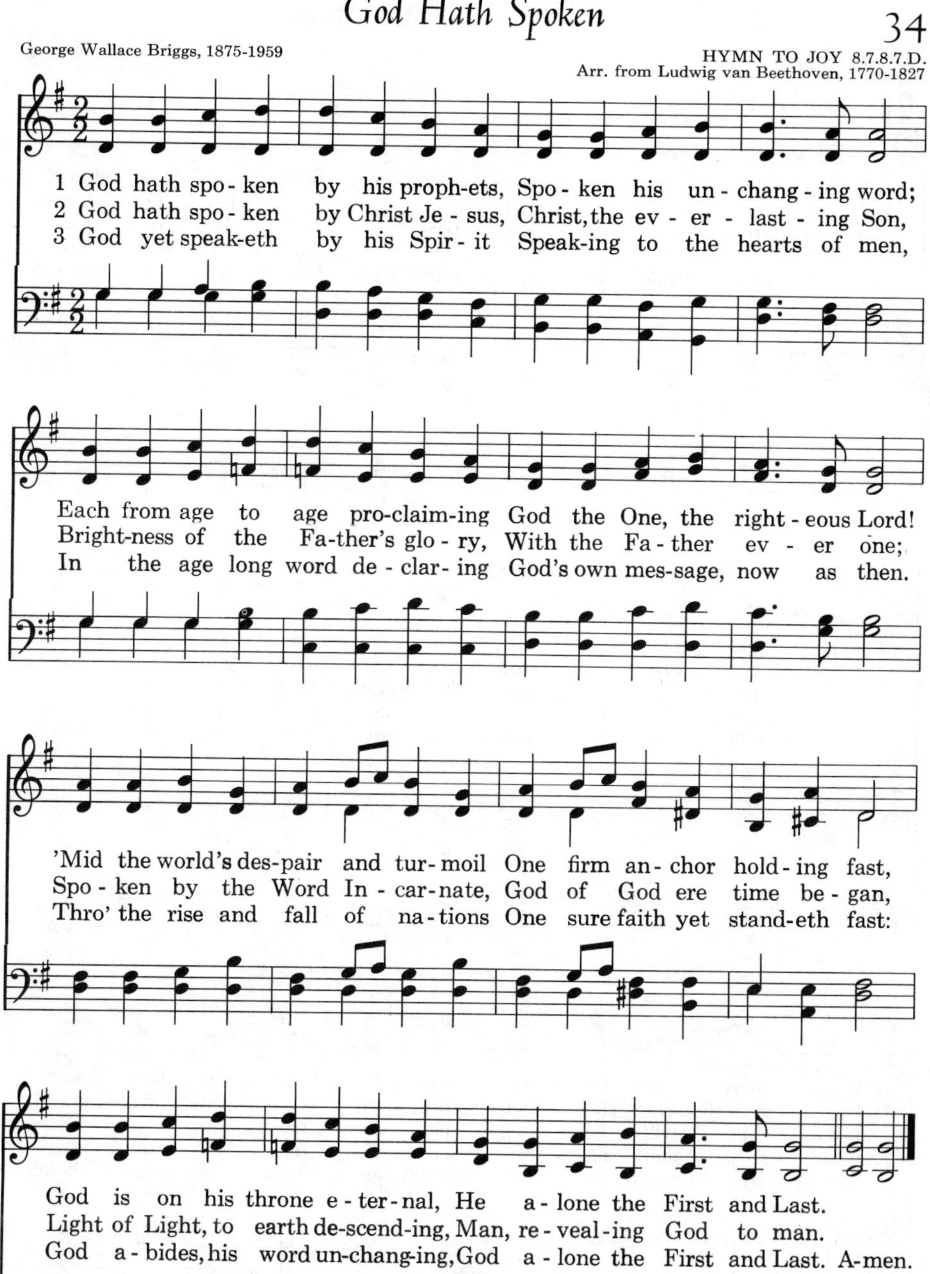

35 *How Firm a Foundation*

"K" in John Rippon's *Selection of Hymns*, 1787, alt.

FOUNDATION 11.11.11.11.
Early American Melody
Harm. Charles H. Heaton, 1928-

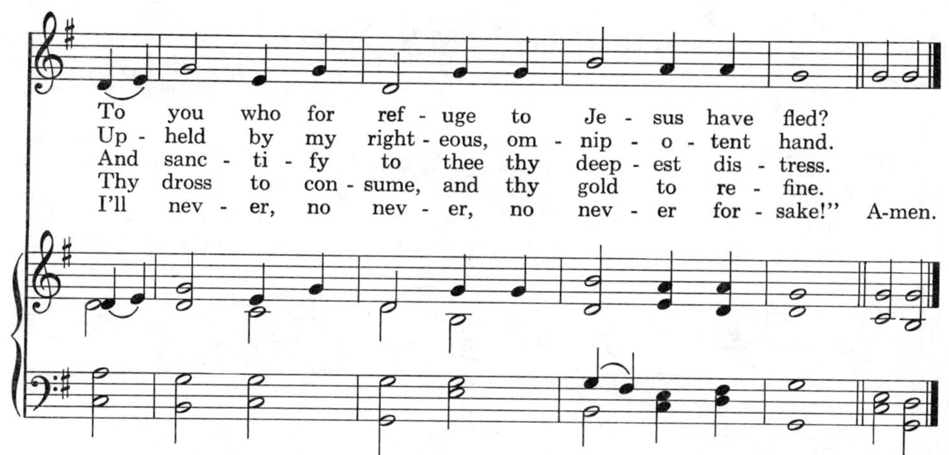

Father, Lead Me Day by Day 36

John P. Hopps, 1834-1912

ORIENTIS PARTIBUS 7.7.7.7.
Adapted from? Pierre de Corbeil, d. 1222

1 Fa - ther, lead me day by day, Ev - er in thine own strong way;
2 When in dan - ger, make me brave, Make me know that thou canst save;
3 When I'm tempt - ed to do wrong, Make me stead - fast, wise and strong;

Teach me to be pure and true, Show me what I ought to do.
Keep me safe - ly by thy side; Let me in thy love a - bide.
And when all a - lone I stand, Shield me with thy might - y hand. A-men.

37

God of the Moving Years

Kenneth Morse, 1913-

CENTRALIA 6.6.12.6.6.6.6.6.4.
George Brandon, 1924-, based on a tune in *The Christian Psalmist*, revised (1854)

si - lent voice, Thy beau - ty stands a - part, a - bove, be -
search-ing mind, Thy laws a - lone con - trol the power to
yond all art. Ac - cept the song we raise; let
make us whole. Thou art the light of life for
men re - joice.
all man - kind! A - - men.
Unison or Harmony
A - - men.

38 The Day Thou Gavest, Lord, Is Ended

First Tune

The Day Thou Gavest, Lord, Is Ended

Second Tune

John Ellerton, 1826-1893

LES COMMANDEMENS DE DIEU 9.8.9.8.
Attr. to Louis Bourgeois, c. 1510-c. 1561
Genevan Psalter, 1547

40 The Lord's My Shepherd

O God, in Whom We Live and Move

George Wallace Briggs, 1875-1959

SALVATION C.M.D.
Ananias Davisson's *Kentucky Harmony*, c. 1815

1 O God, in whom we live and move, In whom we draw each breath,
Who fill - est all the height a - bove, And all the depths be - neath;
Our hands may build thy hal - lowed fane, No bound thy pres - ence owns;
The heaven of heavens can - not con - tain, The low - ly heart en - thrones.

2 And when we ga - ther in thy name, To pray with one ac - cord,
A - round, with - in us, still the same, We find thy pres - ence, Lord.
Thou art a - bout our path, wher - e'er We seek to tread thy ways;
All life is sa - cra - ment and prayer, And ev - ery thought is praise. A-men.

43 God Be with You Till We Meet Again

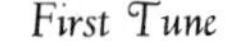

First Tune

Jeremiah E. Rankin, 1828-1904

RANDOLPH 9.8.8.9.
R. Vaughan Williams, 1872-1958

1 God be with you till we meet a-gain; By his coun - sels guide, up - hold you,
2 God be with you till we meet a-gain; 'Neath his wings pro - tect - ing hide you,
3 God be with you till we meet a-gain; When life's per - ils thick con-found you,
4 God be with you till we meet a-gain; Keep love's ban - ner float - ing o'er you,

With his sheep se - cure - ly fold you: God be with you till we meet a-gain.
Dai - ly man - na still pro-vide you: God be with you till we meet a-gain.
Put his arms un - fail-ing round you: God be with you till we meet a-gain.
Smite death's threat-ening wave be-fore you: God be with you till we meet a-gain. A-men.

Music from *The English Hymnal* by permission of Oxford University Press.

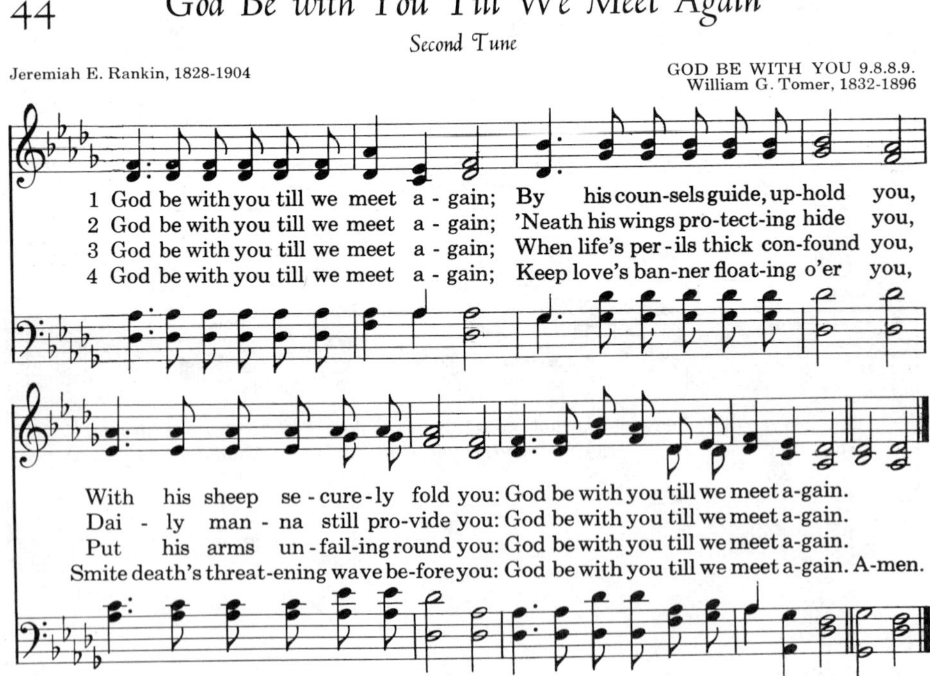

He Leadeth Me, O Blessed Thought

Joseph H. Gilmore, 1834-1918

HE LEADETH ME L.M. with Refrain
William B. Bradbury, 1816-1868

1 He lead-eth me, O bless-ed thought! O words with heaven-ly com-fort fraught!
What-e'er I do, wher-e'er I be, Still 'tis God's hand that lead-eth me.

2 Lord, I would clasp thy hand in mine, Nor ev-er mur-mur nor re-pine;
Con-tent, what-ev-er lot I see, Since 'tis my God that lead-eth me.

3 And when my task on earth is done, When, by thy grace, the vic-tory's won,
E'en death's cold wave I will not flee, Since God through Jor-dan lead-eth me.

He lead-eth me, he lead-eth me, By his own hand he lead-eth me;
His faith-ful fol-lower I would be, For by his hand he lead-eth me. A-men.

46 Lead, Kindly Light

John H. Newman, 1801-1890

SANDON 10.4.10.4.10.10.
Charles H. Purday, 1799-1885

Abide with Me

47

Henry F. Lyte, 1793-1847, alt.

EVENTIDE 10.10.10.10.
William H. Monk, 1823-1889

1 A - bide with me; fast falls the e - ven - tide;
2 I need thy pres - ence ev - ery pass - ing hour;
3 I fear no foe, with thee at hand to bless;
4 Hold thou thy cross be - fore my clos - ing eyes;

The dark - ness deep - ens, Lord, with me a - bide;
What but thy grace can foil the temp - ter's power?
Ills have no weight, and tears no bit - ter - ness;
Shine through the gloom, and point me to the skies;

When oth - er help - ers fail, and com - forts flee,
Who like thy - self my guide and stay can be?
Where is death's sting? where, grave, thy vic - to - ry?
Heaven's morn - ing breaks, and earth's vain shad - ows flee;

Help of the help - less, O a - bide with me.
Through cloud and sun - shine, O a - bide with me.
I tri - umph still if thou a - bide with me.
In life, in death, O Lord, a - bide with me. A-men.

48 Before Jehovah's Aweful Throne

Based on Psalm 100
Isaac Watts, 1674-1748
Alt. by John Wesley, 1703-1791

WINCHESTER NEW L.M.
Adapted from
Musicalisches Handbuch, Hamburg, 1690

1 Be - fore Je - ho - vah's awe - ful throne, Ye
2 His sov - ereign power with - out our aid, Made
3 We are his peo - ple, we his care, Our
4 We'll crowd thy gates with thank - ful songs, High
5 Wide as the world is thy com - mand, Vast

na - tions bow with sa - cred joy; Know that the Lord is
us of clay, and formed us men; And when, like wan - dering
souls, and all our mor - tal frame; What last - ing hon - ors
as the heavens our voic - es raise; And earth, with her ten
as e - ter - ni - ty thy love; Firm as a rock thy

God a - lone, He can cre - ate, and he de - stroy.
sheep, we strayed, He brought us to his fold a - gain.
shall we rear, Al - might - y Mak - er, to thy name?
thou-sand tongues, Shall fill thy courts with sound - ing praise.
truth must stand, When roll - ing years shall cease to move. A - men.

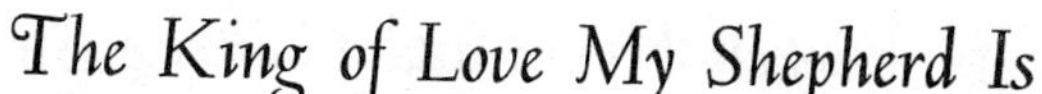

The King of Love My Shepherd Is

49

Based on Psalm 23
Henry W. Baker, 1821-1877

DOMINUS REGIT ME 8.7.8.7.
John B. Dykes, 1823-1876

1 The King of love my shep - herd is, Whose
good - ness fail - eth nev - er; I noth - ing lack if
I am his, And he is mine for - ev - er.

2 Where streams of liv - ing wa - ter flow, My
ran - somed soul he lead - eth, And where the ver - dant
pas - tures grow, With food ce - les - tial feed - eth.

3 Per - verse and fool - ish oft I strayed, But
yet in love he sought me, And on his shoul - der
gen - tly laid, And home re - joic - ing brought me.

4 In death's dark vale I fear no ill, With
thee, dear Lord, be - side me: Thy rod and staff my
com - fort still, Thy cross be - fore to guide me. A - men.

5 Thou spread'st a table in my sight,
Thy unction grace bestoweth,
And O what transport of delight
From thy pure chalice floweth!

6 And so through all the length of days
Thy goodness faileth never;
Good Shepherd, may I sing thy praise
Within thy house forever.

50 With Broken Heart and Contrite Sigh

Cornelius Elven, 1797-1873

BABYLON'S STREAMS L.M.
Thomas Campian, 1567-1620

1 With bro - ken heart and con - trite sigh,
2 Far off I stand with tear - ful eyes,
3 Nor alms, nor deeds that I have done,

A trem - bling sin - ner, Lord, I cry:
Nor dare up - lift them to the skies;
Can for a sin - gle sin a - tone;

Thy par - d'ning grace is rich and free;
But thou dost all my an - guish see:
To Cal - va - ry a - lone I flee:

If Thou but Suffer God to Guide Thee

Wer nur den lieben Gott lässt walten
Georg Neumark, 1621-1681
Tr. Catherine Winkworth, 1827-1878

WER NUR DEN LIEBEN GOTT 9.8.9.8.8.8.
Georg Neumark, 1621-1681

52 Depth of Mercy

Charles Wesley, 1707-1788

HEINLEIN 7.7.7.7.
Attr. to Martin Herbst, 1654-1681

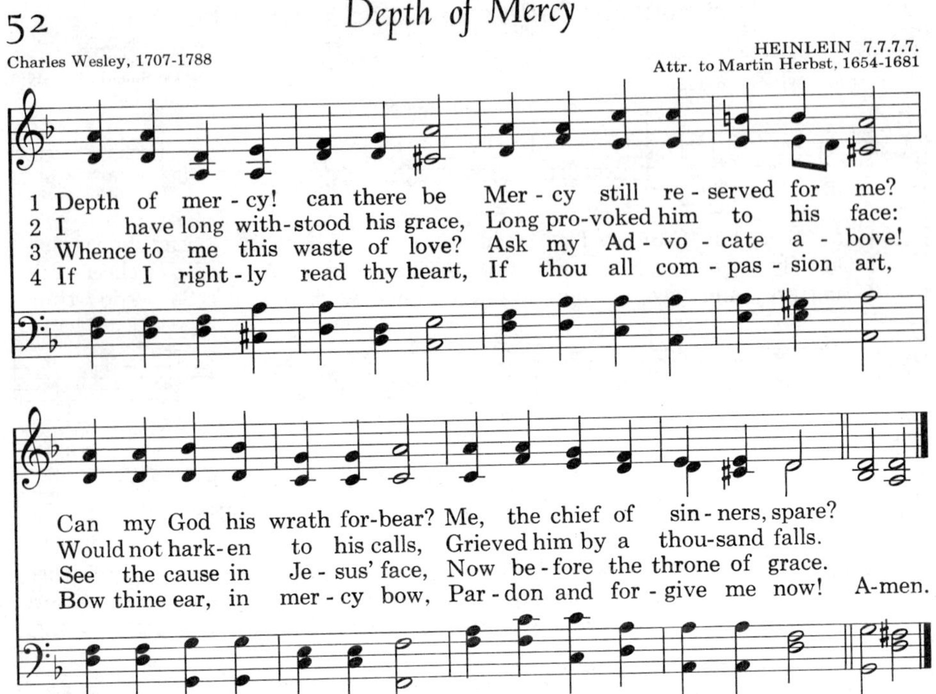

53 Day Is Dying in the West

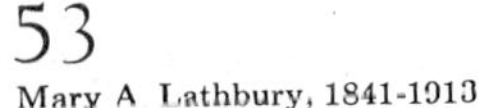
Mary A Lathbury, 1841-1913

CHAUTAUQUA 7.7.7.7.4. with Refrain
William F. Sherwin, 1826-1888

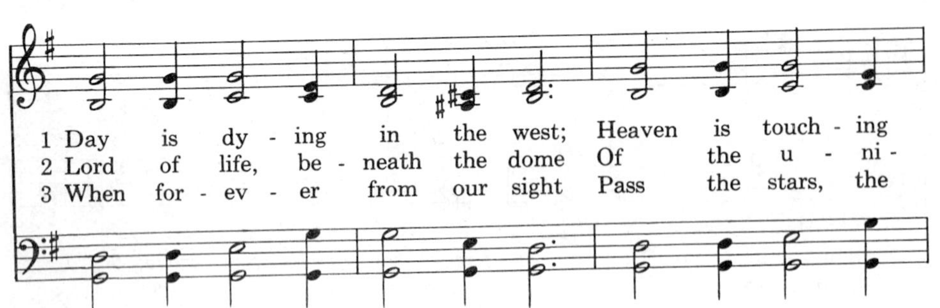

earth with rest; Wait and wor - ship while the night
verse, thy home, Gath - er us who seek thy face
day, the night, Lord of an - gels, on our eyes
Sets her eve - ning lamps a - light Through all the sky.
To the fold of thy em - brace, For thou art nigh.
Let e - ter - nal morn - ing rise, And shad - ows end.
Ho - ly, ho - ly, ho - ly, Lord God of Hosts! Heaven and earth are full of thee!
Heaven and earth are prais - ing thee, O Lord most high! A - men.

54 All Creatures of Our God and King

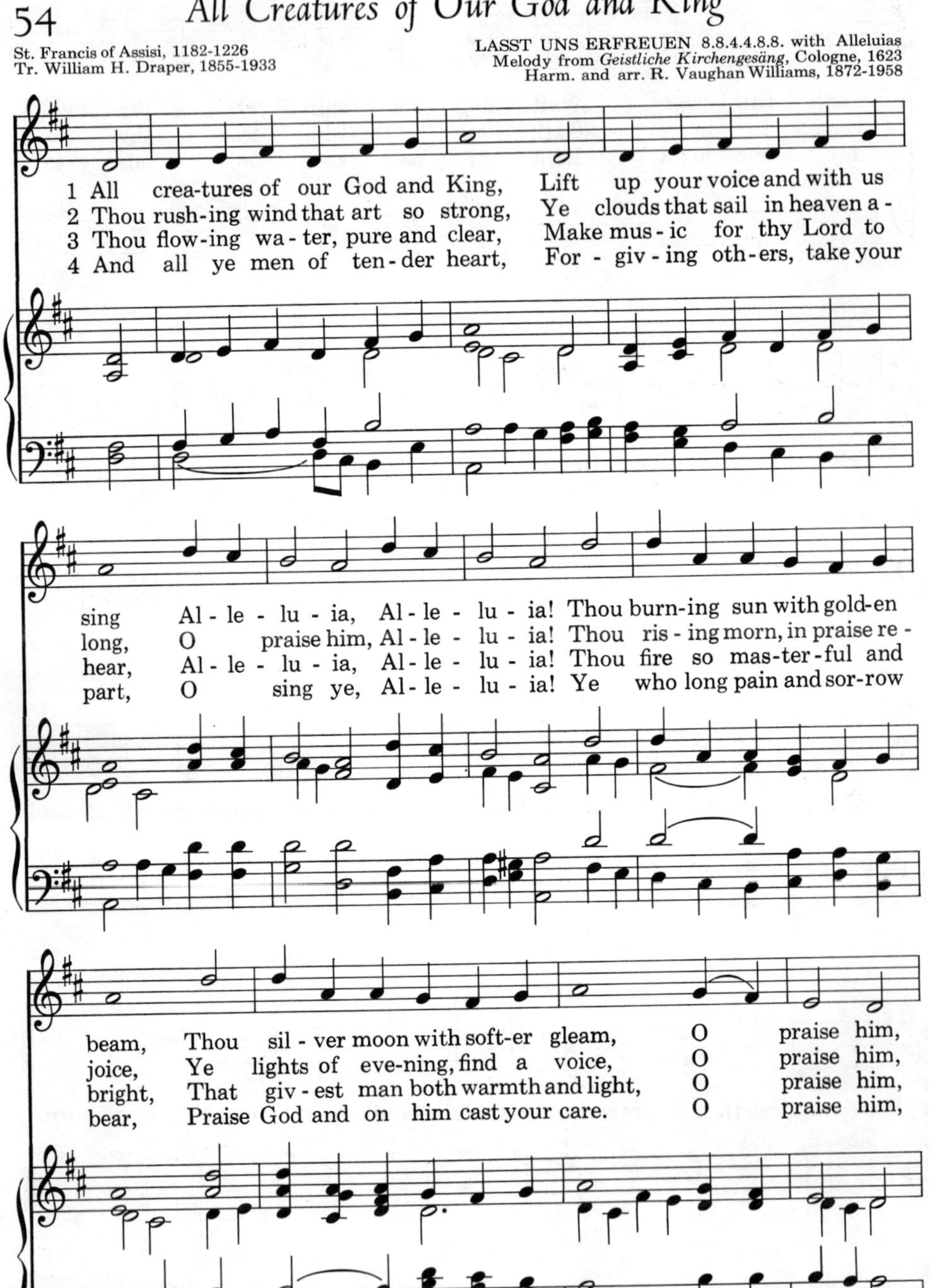

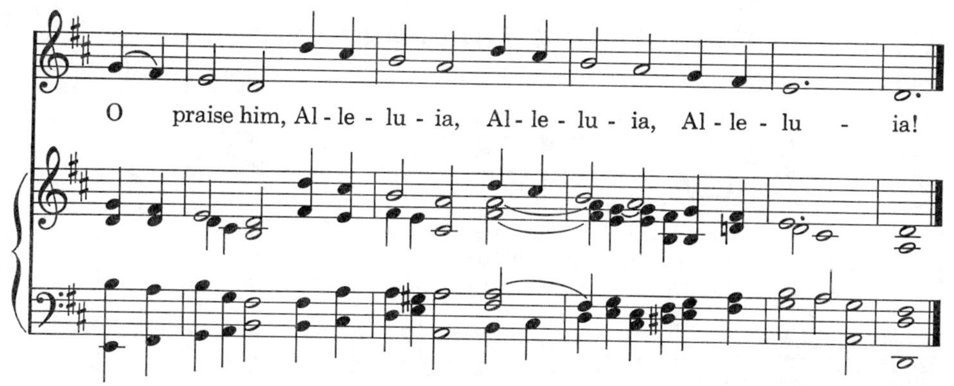

O God, We Praise Thee, and Confess

55

Based on *Te Deum Laudamus*, 5th century?
A Supplement to the New Version, 1700, alt.

TALLIS' ORDINAL C.M.
Thomas Tallis, c. 1505-1585

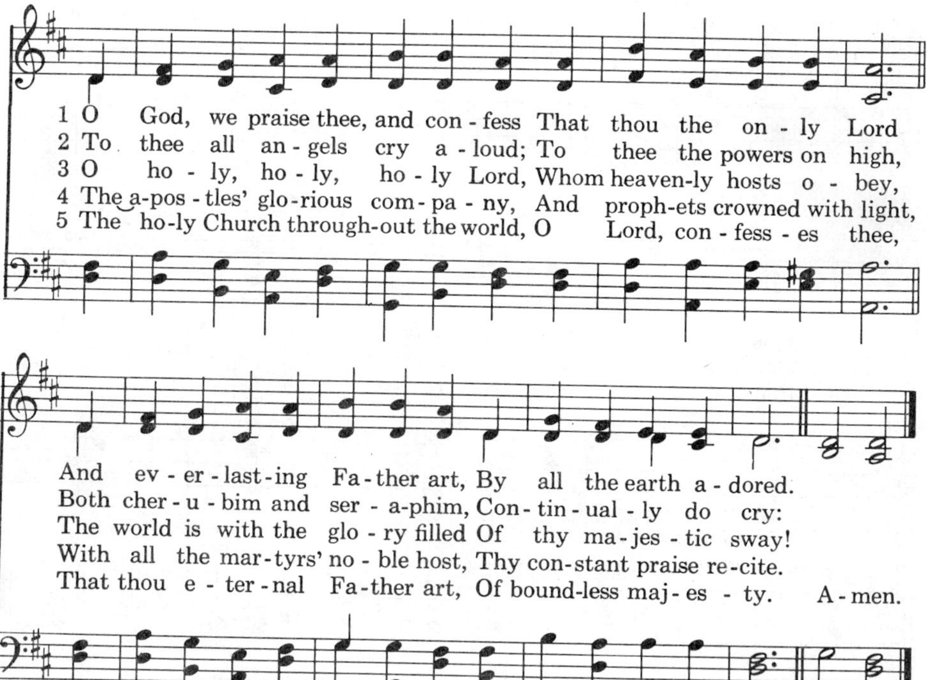

56 *Praise the Lord, His Glories Show*

Henry F. Lyte, 1793-1847

GWALCHMAI 7.7.7.7. with Alleluias
Joseph D. Jones, 1827-1870

1 Praise the Lord, his glo - ries show, Al - le - lu - ia!
2 Earth to heaven, and heaven to earth, Al - le - lu - ia!
3 Praise the Lord, his mer - cies trace, Al - le - lu - ia!

Saints with - in his courts be - low, Al - le - lu - ia!
Tell his won - ders, sing his worth, Al - le - lu - ia!
Praise his prov - i - dence and grace, Al - le - lu - ia!

An - gels round his throne a - bove, Al - le - lu - ia!
Age to age, and shore to shore, Al - le - lu - ia!
All that he for man hath done, Al - le - lu - ia!

All that see and share his love, Al - le - lu - ia!
Praise him, praise him ev - er - more! Al - le - lu - ia!
All he sends us through his Son. Al - le - lu - ia! A-men.

Praise to the Lord, the Almighty

57

58 All Glory Be to God on High

Allein Gott in der Höh' sei Ehr'
Nikolaus Decius, d. 1541
Tr. Catherine Winkworth, 1827-1878, alt.

ALLEIN GOTT IN DER HÖH' 8.7.8.7.8.8.7.
Geistliche Lieder, Leipzig, 1539
Harm. Hieronymus Praetorius, 1560-1629

O thank him for his good - ness!
'Tis well thou art our rul - er!
Have mer - cy on us, Je - sus!
Do thou in faith sus - tain us! A - men.
All Praise to Thee, for Thou, O King Divine
59
F. Bland Tucker, 1895-
NATIONAL CITY 10.10.10. with Alleluia
Lawrence P. Schreiber, 1933-
1 All praise to thee, for thou, O King di - vine, Didst
2 Thou cam'st to us in low - li - ness of thought; By
3 Let this mind be in us which was in thee, Who
4 Let ev - ery tongue con - fess with one ac - cord In
yield the glo - ry that of right was thine, That
thee the out - cast and the poor were sought, And
wast a ser - vant that we might be free, Then
heaven and earth that Je - sus Christ is Lord; And
in our dark-ened hearts thy grace might shine. Al - le - lu - ia!
by thy death was God's sal - va - tion wrought. Al - le - lu - ia!
hum-bling thy-self to death on Cal - va - ry. Al - le - lu - ia!
God the Fa - ther be by all a - dored. Al - le - lu - ia! A-men.

60 Come, O Come, in Pious Lays

George Wither, 1588-1667, alt.

ALLE MENSCHEN 7.7.7.7.D.
Jakob Hintze, 1622-1702
Harm. J. S. Bach, 1685-1750

God Himself Is with Us

62 *Father, We Praise Thee, Now the Night Is Over*

Latin: *Nocte surgentes*
Attr. to Gregory the Great, 540-604
Tr. Percy Dearmer, 1867-1936

CHRISTE SANCTORUM 11.11.11.5.
La Feillée's *Méthode du Plain-chant*, 1781

Thus we a - dore thee.
Joy with - out end - ing.
Through all cre - a - tion. A - men.
Words from The English Hymnal by permission of Oxford University Press. Music from The Revised Church Hymnal by permission of Oxford University Press.
Sing to the Lord a Joyful Song
63
John Samuel Bewley Monsell, 1811-1875
SCHÜTZ 81 L.M.
Heinrich Schütz, 1585-1672
1 Sing to the Lord a joy - ful song, Lift up your hearts, your voic - es raise; To us his gra - cious gifts be - long, To him our songs of love and praise.
2 For life and love, for rest and food, For dai - ly help and night - ly care, Sing to the Lord, for he is good, And praise his name, for it is fair.
3 For joys un - told, that from a - bove Cheer those who love his sweet em - ploy, Sing to our God, for he is love, Ex - alt his name, for it is joy. A-men.

64
Come, Thou Almighty King
Anonymous, c. 1757
ITALIAN HYMN 6.6.4.6.6.6.4.
Felice de Giardini, 1716-1796
1 Come, thou al - might - y King, Help us thy
2 Come, thou in - car - nate Word, Gird on thy
3 Come, ho - ly Com - fort - er, Thy sa - cred
4 To thee, great One in Three E - ter - nal
name to sing; Help us to praise: Fa - ther, all
might - y sword; Our prayer at - tend: Come, and thy
wit - ness bear In this glad hour! Thou who al -
prais - es be Hence ev - er - more! His sov - ereign
glo - ri - ous, O'er all vic - to - ri - ous, Come, and reign
peo - ple bless, And give thy word suc - cess; Spir - it of
might - y art, Now rule in ev - ery heart, And ne'er from
maj - es - ty May we in glo - ry see, And to e -
o - ver us, An - cient of Days.
ho - li - ness, On us de - scend.
us de - part, Spir - it of power.
ter - ni - ty Love and a - dore. A - men.

It Is Good to Sing Thy Praises

From Psalm 92
The Psalter, 1912

HASTINGS-ON-HUDSON 8.7.8.7.D.
Harold W. Friedell, 1905-1958

Glad Hymns and Songs Will I Recite

Author unknown, 13th Century
Tr. from the Hebrew by Alice Lucas

OMNOM KAYN L.M.
Traditional Hebrew Melody

O Worship the King 67

68 *All Praise to Thee, My God*

Holy God, Thy Name We Bless

Attr. to Ignaz Franz, 1719-1790
Tr. R. Birch Hoyle, 1875-1939
Stanza 2 tr. Clarence Walworth, 1820-1900

GROSSER GOTT, WIR LOBEN DICH 7.8.7.8.7.7.
Katholisches Gesangbuch, Vienna, *c.* 1774

70 Holy, Holy, Holy! Lord God Almighty

Reginald Heber, 1783-1826

NICAEA 11.12.12.10.
John B. Dykes, 1823-1876

1 Ho - ly, ho - ly, ho - ly! Lord God Al - might - y!
2 Ho - ly, ho - ly, ho - ly! all the saints a - dore thee,
3 Ho - ly, ho - ly, ho - ly! though the dark - ness hide thee,
4 Ho - ly, ho - ly, ho - ly! Lord God Al - might - y!

Ear - ly in the morn - ing our song shall rise to thee;
Cast - ing down their gold - en crowns a - round the glass - y sea;
Though the eye of sin - ful man thy glo - ry may not see;
All thy works shall praise thy name in earth and sky and sea;

Ho - ly, ho - ly, ho - ly! mer - ci - ful and might - y;
Cher - u - bim and ser - a - phim fall - ing down be - fore thee,
On - ly thou art ho - ly; there is none be - side thee,
Ho - ly, ho - ly, ho - ly! mer - ci - ful and might - y;

God in three per - sons, bless - ed Trin - i - ty!
Which wert, and art, and ev - er - more shalt be.
Per - fect in power, in love, and pur - i - ty.
God in three per - sons, bless - ed Trin - i - ty! A - men.

71 All People That on Earth Do Dwell

Paraphrase of Psalm 100
William Kethe, *d.* 1593

OLD HUNDREDTH L.M.
Genevan Psalter, 1551

72 O for a Thousand Tongues to Sing

Charles Wesley, 1707-1788

AZMON C.M.
Carl G. Gläser, 1784-1829
Mason's *Modern Psalmody*, 1839

73 Praise, My Soul, the King of Heaven

Based on Psalm 103
Henry Francis Lyte, 1793-1847, alt.

PRAISE MY SOUL 8.7.8.7.8.7.
John Goss, 1800-1880

1 Praise, my soul, the King of heav - en, To his feet thy
2 Praise him for his grace and fa - vor To our fa - thers
3 Fa - ther - like, he tends and spares us; Well our fee - ble
4 An - gels, help us to a - dore him, Ye be - hold him

trib - ute bring; Ran - somed, healed, re - stored, for - giv - en,
in dis - tress; Praise him, still the same for - ev - er,
frame he knows; In his hands he gen - tly bears us,
face to face; Sun and moon, bow down be - fore him;

Who, like me, his praise should sing? Praise him! praise him!
Slow to chide, and swift to bless. Praise him! praise him!
Res - cues us from all our foes. Praise him! praise him!
Dwell - ers all in time and space, Praise him! praise him!

Praise him! praise him! Praise the ev - er - last - ing King!
Praise him! praise him! Glo - rious in his faith - ful - ness!
Praise him! praise him! Wide - ly yet his mer - cy flows!
Praise him! praise him! Praise with us the God of grace! A - men.

I'll Praise My Maker While I've Breath

74

Psalm 146
Isaac Watts, 1674-1748
Alt. by John Wesley, 1703-1791

OLD 113TH 8.8.8.8.8.8.
Strassburger Kirchenamt, 1525
Probably by Matthäus Greiter, *c.* 1500-1552
Harm. V. Earle Copes, 1921-

Unison

1 I'll praise my Mak - er while I've breath; And when my voice
2 Hap - py the man whose hopes re - ly On Is - rael's God;
3 The Lord pours eye - sight on the blind; The Lord sup - ports
4 I'll praise him while he lends me breath; And when my voice

is lost in death, Praise shall em - ploy my no - bler powers.
he made the sky And earth and seas, with all their train.
the faint - ing mind; He sends the la - boring con-science peace.
is lost in death, Praise shall em - ploy my no - bler powers.

My days of praise shall ne'er be past, While life, and thought,
His truth for - ev - er stands se - cure, He saves th'op-pressed
He helps the stran - ger in dis - tress, The wid - ow and
My days of praise shall ne'er be past, While life, and thought,

and be - ing last, Or im - mor - tal - i - ty en - dures.
he feeds the poor, And none shall find his prom - ise vain.
the fa - ther - less, And grants the pris - oner sweet re - lease.
and be - ing last, Or im - mor - tal - i - ty en - dures. A-men.

75 Immortal, Invisible, God Only Wise

Walter Chalmers Smith, 1824-1908, alt.

ST. DENIO 11.11.11.11.
Welsh hymn melody
John Roberts' *Caniadau y Cyssegr*, 1839

Ye Servants of God, Your Master Proclaim 76

Charles Wesley, 1707-1788

HANOVER 10.10.11.11.
William Croft, 1678-1727

1 Ye serv - ants of God, your Mas - ter pro - claim,
2 God rul - eth on high, al - might - y to save,
3 Sal - va - tion to God who sits on the throne!
4 Then let us a - dore and give him his right,

And pub - lish a - broad his won - der - ful name.
And still he is nigh, his pres - ence we have;
Let all cry a - loud and hon - or the Son;
All glo - ry and power, all wis - dom and might,

The name, all vic - to - rious, of Je - sus ex - tol;
The great con - gre - ga - tion his tri - umph shall sing,
The prais - es of Je - sus the an - gels pro - claim,
All hon - or and bless - ing with an - gels a - bove,

His king - dom is glo - rious, he rules o - ver all.
As - crib - ing sal - va - tion to Je - sus, our King.
Fall down on their fa - ces and wor - ship the Lamb.
And thanks nev - er ceas - ing and in - fi - nite love. A - men.

77
O Be Joyful in the Lord!
Based on Psalm 100
Curtis Beach, 1914-
FINLAY 7.7.7.7.5.7.6.7.
Harold W. Friedell, 1905-1958
1 O be joy - ful in the Lord! Sing be - fore him, all the earth!
2 Know ye that the Lord is King! All his works his wis - dom prove!
3 En - ter now his ho - ly gate; Let our bur-dened hearts be still;
4 For the Lord our God is kind, And his love shall con - stant be;
Praise him with a glad ac - cord And with lives of no - blest worth.
By his might the heav-ens ring; In his love we live and move.
In the sa - cred si - lence wait, As we seek to know his will.
In his will our peace we find; In his ser-vice, lib - er - ty.
Sons of ev - ery land, Hum - bly now be - fore him stand!
By him we are made, So we trust him un - a - fraid.
Let our lives ex - press Our a - bun-dant thank-ful - ness;
Yea, his law is sure; In his light we walk se - cure;

With the Morn in Radiance Breaking 78

Karpínski, 1741-1825
Tr. W. J. Rose, 1922

SANDELL (TRYGGARE KAN INGEN VARA) L.M.
Swedish Melody

79 *Praise the Lord! Ye Heavens*

Based on Psalm 148
Stanzas 1, 2. Foundling Hospital Collection, c. 1801
Stanza 3: Edward Osler, 1798-1863

HYFRYDOL 8.7.8.7.D.
Rowland Hugh Prichard, 1811-1887

As Pants the Hart 80

Based on Psalm 42
A New Version of the Psalms, 1696, alt.

IRISH C.M.
Hymns and Sacred Poems, Dublin, 1749

1 As pants the hart for cool - ing streams When
2 For thee, my God, the liv - ing God, My
3 Why rest - less, why cast down, my soul? Hope

heat - ed in the chase, So longs my soul, O
thirst - y soul doth pine. O when shall I be -
still, and thou shalt sing The praise of him who

God, for thee, And thy re - fresh - ing grace.
hold thy face, Thou maj - es - ty di - vine?
is thy God, Thy health's e - ter - nal spring. A - men.

81 The God of Abraham Praise

Savior, Again to Thy Dear Name

83 *Let All the World in Every Corner Sing*

George Herbert, 1593-1632

ALL THE WORLD 10.4.6.6.6.6.10.4.
Robert G. McCutchan, 1877-1958

My God, I Love Thee

84

No me mueve, mi Dios
Attr. to Francis Xavier, 1506-1552
Tr. Edward Caswall, 1814-1878, alt.

ABBEY C.M.
Scottish Psalter, 1615

1 My God, I love thee: not be-cause I hope for heaven there-by,
2 Not with the hope of gain-ing aught; Not seek-ing a re-ward;
3 E'en so I love thee, and will love, And in thy praise will sing,

Nor yet be-cause who love thee not Are lost e-ter-nal-ly.
But as thy-self hast lov-ed me, O ev-er-lov-ing Lord,
Sole-ly be-cause thou art my God, And my e-ter-nal King. A-men.

85 *Dear Lord and Father of Mankind*

First Tune

John Greenleaf Whittier, 1807-1892

SALVATION 8.6.8.8.6.
Ananias Davisson's *Kentucky Harmony*, c. 1815, adapted

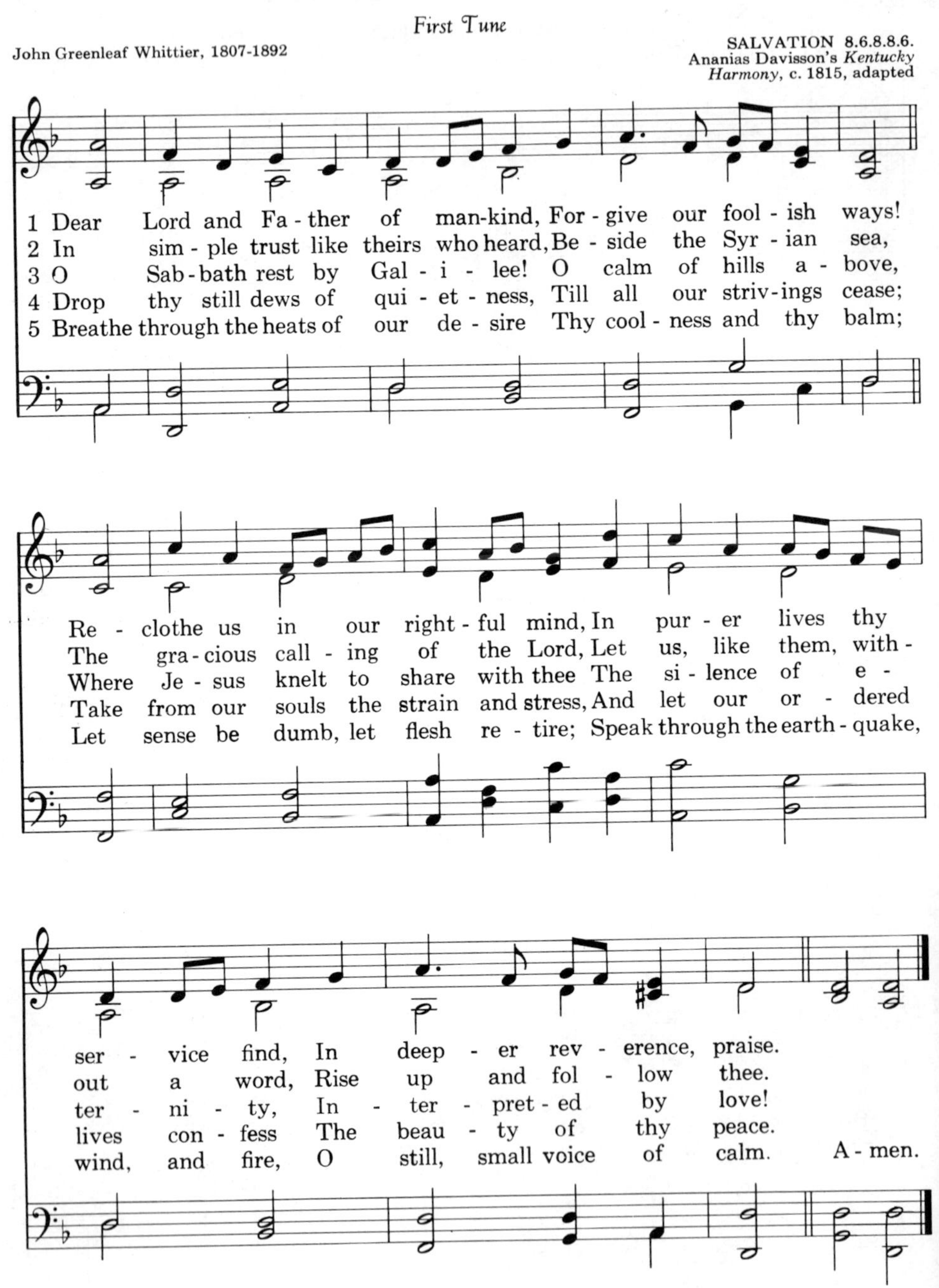

CONFESSION AND COMMITMENT

Dear Lord and Father of Mankind 86

Second Tune

John Greenleaf Whittier, 1807-1892

REST 8.6.8.8.6.
Frederick C. Maker, 1844-1927

87 Declare, O Heavens, the Lord of Space

New realms we find he first hath made,
No soar - ing flight can e'er out - run
Stir deeds of grace to serve thy plan,
All be - ing is his power dis - played; Al - le - lu - ia!
Truth God has shown us in his Son; Al - le - lu - ia!
Wake joy the morn - ing stars be - gan; Al - le - lu - ia!
Al - le - lu - ia! Al - le - lu - ia! Al - le - lu - ia! Al - le - lu - ia!

Creator of the Universe

J. Donald Hughes, 1882-

WEYMOUTH C.M.D.
Theodore P. Ferris, 1908-

1 Cre - a - tor of the u - ni - verse, We lift our minds to thee;
2 Let not the love of eas - y ways Leave deep - er truth un - known;

En - light - en them and lead our thought In fear - less lib - er - ty.
Teach us that power to learn and grow Is found in thee a - lone.

Let not our search for truth in things From thee our souls di - vide;
Let sci - ence find in thee its truth; Tech nol - o - gy, its Goal;

Thou art the liv - ing Lord of truth; Thy Spir - it be our guide!
Phi - los - o - phy, its no - blest thought: Thy light makes know - ledge whole! A - men.

Out of the Depths I Cry to Thee

Aus tiefer Not schrei ich zu dir
Martin Luther, 1483-1546
Tr. Catherine Winkworth, 1827-1878

AUS TIEFER NOT 8.7.8.7.8.8.7.
Martin Luther? 1483-1546
Harm. J. S. Bach, 1685-1750

90 Be Thou My Vision, O Lord of My Heart

Rob tu mo bhoile, a Comdi cride
Irish text, 8th cent.?
Tr. Mary Elizabeth Byrne, 1880-1931
Versified by Eleanor Henrietta Hull, 1860-1935

SLANE 10.10.9.10.
Trad. Irish melody
Harm. David Evans, 1874-1948

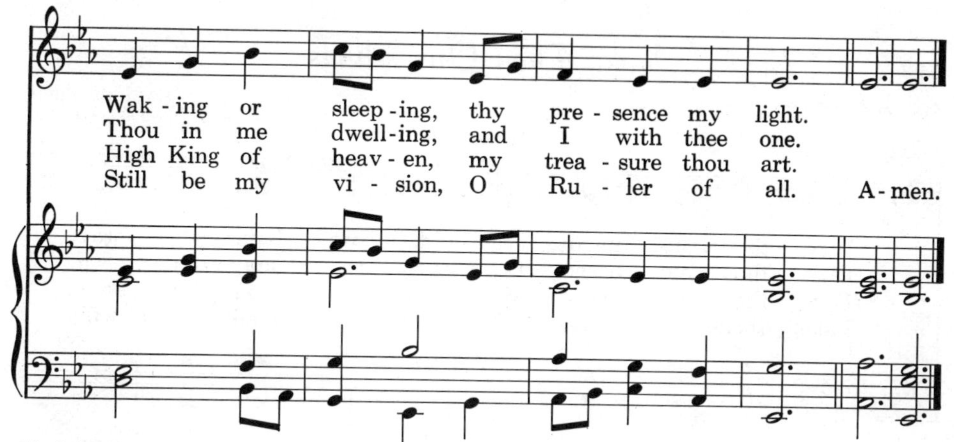

Words from *The Poem Book of the Gael;* Selected and Edited by Eleanor Hull. Used by permission of the Editor's Literary Estate and Chatto and Windus, Ltd. Music from *The Revised Church Hymnary* by permission of Oxford University Press.

On This Day, the First of Days 91

Die parente temporum
Breviary of Le Mans, 1748
Tr. Henry W. Baker, 1821-1877

SCHÜTZ 19 7.7.7.7.
Heinrich Schütz, 1585-1672

1 On this day, the first of days, God the Fa - ther's name we praise,
2 On this day the e - ter - nal Son O - ver death his tri - umph won;
3 Fa - ther, who didst fash - ion me Im - age of thy - self to be,
4 Thou who dost all gifts im - part, Shine, good Spir - it, in my heart;

Who, cre - a - tion's Lord and spring, Did the world from dark - ness bring.
On this day the Spir - it came With his gifts of liv - ing flame.
Fill me with thy love di - vine; Let my ev - ery thought be thine.
Best of gifts, thy - self be - stow; Make me burn thy love to know. A - men.

92 Take Thou Our Minds

Rise Up, O Men of God! 93

William P. Merrill, 1867-1954

FESTAL SONG S.M.
William H. Walter, 1825-1893

95 Praise to God, Immortal Praise

Anna Laetitia Barbauld, 1743-1825, alt.

DIX 7.7.7.7.7.7.
Adapted from a chorale by
Conrad Kocher, 1786-1872

1 Praise to God, im - mor - tal praise, For the love that crowns our days;
Boun - teous source of ev - ery joy, Let thy praise our tongues em - ploy:
All to thee, our God, we owe, Source whence all our bless-ings flow.

2 All the plen - ty sum-mer pours; Au-tumn's rich o'er - flow - ing stores;
Flocks that whi - ten all the plain; Yel - low sheaves of rip - ened grain:
Lord, for these our souls shall raise Grate-ful vows and sol - emn praise.

3 As thy pros-p'ring land hath blest, May we give thee of our best;
And by deeds of kind - ly love For thy mer - cies grate - ful prove;
Sing - ing thus through all our days Praise to God, im - mor - tal praise. A-men.

96 When Thy Heart with Joy O'erflowing

Theodore C. Williams, 1855-1915

BULLINGER 8.5.8.3.
Ethelbert W. Bullinger, 1837-1913

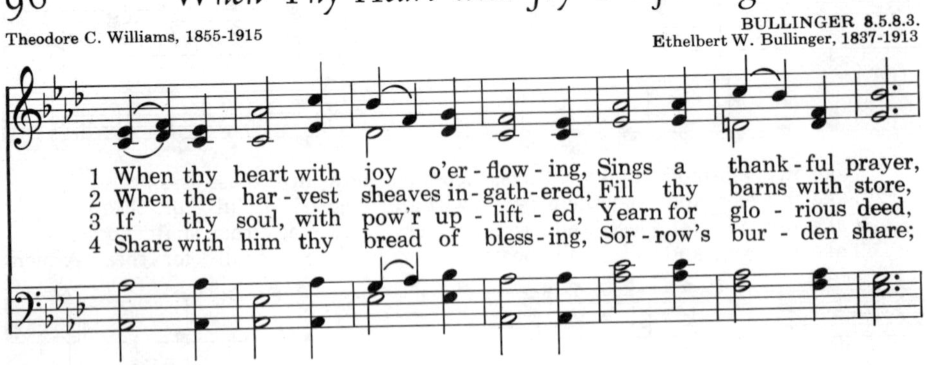

Rejoice, Ye Pure in Heart 97

Edward H. Plumptre, 1821-1891

MARION S.M. with Refrain
Arthur H. Messiter, 1834-1916

1 Re - joice, ye pure in heart; Re - joice, give thanks and sing;
2 With voice as full and strong As o - cean's surg - ing praise,
3 Then on through life's long path, Still chant - ing as ye go,
4 Still lift your stand - ard high, Still march in firm ar - ray,

Your fes - tal ban - ner wave on high, The cross of Christ your King!
Send forth the hymns our fa - thers loved, The psalms of an - cient days.
From youth to age, by night and day, In glad - ness and in woe.
As war - riors through the dark - ness toil Till dawns the gold - en day!

Re - joice, re - joice, Re - joice, give thanks and sing. A-men.

Re - joice, re - joice,

THANKSGIVING

98 As Men of Old Their First Fruits Brought

Frank von Christierson, 1900-

FOREST GREEN C.M.D.
English melody
Arr. R. Vaughan Williams, 1872-1958

1 As men of old their first fruits brought Of orch - ard, flock, and field
2 A world in need now sum - mons us To la - bor, love and give;
3 In gra - ti - tude and hum - ble trust We bring our best to thee

To God the Giv - er of all good, The Source of boun-teous yield;
To make our life an of - fer - ing To God, that man may live;
To serve thy cause and share thy love With all hu - man - i - ty.

So we to - day first fruits would bring The wealth of this good land,
The Church of Christ is call - ing us To make the dream come true:
O thou who gav - est us thy - self In Je - sus Christ thy Son,

Of farm and mar - ket, shop and home, Of mind, and heart, and hand.
A world re-deemed by Christ-like love; All life in Christ made new.
Teach us to give our - selves each day Un - til life's work is done. A-men.

THANKSGIVING

Now Thank We All Our God

99

First Tune

Nun danket alle Gott
Martin Rinckart, 1586-1649
Tr. Catherine Winkworth, 1827-1878

NUN DANKET 6.7.6.7.6.6.6.6.
Melody by Johann Crüger, 1598-1662

THANKSGIVING

100 Now Thank We All Our God

THANKSGIVING

Music taken from *Three Hymn Tunes* from 20th Century Folk Mass by permission of the publishers, W. Paxton & Co. Ltd., London; W. 1., England.

THANKSGIVING

Come, Ye Thankful People, Come

Henry Alford, 1810-1871
Anna L. Barbauld, 1743-1825, and others

ST. GEORGE'S WINDSOR 7.7.7.7.D.
George J. Elvey, 1816-1893

1 Come, ye thank-ful peo - ple, come, Raise the song of har - vest home;
2 All the bless-ings of the field, All the stores the gar - dens yield,
3 These to thee, our God, we owe, Source whence all our bless - ings flow;

All is safe - ly gath - ered in, Ere the win - ter storms be - gin;
All the fruits in full sup - ply, Rip - ened 'neath the sum - mer sky,
And for these our souls shall raise Grate-ful vows and sol - emn praise.

God, our Mak - er, doth pro - vide For our wants to be sup - plied;
All that spring with boun-teous hand Scat - ters o'er the smil - ing land,
Come, then, thank-ful peo - ple, come, Raise the song of har - vest home;

Come to God's own tem - ple, come, Raise the song of har - vest home.
All that lib - eral au-tumn pours From her rich o'er - flow - ing stores,
Come to God's own tem - ple, come, Raise the song of har - vest home. A-men.

THANKSGIVING

We Gather Together

Wilt heden nu treden
Anonymous, 16th cent.
Tr. Theodore Baker, 1851-1934

KREMSER 12.11.12.11.
Nederlandtsche Gedenckelanck, 1626
Arr. Edward Kremser, 1838-1914

1 We gath - er to - geth - er to ask the Lord's bless - ing;
2 Be - side us to guide us, our God with us join - ing,
3 We all do ex - tol thee, thou lead - er tri - um-phant

He chast - ens and hast - ens his will to make known;
Or - dain - ing, main - tain - ing his king - dom di - vine;
And pray that thou still our de - fend - er wilt be.

The wick - ed op - press - ing now cease from dis - tress - ing:
So from the be - gin - ning the fight we were win - ning:
Let thy con - gre - ga - tion es - cape tri - bu - la - tion;

Sing prais - es to his name; He for - gets not his own.
Thou, Lord, wast at our side: all glo - ry be thine!
Thy name be ev - er praised! O Lord, make us free! A - men.

Creator of the Stars of Night

First Tune

Conditor alme siderum
9th century
Tr. John Mason Neale, 1818-1866, alt.
Version in *The Hymnal 1940*

CONDITOR ALME L.M.
Sarum plainsong, Mode IV
Harm. J. H. Arnold, 1887-1956

1 Cre - a - tor of the stars of night, Thy
2 To thee the trav - ail deep was known That
3 When the old world drew on toward night, Thou
4 At thy great name ex - alt - ed now All

peo - ple's ev - er - last - ing light, O Christ, thou Sav - ior
made the whole cre - a - tion groan, Till thou, Re - deem - er,
cam - est, not in splen - dor bright As mon - arch, but the
knees must bend, all hearts must bow; And things ce - les - tial

of us all, We pray thee, hear us when we call.
should - est free Thine own in glo - rious lib - er - ty.
hum - ble child Of Mar - y, blame - less moth - er mild.
thee shall own, And things ter - res - trial, Lord a - lone. A - men.

ADVENT

Creator of the Stars of Night

Second Tune

105 Lift Up Your Heads, Ye Mighty Gates

Based on Psalm 24
Georg Weissel, 1590-1635
Tr. Catherine Winkworth, 1829-1878, alt.

TRURO L.M.
Psalmodia Evangelica, 1789

106 Come, Thou Long-Expected Jesus

Charles Wesley, 1707-1788

STUTTGART 8.7.8.7.
Christian F. Witt, 1660-1716
Psalmodia Sacra, Gotha, 1715

1 Come, thou long - ex - pect - ed Je - sus, Born to set thy peo - ple free;
2 Is - rael's strength and con - so - la - tion, Hope of all the earth thou art;
3 Born thy peo - ple to de - liv - er, Born a child, and yet a king,
4 By thine own e - ter - nal Spir - it Rule in all our hearts a - lone;

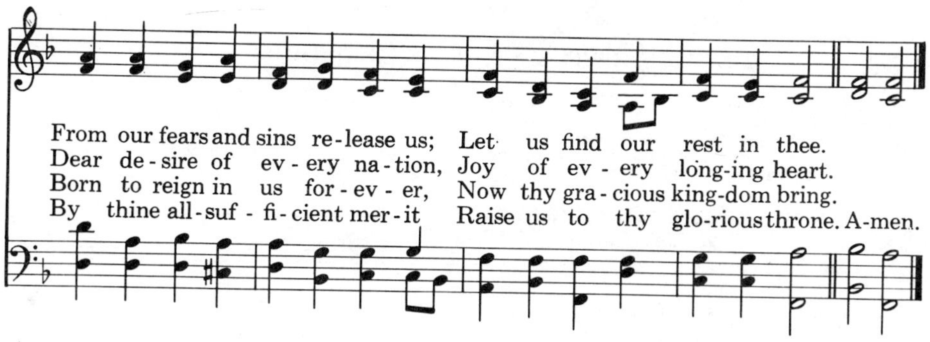

Alternate tune No. 294

Ah! Think Not the Lord Delayeth 107

Percy Dearmer, 1867-1936

ALLES IST AN GOTTES SEGEN 8.8.7.D.
Attr. to J. B. König, 1691-1758
Harmonischer Lieder-Schatz, 1738

1 Ah! think not the Lord de-lay-eth; "I am with you," still he say-eth,
2 For e'en now the reign of heav-en Spreads through-out the world like leav-en,
3 Not for us to find the rea-sons, Or to know the times and sea-sons,

"Do you yet not un-der-stand?" Look not back, the past re-gret-ting;
Un-ob-served, and ver-y near, Like the seed when no man know-eth,
Comes the Lord when strikes the hour; Ours to bear the faith-ful wit-ness

On the dawn your hearts be set-ting; Rise, and join the Lord's com-mand.
Like the shel-tering tree that grow-eth, Comes the life e-ter-nal here.
Which can shape the world to fit-ness, Thine, O God, to give the power. A-men.

108 O Come, O Come, Emmanuel

First Tune

Veni, veni Emmanuel
Psalteriolum Cantionum Catholicarum, Cologne, 1710
Sts. 1,2: Tr. John Mason Neale, 1818-1866, alt.
Sts. 3,4: Henry Sloane Coffin, 1877-1954

VENI EMMANUEL 8.8.8.8.8.8.
Adapted from plainsong phrases
by Thomas Helmore, 1811-1890

O Come, O Come, Emmanuel

ADVENT

110 Comfort, Comfort Ye My People

Based on Isaiah 40:1-8
Johann Olearius, 1611-1684
Tr. Catherine Winkworth, 1827-1878, alt.

PSALM 42 8.7.8.7.7.7.8.8.
Genevan Psalter, 1551

Veiled in Darkness Judah Lay

Douglas LeTell Rights, 1891-1956

NICHT SO TRAURIG 7.7.7.7.7.7.
Johann Georg Ebeling, 1637-1676

Words used by permission of Burton J. Rights.

112 Wake, Awake, for Night Is Flying

Wachet auf, ruft uns die Stimme
Philipp Nicolai, 1556-1608
Tr. Catherine Winkworth, 1827-1878, and others

WACHET AUF 8.9.8.8.9.8.6.6.4.8.8.
Philipp Nicolai, 1556-1608
Harm. J. S. Bach, 1685-1750

1 Wake, a-wake, for night is fly - ing; The watch-men on the
2 Zi - on hears the watch-men sing - ing; Her heart with deep de -

heights are cry - ing, A - wake, Je - ru - sa - lem, a - rise!
light is spring - ing, She wakes, she ris - es from her gloom,

Mid-night's sol - emn hour is toll - ing; His char - iot wheels are
For her Lord comes down all glo - rious, In grace ar - rayed, by

near - er roll - ing; He comes! O Church, lift up thine eyes!
truth vic - to - rious; Her star is risen, her light is come!

3 Now let all the heavens adore thee,
And men and angels sing before thee
With harp and cymbal's clearest tone;
Of one pearl each shining portal,
Where we shall join the choirs immortal
In praises round thy glorious throne;
No vision ever brought,
No ear hath ever caught
Such great glory!
Therefore will we, eternally,
Sing hymns of joy and praise to thee.

113 Hail to the Lord's Anointed

Psalm 72
James Montgomery, 1771-1854

WOODBIRD 7.6.7.6.D.
Traditional German Melody

ADVENT

Let All Mortal Flesh Keep Silence

Σιγησάτω πᾶσα σὰρξ βροτεία
Liturgy of St. James
Tr. Gerard Moultrie, 1829-1885

PICARDY 8.7.8.7.8.7.
Traditional French Carol

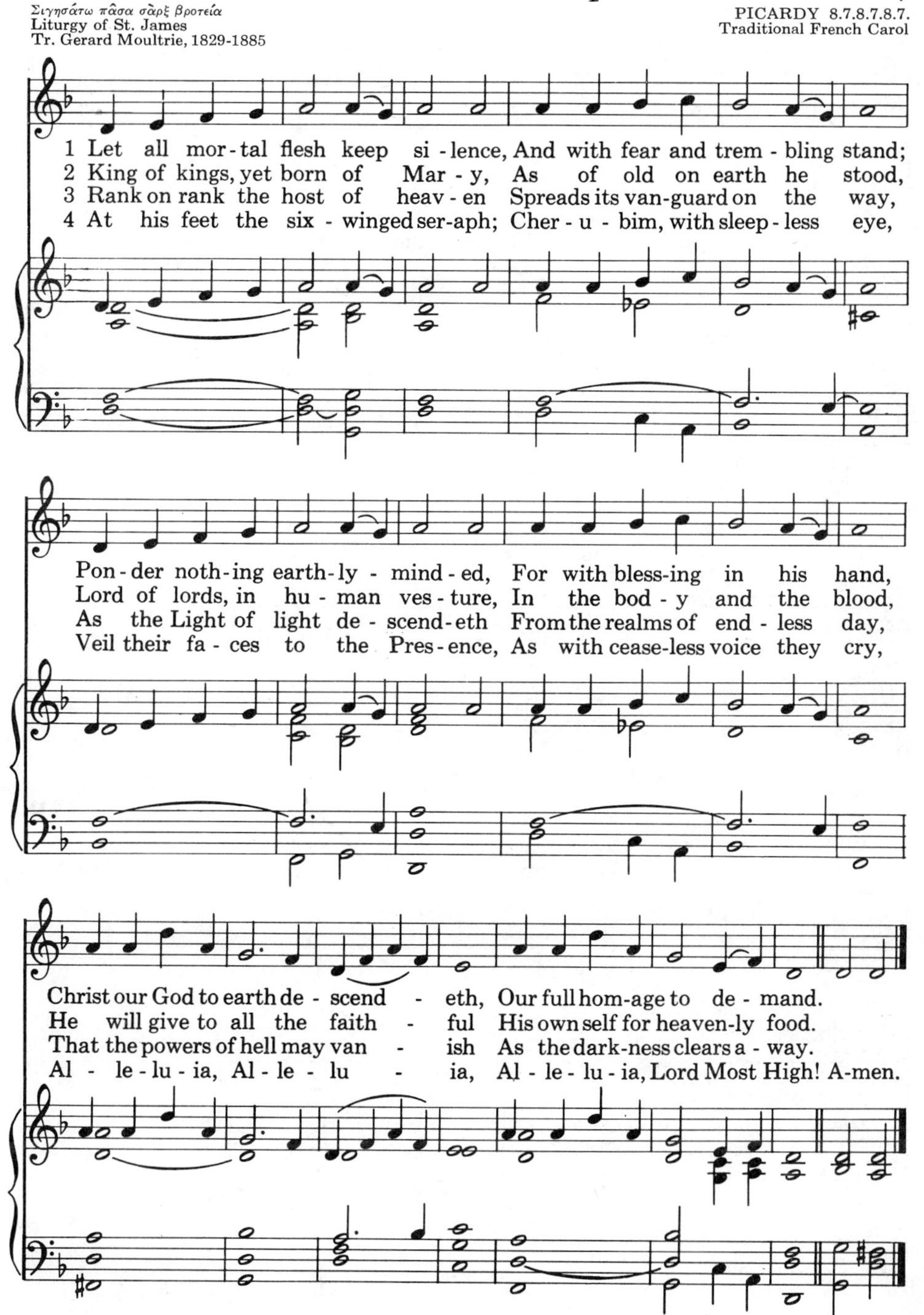

115 On Jordan's Bank the Baptist's Cry

Jordanis oras praeira
Charles Coffin, 1676-1749
Tr. Jonn Chandler, 1806-1876, alt.

ALSTONE L.M.
Christopher Edwin Willing, 1830-1904

ADVENT

Hark! a Thrilling Voice Is Sounding 116

117 The First Nowell

Traditional English Carol

THE FIRST NOWELL Irregular
Traditional English Melody

BIRTH

Silent Night, Holy Night 118

Stille Nacht, heilige Nacht
Joseph Mohr, 1792-1848
Tr. John F. Young, 1820-1865

STILLE NACHT Irregular
Franz Gruber, 1787-1863

1 Si - lent night, ho - ly night, All is calm, all is bright
2 Si - lent night, ho - ly night, Shep - herds quake at the sight,
3 Si - lent night, ho - ly night, Son of God, love's pure light
4 Si - lent night, ho - ly night, Won - drous star, lend thy light;

Round yon vir - gin moth - er and child, Ho - ly in - fant so ten - der and mild,
Glo - ries stream from heav - en a - far, Heaven - ly hosts sing al - le - lu - ia;
Ra - diant beams from thy ho - ly face, With the dawn of re - deem - ing grace,
With the an - gels let us sing, Al - le - lu - ia to our King;

Sleep in heav - en - ly peace, Sleep in heav - en - ly peace.
Christ, the Sav - ior, is born! Christ, the Sav - ior, is born!
Je - sus, Lord, at thy birth, Je - sus, Lord, at thy birth.
Christ, the Sav - ior, is born, Christ, the Sav - ior, is born.

BIRTH

119 It Came Upon the Midnight Clear

Edmund H. Sears, 1810-1876, alt.

CAROL C.M.D.
Richard S. Willis, 1819-1900

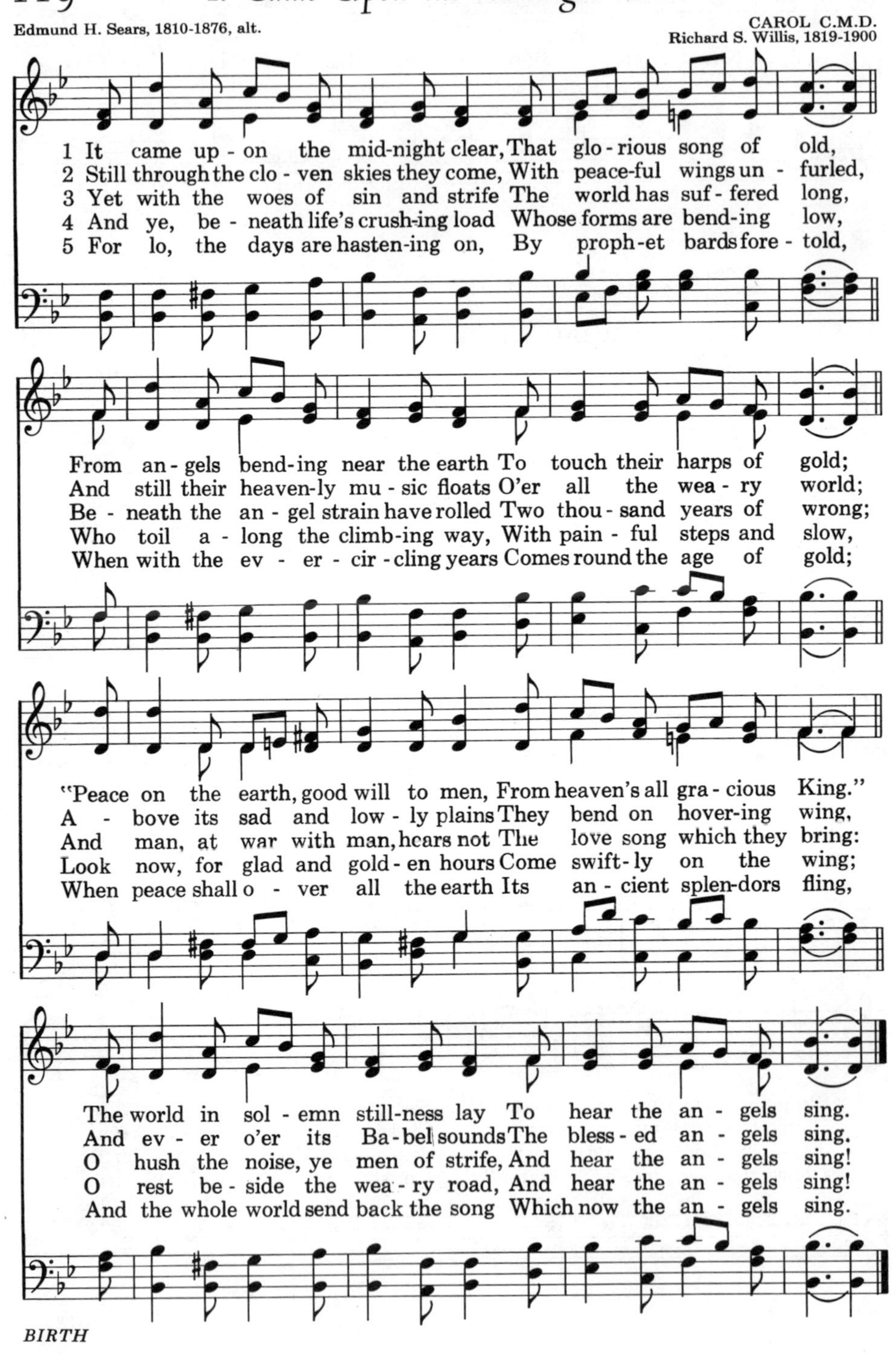

BIRTH

O Little Town of Bethlehem

121

O Come, All Ye Faithful

Adeste fideles
John Francis Wade?, *c.* 1711-1786
Tr. Frederick Oakeley, 1802-1880, and others

ADESTE FIDELES Irregular
John Francis Wade?, *c.* 1711-1786

BIRTH

Joy to the World! the Lord Is Come

Psalm 98
Isaac Watts, 1674-1748

ANTIOCH C.M.
Adapted from G. F. Handel, 1685-1759
Arr. Lowell Mason, 1792-1872

123 Hark! the Herald Angels Sing

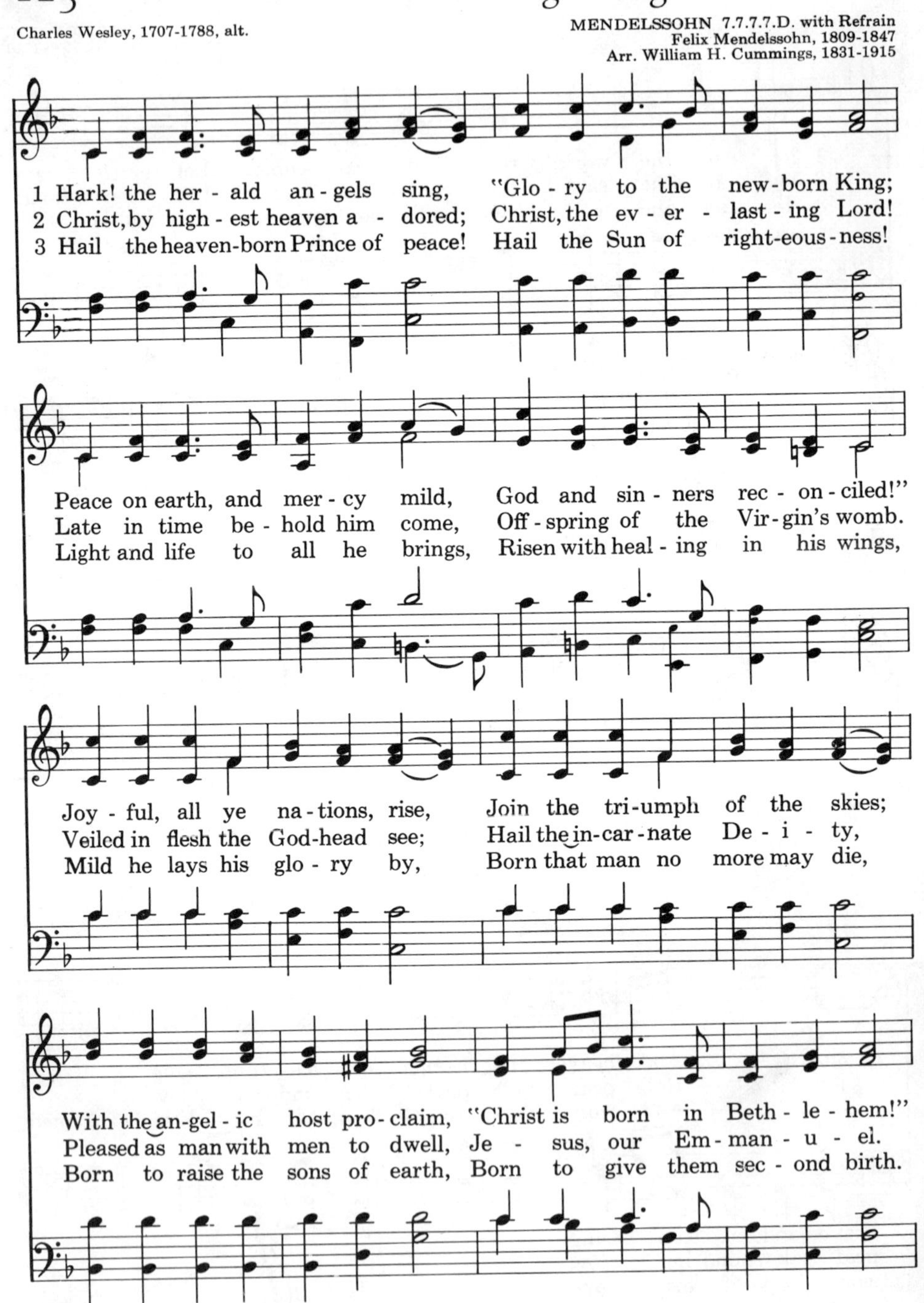

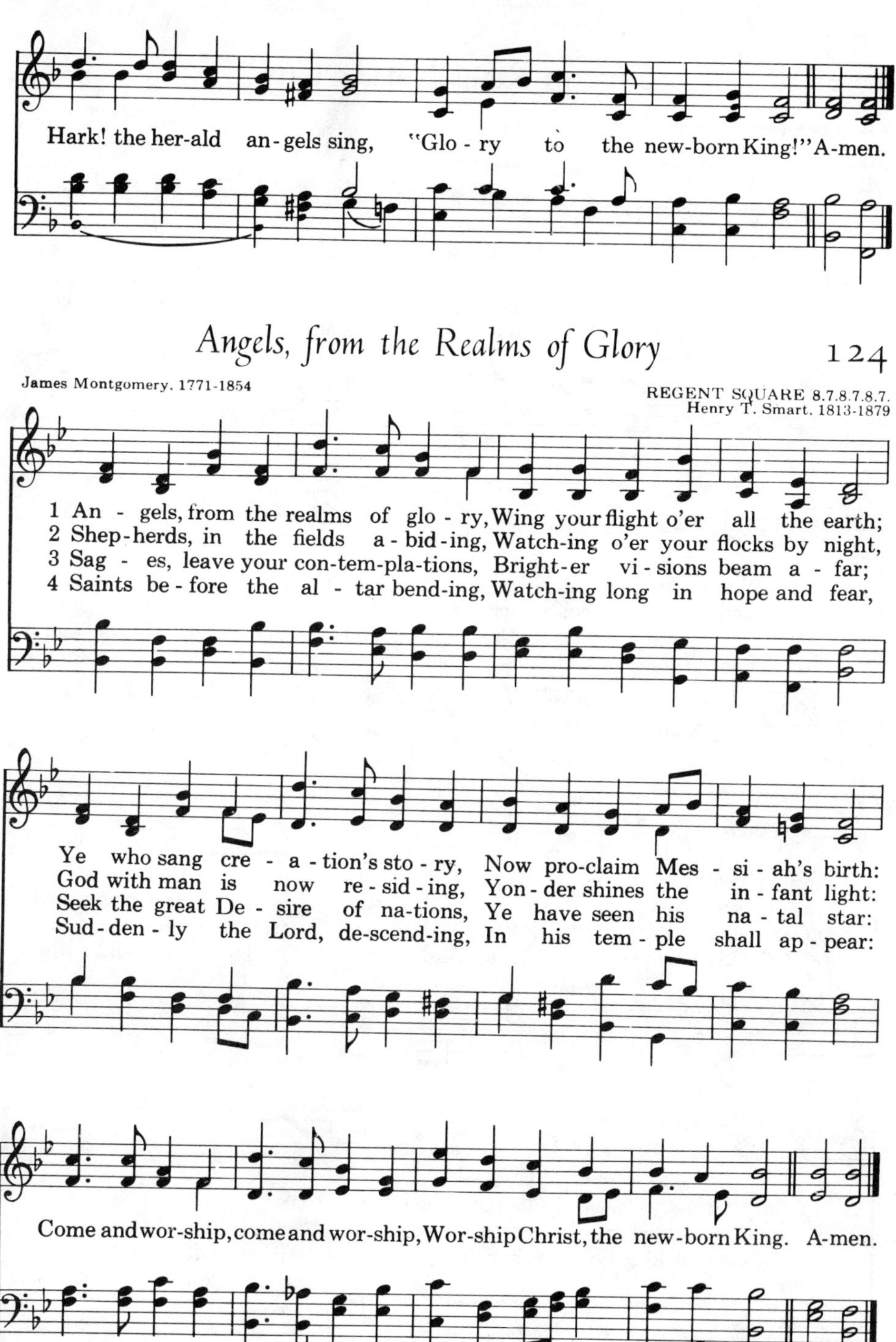
Hark! the her-ald an-gels sing, "Glo - ry to the new-born King!" A-men.
Angels, from the Realms of Glory
124
James Montgomery, 1771-1854
REGENT SQUARE 8.7.8.7.8.7.
Henry T. Smart, 1813-1879
1 An - gels, from the realms of glo - ry, Wing your flight o'er all the earth;
2 Shep-herds, in the fields a - bid - ing, Watch-ing o'er your flocks by night,
3 Sag - es, leave your con-tem-pla-tions, Bright-er vi - sions beam a - far;
4 Saints be - fore the al - tar bend-ing, Watch-ing long in hope and fear,
Ye who sang cre - a - tion's sto - ry, Now pro-claim Mes - si - ah's birth:
God with man is now re - sid - ing, Yon - der shines the in - fant light:
Seek the great De - sire of na-tions, Ye have seen his na - tal star:
Sud - den - ly the Lord, de-scend-ing, In his tem - ple shall ap - pear:
Come and wor-ship, come and wor-ship, Wor-ship Christ, the new-born King. A-men.

125 Once in Royal David's City

BIRTH

While Shepherds Watched Their Flocks

5 Thus spake the seraph, and forthwith
Appeared a shining throng
Of angels praising God, who thus
Addressed their joyful song:

6 "All glory be to God on high
And on the earth be peace;
Good will henceforth from heaven to men
Begin and never cease."

On This Day Earth Shall Ring

Piae Cantiones, 1582
Tr. Jane M. Joseph, *c.* 1894-1929

PERSONENT HODIE 6.6.6.6.6. with Refrain
Piae Cantiones, 1582
Arr. Gustav T. Holst, 1874-1934

1 On this day earth shall ring With the song children sing To the Lord, Christ our King, Born on earth to save us; Him the Father gave us.

2 His the doom, ours the mirth; When he came down to earth, Bethlehem saw his birth; Ox and ass beside him From the cold would hide him.

3 God's bright star, o'er his head, Wise men three to him led, Kneeling low by his bed, Lay their gifts before him, Praise him and adore him.

4 On this day angels sing; With their song earth shall ring, Praising Christ, heaven's King, Born on earth to save us. Peace and love he gave us.

REFRAIN

Id-e-o - o - o,

R.H. L.H.

BIRTH

Words and music used by permission of J. Curwen & Sons, Ltd.

Away in a Manger 128

Anonymous

CRADLE SONG 11.11.11.11.
W. J. Kirkpatrick, 1838-1921

1 A - way in a man-ger, no crib for a bed, The lit - tle Lord
2 The cat - tle are low-ing, the ba - by a - wakes, But lit - tle Lord

Je - sus laid down his sweet head. The stars in the bright sky looked
Je - sus, no cry - ing he makes. I love thee, Lord Je - sus, look

down where he lay, The lit - tle Lord Je - sus, a - sleep on the hay.
down from the sky, And stay by my cra - dle till morn-ing is nigh.

129 Angels We Have Heard on High

French carol
Version by Earl Marlatt, 1892-

GLORIA 7.7.7.7. with Refrain
French carol

1 Angels we have heard on high
Sweetly singing o'er the plains.
And the mountains in reply
Echoing their joyous strains.

2 Shepherds, why this jubilee?
Why these songs of happy cheer?
What great brightness did you see?
What glad tidings did you hear?

3 Come to Bethlehem and see
Him whose birth the angels sing;
Come, adore on bended knee,
Christ, the Lord, the newborn King.

Refrain:
Glo - - - - - - - ri - a in ex - cel - sis De - o. De - o.

BIRTH

Come Hither, Ye Children

131 Break Forth, O Beauteous Heavenly Light

St. 1, Johann Rist, 1607-1667
Tr. John Troutbeck, 1832-1899
St. 2 Arthur Tozer Russell, 1806-1874

ERMUNTRE DICH, MEIN SCHWACHER GEIST 8.7.8.7.8.8.7.7.
Johann Schop, c. 1590-1664
Harm. J. S. Bach, 1685-1750

BIRTH

From Heaven Above to Earth I Come 132

Vom Himmel Hoch
Martin Luther, 1483-1546
Tr. Catherine Winkworth, 1827-1878

VOM HIMMEL HOCH L.M.
Valentin Schumann's *Geistliche Leider*, 1539

1 From heaven a - bove to earth I come To bear good news to
2 To you this night is born a child Of Ma - ry, cho - sen
3 Ah, dear - est Je - sus, ho - ly Child, Make thee a bed, soft,
4 Glo - ry to God in high - est heaven, Who un - to man his

ev - ery home; Glad ti - dings of great joy I bring, Where-
moth - er mild; This lit - tle child, of low - ly birth, Shall
un - de - filed, With - in my heart, that it may be A
Son hath given, While an - gels sing with pi - ous mirth A

of I now will say and sing.
be the joy of all the earth.
qui - et cham - ber kept for thee.
glad new year to all the earth.

133 What Child Is This

William Chatterton Dix, 1837-1898

GREENSLEEVES 8.7.8.7. with Refrain
English Folk Song

BIRTH

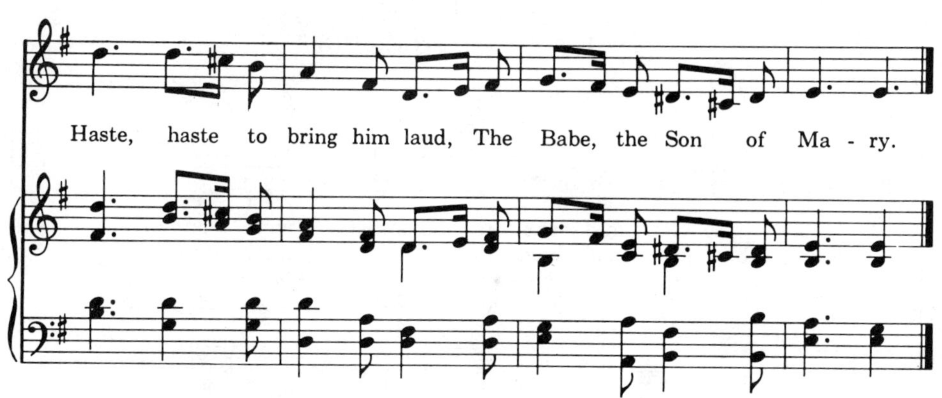

Love Came Down at Christmas 134

Christina G. Rossetti, 1830-1894

GARTAN 6.7.6.7.
Irish Traditional Air
Harm. David Evans, 1874-1948

1 Love came down at Christ-mas, Love all love - ly, Love di - vine;
Love was born at Christ - mas, Star and an - gels gave the sign.

2 Wor - ship we the God-head, Love in - car - nate, Love di - vine;
Wor - ship we our Je - sus: But where-with for sa - cred sign?

3 Love shall be our to - ken, Love be yours and love be mine,
Love to God and all men, Love for plea and gift and sign.

135 *In the Bleak Midwinter*

Christina G. Rossetti, 1830-1894, alt.

CRANHAM Irregular
Gustav T. Holst, 1874-1934

1 In the bleak mid - win - ter, Frost - y wind made moan,
2 Our God, heaven can - not hold him, Nor earth sus - tain;
3 An - gels and arch - an - gels May have gath - ered there,
4 What can I give him, Poor as I am?

Earth stood hard as i - ron, Wa - ter like a stone;
Heaven and earth shall flee a - way When he comes to reign;
Cher - u - bim and ser - a - phim Throng-ed the air;
If I were a shep - herd, I would bring a lamb;

Snow had fall - en, snow on snow, Snow on snow,
In the bleak mid - win - ter A sta - ble place suf - ficed The
But his moth - er on - ly, In her maid - en bliss,
If I were a wise man, I would do my part; Yet

In the bleak mid - win - ter, Long a - go.
Lord God al - might - y, Je - sus Christ.
Wor-shipped the be - lov - ed With a kiss.
what I can I give him — Give my heart.

BIRTH

Infant Holy, Infant Lowly

137 Good Christian Men, Rejoice

Latin, 14th century
Tr. John Mason Neale, 1818-1866

IN DULCI JUBILO 6.6.7.7.7.8.5.5.
14th Century Melody

BIRTH

Let All Together Praise Our God

Lobt Gott, ihr Christen allzugleich
Nikolaus Herman, *c.* 1485-1561
Tr. Arthur Tozer Russell, 1806-1874

LOBT GOTT, IHR CHRISTEN C.M.
Nikolaus Herman, *c.* 1485-1561
Harm. J. S. Bach, 1685-1750

BIRTH

139 Of the Father's Love Begotten

Corde natus ex Parentis
Aurelius Prudentius Clemens, 348-*c.* 413
Tr. John Mason Neale, 1818-1866
and Henry W. Baker, 1821-1877

DIVINUM MYSTERIUM 8.7.8.7.8.7.7.
13th century plainsong Mode V
Harm. Winfred Douglas, 1867-1944

1 Of the Fa-ther's love be - got - ten, Ere the worlds be - gan to be,
2 O ye heights of heaven a - dore him; An - gel hosts, his prais - es sing;
3 Christ, to thee with God the Fa - ther, And, O Ho - ly Ghost, to thee,

He is Al-pha and O - me - ga, He the source, the end - ing he;
Powers, do-min-ions, bow be - fore him, And ex - tol our God and King;
Hymn and chant and high thanks-giv - ing, And un - wea - ried prais - es be:

Of the things that are, that have been, And that
Let no tongue on earth be si - lent, Ev - ery
Hon - or, glo - ry, and do - min - ion, And e -

fu - ture years shall see, Ev - er-more and ev - er - more!
voice in con-cert ring, Ev - er-more and ev - er - more!
ter - nal vic - to - ry, Ev - er-more and ev - er - more! A - men.
Earth Has Many a Noble City
140
Aurelius Prudentius Clemens, 348-c.413
Tr. Edward Caswall, 1814-1878
LIEBEN IST MEIN LEBEN 8.7.8.7.
Heil und Hülfsmittel, Dresden, 1767
1 Earth has man - y a no - ble cit - y; Beth - lehem thou dost
2 Fair - er than the sun at morn - ing Was the star that
3 East - ern sag - es at his cra - dle Make o - bla - tions
4 Sa - cred gifts of mys - tic mean - ing: In - cense doth their
5 Je - sus, whom the Gen - tiles wor - shiped At thy glad E -
all ex - cel: Out of thee the Lord from heav - en
told his birth, To the world its God an - nounc - ing
rich and rare; See them give, in deep de - vo - tion,
God dis - close, Gold the King of kings pro - claim - eth,
pi - phan - y, Un - to thee, with God the Fa - ther
Came to rule his Is - ra - el.
Seen in flesh - ly form on earth.
Gold and frank - in - cense, and myrrh.
Myrrh his sep - ul - chre fore - shows.
And the Spir - it, glo - ry be. A - men.

141 As with Gladness Men of Old

William C. Dix, 1837-1898, alt.

DIX 7.7.7.7.7.7.
Abridged from a chorale by Conrad Kocher, 1786-1872

EPIPHANY

What Star Is This, with Beams So Bright

Charles Coffin, 1676-1749
Tr. John Chandler, 1806-1876, alt.

PUER NOBIS NASCITUR L.M.
Adapt. Michael Praetorius, 1571-1621
Harm. George R. Woodward, 1848-1934

Our Faith Is in the Christ Who Walks

Thomas Curtis Clark, 1877-1953

WAREHAM L.M.
William Knapp, 1698?-1768

1 Our faith is in the Christ who walks
2 His gos - pel calls for liv - ing men,
3 We serve no God whose work is done,
4 God was and is and e'er shall be;

With men to - day, in street and mart;
With sing - ing blood and minds a - lert;
Who rests with - in his firm - a - ment;
Christ lived and loved and loves us still;

The con - stant Friend who thinks and talks
Strong men, who fall to rise a - gain,
Our God, his la - bor but be - gun,
And man goes for - ward, proud and free,

With those who seek him with the heart.
Who strive and bleed, with cour - age girt.
Toils ev - er - more, with power un - spent.
God's pres - ent pur - pose to ful - fill. A - men.

Jesus, Friend of Thronging Pilgrims

W. Nantlais Williams, 1874-1959

REGENT SQUARE 8.7.8.7.8.7.
Henry T. Smart, 1813-1879

1 Jesus, Friend of thronging pilgrims,
As of those who walk alone,
Look upon our crowded cities
With compassion from thy throne;
Loving Shepherd, Loving Shepherd,
Move among us as thine own.

2 Thou didst know the market places
And the streets in days of yore;
Thou could'st see beneath the pleasures
Broken hearts and spirits sore;
Gracious Healer, Gracious Healer,
How we need thy touch once more!

3 Send thy servants to the highways
Where are heard the doleful cries;
Call again the hungry masses
To the feast that satisfies;
For the supper, For the supper
Now is spread before their eyes.

4 By thy power be streets transfigured,
Haunts of sin be purified;
Rich and poor be found in concord,
Zion's courts their hope and pride;
Lord of cities, Lord of cities,
Here make healing peace abide. Amen.

145 Lord, Whose Love Through Humble Service

Albert F. Bayly, 1901-

IN BABILONE 8.7.8.7.D.
Oude en Nieuwe Hollantse Boerenlities, c. 1710

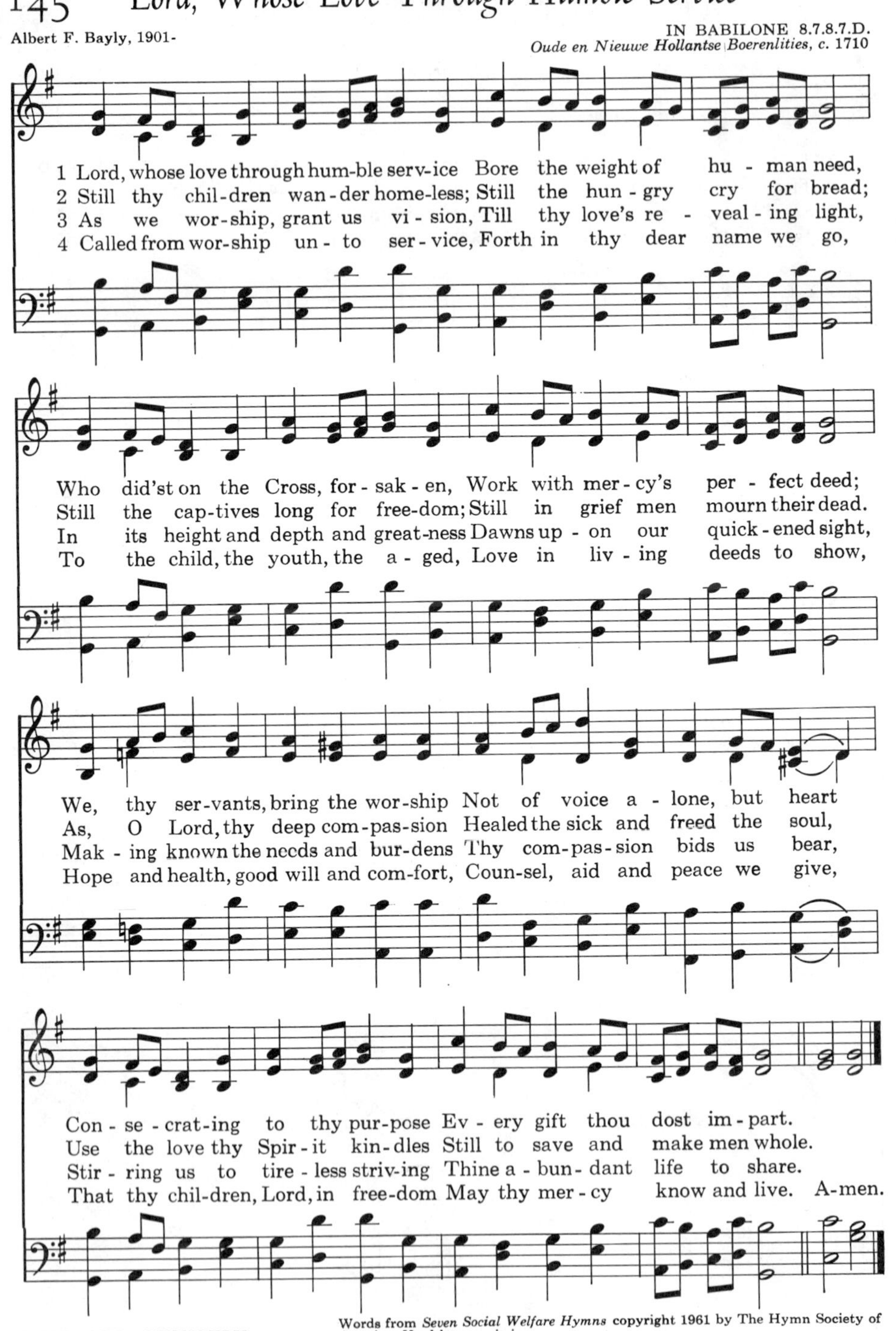

LIFE AND MINISTRY

O Love, How Deep, How Broad, How High
146
O amor quam ecstaticus
Latin, 15th century
Tr. Benjamin Webb, 1819-1885, alt.
DEO GRACIAS L.M.
Arr. for The Hymnal 1933
1 O love, how deep, how broad, how high, How pass - ing
2 For us bap - tized, for us he bore His ho - ly
3 For us he prayed, for us he taught, For us his
4 For us to wick - ed men be - trayed, Scourged, mocked, in
5 For us he rose from death a - gain, For us he
thought and fan - ta - sy, That God, the Son of God, should
fast, and hun-gered sore; For us temp - ta - tions sharp he
dai - ly works he wrought, By words and signs and ac - tions,
pur - ple robe ar - rayed, He bore the shame - ful cross and
went on high to reign; For us he sent his Spir - it
take Our mor - tal form for mor - tals' sake.
knew; For us the temp - ter o - ver - threw.
thus Still seek - ing not him - self, but us.
death; For us gave up his dy - ing breath.
here To guide, to strength - en, and to cheer. A - men.

147 O Son of Man, Our Hero Strong and Tender

Frank Fletcher, 1870-1954

CHARTERHOUSE 11.10.11.10.
David Evans, 1874-1948

Words by permission of Oxford University Press. Music from *The Revised Church Hymnary* by permission of Oxford University Press.

Jesus, with Thy Church Abide 148

Thomas B. Pollock, 1836-1896

ST. KATRINE 7.7.7.6.
J. Williamson, 1868-1947

1 Je - sus, with thy church a - bide; Be her Sav - ior, Lord, and guide,
2 May her voice be ev - er clear, Warn-ing of a judg-ment near,
3 May her lamp of truth be bright; Bid her bear a - loft its light
4 Judge her not for work un - done, Judge her not for fields un - won,

While on earth her faith is tried: We be - seech thee, hear us.
Tell - ing of a Sav - ior dear: We be - seech thee, hear us.
Through the realms of pa - gan night: We be - seech thee, hear us.
Bless her works in thee be - gun: We be - seech thee, hear us. A-men.

149 The Son of God, Our Christ

Edward M. Blumenfeld, 1927-

TOULON 10.10.10.10.
Abridged from *Genevan Psalter*, 1551

Thou Didst Leave Thy Throne 150

Emily E. S. Elliott, 1836-1897, alt.

MARGARET Irregular
Timothy R. Matthews, 1826-1910

1 Thou didst leave thy throne and thy king - ly crown When thou
2 Heav - en's arch - es rang when the an - gels sang, Pro -
3 Thou didst come, O Lord, with the liv - ing word That should
4 When the heavens shall ring and the an - gels sing At thy

cam - est to earth for me, But in Beth - le - hem's home there was
claim - ing thy roy - al de - gree, But in low - ly birth didst thou
set thy peo - ple free, But with mock - ing scorn and with
com - ing to vic - to - ry, Let thy voice call me home, say - ing,

found no room For thy ho - ly na - tiv - i - ty. O
come to earth, And in great hu - mil - i - ty. O
crown of thorn They bore thee to Cal - va - ry. O
"Yet there is room, There is room at my side for thee." And my

come to my heart, Lord Je - sus; There is room in my heart for thee!
come to my heart, Lord Je - sus; There is room in my heart for thee!
come to my heart, Lord Je - sus; There is room in my heart for thee!
heart shall re - joice, Lord Je - sus; When thou com - est and call - est me. A - men.

151 Take Up Thy Cross

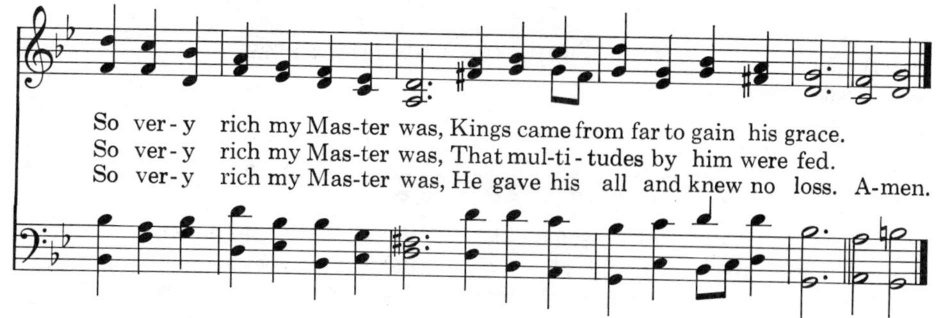

Most Wondrous Is of All on Earth 153

N. F. S. Grundtvig, 1783-1872
Tr. Jean Fraser, 1951

8.7.8.7.
Danish Folk Song

1 Most won-drous is of all on earth The king-dom Je-sus found-ed, Its glo-ry, peace and pre-cious worth No tongue has ev-er sound-ed.

2 As breath of wind in-vis-i-ble, Its signs are yet re-vealed: A cit-y set up-on a hill From men is not con-ceal-ed.

3 Its se-cret: God's al-might-y word Which heaven and earth cre-a-ted, The val-leys when his voice they heard Were filled, the floods a-bat-ed.

4 The tempt-er by his e-vil power The king-dom is dis-tress-ing. God crowns in his ap-point-ed hour With joy and fruit-ful bless-ing.

5 Its glo-rious King is he who died Up-on the Cross to save us, New joy un-to the world to bring His ver-y life he gave us. A-men.

154 Draw Nigh to Thy Jerusalem

Jeremy Taylor, 1613-1667, alt.

FARLEY CASTLE 10.10.10.10.
Henry Lawes, 1596-1662

TRIUMPHAL ENTRY

Music from *Hymnal for Colleges and Schools*, edited by E. Harold Geer. Used by permission of Yale University Press.

All Glory, Laud, and Honor

Gloria, laus, et honor
Theodulph of Orleans, *c.* 760-*c.* 821
Tr. John M, Neale, 1818-1866

ST. THEODULPH 7.6.7.6.D.
Melchior Teschner, 1584-1635

Ride On, Ride On in Majesty!

Henry H. Milman, 1791-1878, alt.

THE KING'S MAJESTY L.M.
Graham George, 1912-

1 Ride on, ride on in majesty! Hark! all the tribes hosanna cry; Thy humble beast pursues his road With palms and scattered garments strowed.

2 Ride on, ride on in majesty! In lowly pomp ride on to die; O Christ, thy triumphs now begin O'er captive death and conquered sin.

3 Ride on, ride on in majesty! The winged squadrons of the sky Look down with sad and wondering eyes To see the approaching sacrifice.

4 Ride on, ride on in majesty! Thy last and fiercest strife is nigh; Bow thy meek head to mortal pain, Then take, O Christ, thy power, and reign. Amen.

TRIUMPHAL ENTRY

What Wondrous Love Is This

American Folk Hymn

WONDROUS LOVE 12.9.12.9
Southern Harmony, 1835
Arr. Paul Christiansen, 1914-

Into the Woods My Master Went

Sidney Lanier, 1842-1881

RIDGEFIELD Irregular
Harold W. Friedell, 1905-1958

1 In - to the woods my Mas - ter went, Clean for - spent,
2 Out of the woods my Mas - ter went, And he was well con-

for - spent, In - to the woods my Mas - ter came, For -
tent, con - tent, Out of the woods my Mas - ter came, Con -

spent with love and shame. But the o - lives they were not
tent with death and shame. When death and shame would

PASSION

Music from *New Songs for the Junior Choir* by permission of Concordia Publishing House.

159 *Beneath the Cross of Jesus*

Elizabeth C. Clephane, 1830-1869

ST. CHRISTOPHER 7.6.8.6.8.6.8.6.
Frederick C. Maker, 1844-1927

1 Be-neath the cross of Je - sus I fain would take my stand,
2 Up - on that cross of Je - sus Mine eye at times can see
3 I take, O cross, thy shad - ow For my a - bid - ing place;

The shad - ow of a might - y rock With - in a wea - ry land;
The ver - y dy - ing form of one Who suf - fered there for me;
I ask no oth - er sun - shine than The sun - shine of his face;

A home with - in the wild - er - ness, A rest up - on the way,
And from my smit - ten heart with tears Two won - ders I con - fess—
Con - tent to let the world go by, To know no gain nor loss,

From the burn - ing of the noon - tide heat, And the bur - den of the day.
The won - ders of his glo - rious love And my un - wor - thi - ness.
My sin - ful self my on - ly shame, My glo - ry all the cross. A - men.

Before the Cross of Jesus

Ferdinand Q. Blanchard, 1876-

ST. CHRISTOPHER 7.6.8.6.7.6.8.6.
Frederick C. Maker, 1844-1927

161 Were You There When They Crucified My Lord?

Anonymous

WERE YOU THERE Irregular
Negro Spiritual

trem - ble. Were you there when they cru - ci - fied my Lord?
trem - ble. Were you there when they nailed him to the tree?
trem - ble. Were you there when they laid him in the tomb?
Ah, Holy Jesus, How Hast Thou Offended
162
Herzliebster Jesu, was hast du verbrochen?
Johann Heerman, 1585-1647
Tr. Robert S. Bridges, 1844-1930
HERZLIEBSTER JESU 11.11.11.5.
Johann Crüger, 1598-1662
1 Ah, ho - ly Je - sus, how hast thou of - fend - ed,
2 Who was the guilt - y? Who brought this up - on thee?
3 For me, kind Je - sus, was thy in - car - na - tion,
4 There - fore, kind Je - sus, since I can - not pay thee,
That man to judge thee hath in hate pre - tend - ed? By foes de -
A - las, my trea - son, Je - sus, hath un - done thee! 'Twas I, Lord
Thy mor - tal sor - row, and thy life's ob - la - tion; Thy death of
I do a - dore thee, and will ev - er pray thee, Think on thy
rid - ed, by thine own re - ject - ed, O most af - flict - ed!
Je - sus, I it was de - nied thee; I cru - ci - fied thee.
an - guish and thy bit - ter pas - sion, For my sal - va - tion.
pit - y and thy love un - swerv - ing, Not my de - serv - ing. A-men.
Words from The Yattendon Hymnal by permission of Oxford University Press.
PASSION

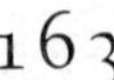

O Sacred Head, Now Wounded

Based on Latin attributed to Bernard of Clairvaux, 1091-1153
German version Paul Gerhardt, 1607-1676
Tr. James Waddell Alexander, 1804-1859

PASSION CHORALE 7.6.7.6.D.
Hans Leo Hassler, 1564-1612
Harm. J. S. Bach, 1685-1750

1 O sa-cred Head, now wound-ed, With grief and shame weighed down;
2 What thou, my Lord, hast suf - fered Was all for sin-ners' gain:
3 What lan-guage shall I bor - row To thank thee, dear-est Friend,

Now scorn-ful-ly sur-round-ed With thorns, thine on-ly crown;
Mine, mine was the trans-gres-sion, But thine the dead-ly pain.
For this thy dy-ing sor-row, Thy pit-y with-out end?

O sa-cred Head, what glo - ry, What bliss till now was thine!
Lo, here I fall, my Sav - ior! 'Tis I de-serve thy place;
O make me thine for-ev - er; And should I faint-ing be,

Yet, though de-spised and gor - y, I joy to call thee mine.
Look on me with thy fa - vor, Vouch-safe to me thy grace.
Lord, let me nev-er, nev - er Out-live my love to thee. A-men.

Near the Cross Her Vigil Keeping

From the Latin, 13th century
Tr. Louis Fitzgerald Benson, 1855-1930

STABAT MATER 8.8.7.8.8.7.
Mechlin Plainsong, Mode IV

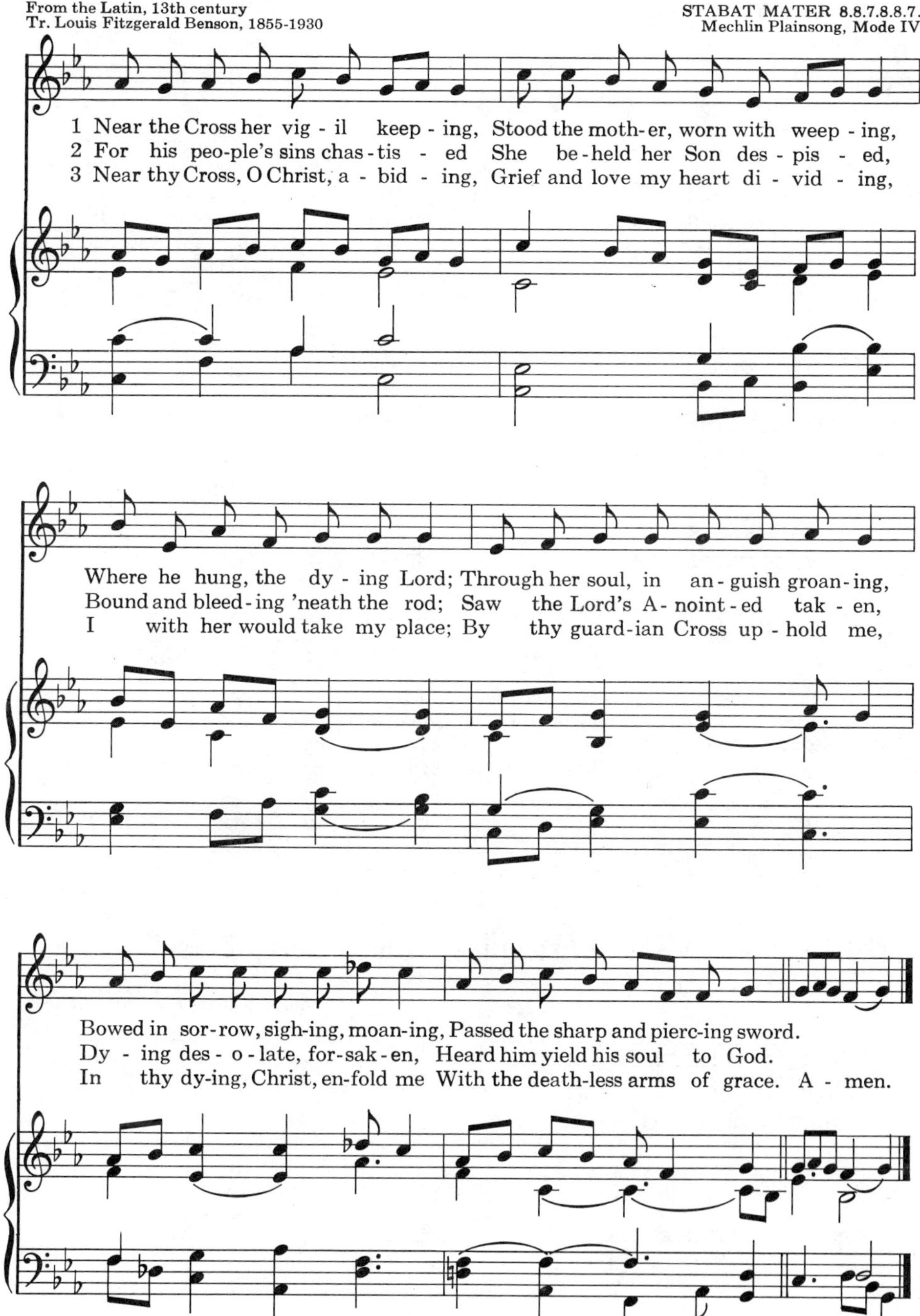

165 'Tis Midnight, and on Olive's Brow

William B. Tappan, 1794-1849, alt.

OLIVE'S BROW L.M.
William B. Bradbury, 1816-1868

1 'Tis mid - night, and on Ol - ive's brow The
2 'Tis mid - night, and, from all re - moved, The
3 'Tis mid - night, and, for oth - ers' guilt, The
4 'Tis mid - night, and from heaven - ly plains Is

star is dimmed that late - ly shone; 'Tis mid-night, in the
Sav - ior wres - tles lone with fears; E'en that dis - ci - ple
Man of Sor - rows weeps in blood; Yet he that hath in
borne the song that an - gels know; Un - heard by mor - tals

gar - den now The suf-fering Sav - ior prays a - lone.
whom he loved Heeds not his Mas-ter's grief and tears.
an - guish knelt Is not for - sak - en by his God.
are the strains That sweet-ly soothe the Sav - ior's woe. A-men.

166 Lord, Who Throughout These Forty Days

Claudia F. Hernaman, 1838-1898

ST. FLAVIAN C.M.
Adapt. from the *English Psalter*, 1562

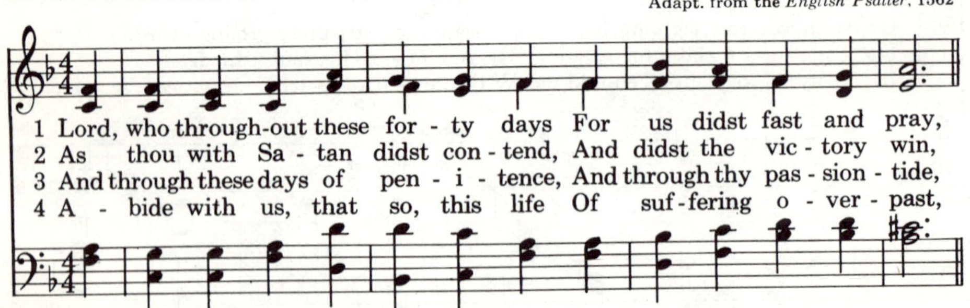

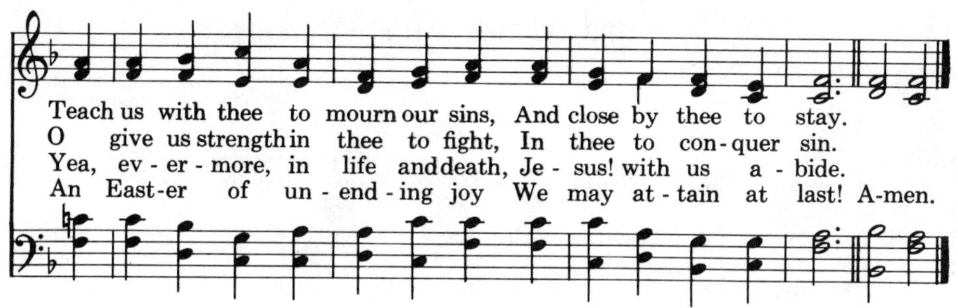

Throned Upon the Awful Tree 167

John Ellerton, 1826-1893, alt.

ARFON 7.7.7.7.7.7.
Welsh Hymn Melody

1 Throned up - on the aw - ful tree, King of grief, I watch with thee.
2 Si - lent through those three dread hours, Wres-tling with the e - vil powers,
3 Hark, that cry that peals a - loud Up-ward through the whelm-ing cloud!
4 Lord, should fear and an-guish roll Dark - ly o'er my sin - ful soul,

Dark - ness veils thine an-guished face; None its lines of woe can trace;
Left a - lone with hu - man sin, Gloom a - round thee and with - in,
Thou, the Fa-ther's on - ly Son, Thou, his own a - noint-ed one,
Thou, who once wast thus be - reft That thine own might ne'er be left,

None can tell what pangs un-known Hold thee si - lent and a - lone.
Till the ap-point-ed time is nigh, Till the Lamb of God may die.
Thou dost ask him can it be? "Why hast thou for - sak - en me?"
Teach me by that bit - ter cry In the gloom to know thee nigh. A-men.

168 O Come and Mourn with Me Awhile

Frederick William Faber, 1814-1863

COUTANCES L.M.
French Church Melody,
from the *Rouen Antiphoner*, 1728

169 Alone Thou Goest Forth, O Lord

Solus ad victimam procedis, Domine
Peter Abelard, 1079-1142
Tr. F. Bland Tucker, 1895-

BANGOR C.M.
William Tans'ur, 1706-1783

1 A - lone thou go - est forth, O Lord, In sac - ri - fice to die;
2 Our sins, not thine, thou bear - est, Lord, Make us thy sor - row feel,
3 This is earth's dark-est hour, but thou Dost light and life re - store;
4 Give us com - pas - sion for thee,Lord,That, as we share this hour,

Is this thy sor - row naught to us Who pass un - heed - ing by?
Till through our pit - y and our shame Love an - swers love's ap - peal.
Then let all praise be giv - en thee Who liv - est ev - er - more.
Thy cross may bring us to thy joy And res - ur - rec - tion power. A-men.
Words by permission of The Church Pension Fund.
Go to Dark Gethsemane
170
James Montgomery, 1771-1854
ARFON 7.7.7.7.7.7.
Welsh Hymn Melody
1 Go to dark Geth - se - ma - ne, Ye that feel the temp - ter's pow'r;
2 Fol - low to the judg-ment hall; View the Lord of life ar - raigned.
3 Cal - v'ry's mourn-ful moun-tain climb; There, a - dor - ing at his feet
Your Re - deem - er's con - flict see, Watch with him one bit - ter hour:
O the worm-wood and the gall! O the pangs his soul sus - tained!
Mark that mir - a - cle of time, God's own sac - ri - fice com - plete:
Turn not from his griefs a - way; Learn of Je - sus Christ to pray.
Shun not suf - f'ring, shame or loss; Learn of him to bear the cross.
"It is fin - ished!" hear him cry; Learn of Je - sus Christ to die. A-men.

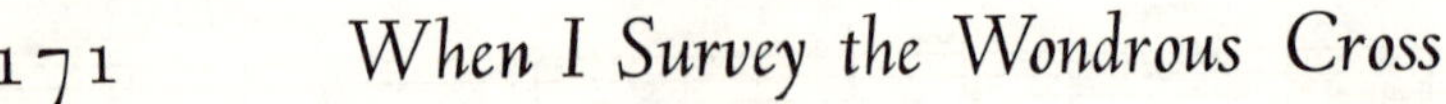

Isaac Watts, 1674-1748

HAMBURG L.M.
Arr. Lowell Mason, 1792-1872

1 When I survey the wondrous cross
On which the Prince of glory died,
My richest gain I count but loss,
And pour contempt on all my pride.

2 Forbid it, Lord, that I should boast,
Save in the death of Christ, my God;
All the vain things that charm me most
I sacrifice them to his blood.

3 See, from his head, his hands, his feet,
Sorrow and love flow mingled down!
Did e'er such love and sorrow meet,
Or thorns compose so rich a crown? A-men.

4 Were the whole realm of nature mine,
That were a present far too small;
Love so amazing, so divine,
Demands my soul, my life, my all.

PASSION

Deep Were His Wounds

William Johnson, 1906-

MARLEE 6.6.6.6.8.8.
Leland B. Sateren, 1913-

1 Deep were his wounds, and red, On cru - el Cal - va - ry,
2 He suf-fered shame and scorn, And wretch-ed, dire dis - grace;
3 His life, his all, he gave When he was cru - ci - fied;

As on the Cross he bled In bit - ter ag - o - ny; But they, whom
For-sak-en and for-lorn, He hung there in our place. But such as
Our burd-ened souls to save, What fear - ful death he died! But each of

sin has wound - ed sore, Find heal-ing in the wounds he bore.
would from sin be free Look to his Cross for vic - to - ry.
us, though dead in sin, Through him e-ter - nal life may win. A-men.

PASSION

173 *Come, Ye Faithful, Raise the Strain*

Attr. to John of Damascus, *c.* 696-*c.* 754
Tr. John M. Neale, 1818-1866, alt.

ST. KEVIN 7.6.7.6.D.
Arthur S. Sullivan, 1842-1900

1 Come, ye faith-ful, raise the strain Of tri-umph-ant glad-ness;
God hath brought his peo-ple forth In-to joy from sad-ness;
Now re-joice, Je-ru-sa-lem, And with true af-fec-tion
Wel-come in un-wea-ried strains Je-sus' res-ur-rec-tion.

2 'Tis the spring of souls to-day; Christ hath burst his pris-on,
And from three days' sleep in death As a sun hath ris-en;
All the win-ter of our sins, Long and dark, is fly-ing
From his light, to whom we give Laud and praise un-dy-ing.

3 Now the queen of sea-sons, bright With the day of splen-dor,
With the roy-al feast of feasts, Comes its joy to ren-der;
Comes to glad Je-ru-sa-lem Who with true af-fec-tion
Wel-comes in un-wea-ried strains Je-sus' res-ur-rec-tion. A-men.

RESURRECTION

Jesus Christ Is Risen Today

174

St. 1: *Surrexit Christus hodie*, 14th century
Tr. in *Lyra Davidica*, 1708
Sts. 2,3: J. Arnold's *Compleat Psalmist*, 1750, alt.
St. 4: Charles Wesley, 1707-1788

LLANFAIR 7.7.7.7. with Alleluias
Robert Williams, *c.* 1781-1821
Harm. John Roberts, 1822-1877

RESURRECTION

175 Alleluia! Alleluia! Hearts to Heaven and Voices Raise

Christopher Wordsworth, 1807-1885

IN BABILONE 8.7.8.7.D.
Oude en Nieuwe Hollantse Boerenlities, c. 1710

RESURRECTION

Je - sus Christ, the King of glo - ry, Now is ris - en from the dead.
We with him to life e - ter - nal By his re - sur - rec - tion rise.
Al - le - lu - ia! Al - le - lu - ia! To the Tri - une Maj - es - ty. A-men.
Christ the Lord Is Risen Again
176
Christ ist erstanden
Michael Weisse, c. 1488-1534
Tr. Catherine Winkworth, 1827-1878
CHRIST IST ERSTANDEN 7.7.7.7.4.
Germany, 12th century
1 Christ the Lord is risen a - gain, Christ hath bro - ken ev - ery chain,
2 He who bore all pain and loss Com - fort - less up - on the cross,
3 He who slum-bered in the grave Is ex - alt - ed now to save;
Hark, the an - gels shout for joy, Sing - ing ev - er - more on high:
Lives in glo - ry now on high, Pleads for us and hears our cry:
Now through Chris-ten-dom it rings That the Lamb is King of kings:
Al - le - lu - ia! A - men.
RESURRECTION

177 Christ Jesus Lay in Death's Strong Bands

Christ lag in Todesbanden
Martin Luther, 1483-1546
Tr. Richard Massie, 1800-1887

CHRIST LAG IN TODESBANDEN 8.7.8.7.7.8.7.4.
Johann Walther's *Geystliche gesangk Buchleyn*, 1524
Harm. Hans Leo Hassler, 1564-1612

RESURRECTION

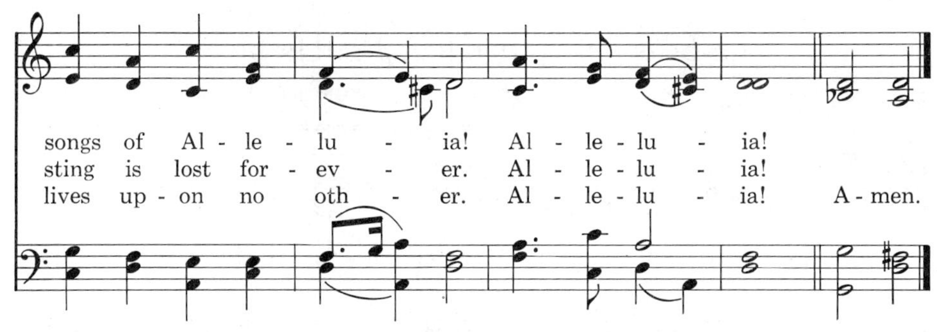

Good Christian Men Rejoice and Sing! 178

Cyril A. Alington, 1872-1955

GELOBT SEI GOTT 8.8.8. with Alleluias
Melody by Melchior Vulpius, *c.* 1560-1616

1 Good Chris - tian men re - joice and sing! Now is the
2 The Lord of life is risen for aye; Bring flowers of
3 Praise we in songs of vic - to - ry That love, that
4 Thy name we bless, O ris - en Lord, And sing to -

tri - umph of our King! To all the world glad
song to strew his way; Let all man - kind re -
life which can - not die, And sing with hearts up -
day with one ac cord The life laid down, the

news we bring:
joice and say:
lift - ed high:
life re - stored:
Al - le - lu - ia! Al - le - lu - ia! Al - le - lu - ia!

179 O Sons and Daughters, Let Us Sing

Jean Tisserand, d. 1494
Tr. John M. Neale, 1818-1866, alt.

O FILII ET FILIAE 8.8.8. with Alleluias
French: 15th century?
Airs sur les hymnes sacres, odes et noels, 1623; adapted

RESURRECTION

Christ the Lord Is Risen Today

Charles Wesley, 1707-1788, and others

EASTER HYMN 7.7.7.7. with Alleluias
From *Lyra Davidica*, 1708

1 Christ the Lord is risen to - day, Al - - - - le - lu - ia!
Sons of men and an - gels say, Al - - - - le - lu - ia!
Raise your joys and tri-umphs high, Al - - - - le - lu - ia!
Sing, ye heavens, and earth re - ply, Al - - - - le - lu - ia!

2 Lives a - gain our glo - rious King, Al - - - - le - lu - ia!
Where, O death, is now thy sting? Al - - - - le - lu - ia!
Once he died, our souls to save, Al - - - - le - lu - ia!
Where thy vic - to - ry, O grave? Al - - - - le - lu - ia!

3 Love's re - deem - ing work is done, Al - - - - le - lu - ia!
Fought the fight, the bat - tle won, Al - - - - le - lu - ia!
Death in vain for - bids him rise, Al - - - - le - lu - ia!
Christ hath o - pened Par - a - dise, Al - - - - le - lu - ia!

4 Soar we now where Christ has led, Al - - - - le - lu - ia!
Fol - lowing our ex - alt - ed Head, Al - - - - le - lu - ia!
Made like him, like him we rise, Al - - - - le - lu - ia!
Ours the cross, the grave, the skies, Al - - - - le - lu - ia!

181

Thine Is the Glory

Edmond L. Budry, 1854-1932
Tr. R. Birch Hoyle, 1875-1939

MACCABEUS 5.5.6.5.6.5.6.5. with Refrain
George Frederick Handel, 1685-1759

1 Thine is the glo - ry, Ris - en, con - quering Son,
End - less is the vic - tory Thou o'er death hast won.
An - gels in bright rai - ment Rolled the stone a - way,
Kept the fold - ed grave-clothes Where thy bod - y lay.

2 Lo! Je - sus meets thee, Ris - en from the tomb;
Lov - ing - ly he greets thee, Scat - ters fear and gloom;
Let his church with glad - ness Hymns of tri - umph sing,
For her Lord now liv - eth; Death hath lost its sting.

3 No more we doubt thee, Glo - rious Prince of life!
Life is nought with - out thee; Aid us in our strife;
Make us more than con - querors, Through thy death - less love.
Bring us safe through Jor - dan To thy home a - bove.

The Strife Is O'er 182

Finita iam sunt praelia
Latin 17th century
Tr. Francis Pott, 1832-1908, alt.

VICTORY 8.8.8. with Alleluia
Arr. from G. P. da Palestrina, 1525-1594
William H. Monk, 1823-1889

1 The strife is o'er, the bat - tle done; The vic - to - ry of life is won; The song of tri - umph has be - gun: Al - le - lu - ia!

2 The powers of death have done their worst, But Christ their le - gions hath dis-persed; Let shouts of ho - ly joy out - burst: Al - le - lu - ia!

3 The three sad days are quick - ly sped, He ris - es glo - rious from the dead; All glo - ry to our ris - en Head! Al - le - lu - ia!

4 Lord, by the stripes which wound-ed thee, From death's dread sting thy serv-ants free, That we may live and sing to thee: Al - le - lu - ia!

The Day of Resurrection

'Αναστάσεως ἡμέρα
John of Damascus, *c.* 696-*c.* 754
Tr. John M. Neale, 1818-1866, alt.

LANCASHIRE 7.6.7.6.D.
Henry T. Smart, 1813-1879

1 The day of res - ur - rec - tion! Earth, tell it out a - broad;
2 Our hearts be pure from e - vil, That we may see a - right
3 Now let the heavens be joy - ful, Let earth her song be - gin,

The Pass - o - ver of glad - ness, The Pass - o - ver of God.
The Lord in rays e - ter - nal Of res - ur - rec - tion light;
The round world keep high tri - umph, And all that is there - in;

From death to life e - ter - nal, From earth un - to the sky,
And, lis-tening to his ac - cents, May hear so calm and plain
Let all things seen and un - seen Their notes of glad - ness blend,

Our Christ hath brought us o - ver With hymns of vic - to - ry
His own "All hail," and, hear - ing, May raise the vic - tor strain.
For Christ the Lord is ris - en, Our joy that hath no end. A-men.

Crown Him with Many Crowns

Matthew Bridges, 1800-1894
Godfrey Thring, 1823-1903, st. 3

DIADEMATA S.M.D.
George J. Elvey, 1816-1893

1 Crown him with man - y crowns, The Lamb up - on his throne;
Hark! how the heaven-ly an - them drowns All mu - sic but its own;
A - wake, my soul, and sing Of him who died for thee,
And hail him as thy match-less King Through all e - ter - ni - ty.

2 Crown him the Lord of love; Be - hold his hands and side,
Rich wounds, yet vis - i - ble a - bove, In beau - ty glo - ri - fied;
No an - gel in the sky Can ful - ly bear that sight,
But down-ward bends his burn-ing eye At mys - ter - ies so bright.

3 Crown him the Lord of life, Who tri-umphed o'er the grave,
And rose vic - to - rious in the strife For those he came to save;
His glo - ries now we sing Who died and rose on high,
Who died, e - ter - nal life to bring, And lives that death may die.

4 Crown him the Lord of years, The po - ten - tate of time,
Cre - a - tor of the roll - ing spheres, In - eff - a - bly sub - lime.
All hail, Re - deem - er, hail! For thou hast died for me;
Thy praise shall nev-er, nev - er fail Through-out e - ter - ni - ty. A - men.

185 *Blessing and Honor and Glory and Power*

Horatius Bonar, 1809-1889

O QUANTA QUALIA 10.10.10.10.
La Feillée's *Méthode du Plain-chant,* 1808

Look, Ye Saints, the Sight Is Glorious

187 Lo! He Comes, with Clouds Descending

Charles Wesley, 1707-1788

ST. THOMAS (Wade) 8.7.8.7.8.7.
John Francis Wade? 1711-1786

Rejoice, the Lord Is King

Charles Wesley, 1707-1788

DARWALL 148 6.6.6.6.8.8.
John Darwall, 1731-1789

1 Re - joice, the Lord is King! Your Lord and King a - dore!
2 The Lord the Sav - ior reigns, The God of truth and love:
3 His king - dom can - not fail; He rules o'er earth and heaven;
4 Re - joice in glo - rious hope! Our Lord the Judge shall come,

Man - kind, give thanks and sing, And tri - umph ev - er - more.
When he had purged our stains, He took his seat a - bove.
The keys of death and hell To Christ the Lord are given.
And take his ser - vants up To their e - ter - nal home.

Lift up your heart! lift up your voice!

Re - joice! a - gain I say, re - joice! A - men.

189 O Holy Spirit, Comforter

I. Ernest Holling, 1867-

PONDEN COTE 8.6.8.6.6.6.6.6.
Charles H. Heaton, 1928-

1 O Ho - ly Spir - it, Com-fort - er, Blest Ad - vo-cate and Friend,
2 O Ho - ly Spir - it, Com-fort - er, Thou prom - ised guide di - vine,
3 O Ho - ly Spir - it, Com-fort - er, Thou search - ing, cleans-ing fire,

Be near us in the stress of life, Thy heaven-ly aid to lend.
On all the journ - ey of our life, Com-mand thy light to shine.
Come purge a - way the dross of sin, Make pure the heart's de - sire;

For thou the Spir - it art Of life and light and love,
So shall we nev - er stray From ways our Mas - ter trod,
Then kin - dle in us zeal, And crown with tongues of flame,

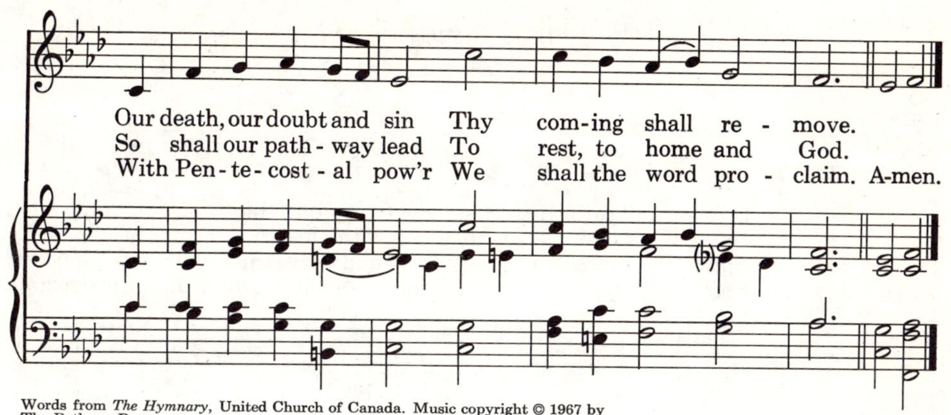

Words from *The Hymnary,* United Church of Canada. Music copyright © 1967 by The Bethany Press.

O Holy Spirit, Come to Me

190

J. M. Blough

ISLEWORTH 8.6.8.6.
Samuel Howard, 1710-1782, alt.

1 O Ho - ly Spir - it, come to me
And take me for thine own;
Come with thy power and with thy grace,
And make my heart thy home.

2 O Ho - ly Spir - it, dwell in me
And cleanse my heart from sin;
Re - deem from ev - ery guilt and stain,
O make me pure with - in.

3 O Ho - ly Spir - it, show to me
The truth that sets men free;
Teach me to love thy work di - vine,
And all its glor - ies see.

4 O Ho - ly Spir - it, quick - en me
And set my soul a - flame;
Urge me to mag - ni - fy the Lord,
And thus pro - claim his name. A - men.

191

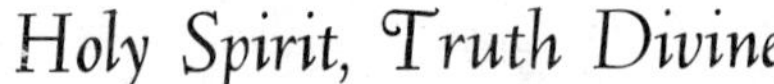

Samuel Longfellow, 1819-1892 | *First Tune* | SONG 13 7.7.7.7. Adapt. Orlando Gibbons, 1583-1625

1 Ho - ly Spir - it, Truth di - vine, Dawn up - on this soul of mine;
2 Ho - ly Spir - it, Love di - vine, Glow with - in this heart of mine;
3 Ho - ly Spir - it, Power di - vine, Fill and nerve this will of mine;
4 Ho - ly Spir - it, Right di - vine, King with - in my con - science reign;

Word of God, and in - ward light, Wake my spir - it, clear my sight.
Kin - dle ev - ery high de - sire; Per - ish self in thy pure fire.
By thee may I strong-ly live, Brave-ly bear, and no - bly strive.
Be my law, and I shall be Firm-ly bound, for - ev - er free. A-men.

192

Holy Spirit, Truth Divine

Samuel Longfellow, 1819-1892 | *Second Tune* | MERCY 7.7.7.7. Louis M. Gottschalk, 1829-1869

1 Ho - ly Spir - it, Truth di - vine, Dawn up - on this soul of mine;
2 Ho - ly Spir - it, Love di - vine, Glow with - in this heart of mine;
3 Ho - ly Spir - it, Power di - vine, Fill and nerve this will of mine;
4 Ho - ly Spir - it, Right di - vine, King with - in my con - science reign;

Word of God, and in - ward light, Wake my spir - it, clear my sight.
Kin - dle ev - ery high de - sire; Per - ish self in thy pure fire.
By thee may I strong-ly live, Brave - ly bear, and no - bly strive.
Be my law, and I shall be Firm - ly bound, for - ev - er free. A-men.

Come, Holy Spirit, God and Lord! 193

Komm, heiliger Geist, Herre Gott
Martin Luther, 1483-1546
Tr. Catherine Winkworth, 1827-1878, alt.
Vs. 3 alt. W. Sherman Skinner, 1906-

DAS NEUGEBORNE KINDELEIN L.M.
Melody by Melchior Vulpius, *c.* 1560-1616
Harm. J. S. Bach, 1685-1750

194 *Gracious Spirit, Dwell with Me*

Thomas T. Lynch, 1818-1871

REDHEAD NO. 76 7.7.7.7.7.7.
Richard Redhead, 1820-1901

1 Gra - cious Spir - it, dwell with me, I my - self would gra - cious be; And with words that help and heal Would thy life in mine re - veal, And with ac - tions bold and meek Would for Christ my Sav - ior speak.

2 Might - y Spir - it, dwell with me, I my - self would might - y be; Might - y so as to pre - vail Where un - aid - ed man must fail; Ev - er by a might - y hope, Press - ing on and bear - ing up.

3 Ho - ly Spir - it, dwell with me, I my - self would ho - ly be; Sep - a - rate from sin, I would Choose and cher - ish all things good, And what - ev - er I can be Give to him who gave me thee! A - men.

Come, Holy Spirit, Heavenly Dove 195

Harmonization from *Gesangbuchs* No. 231 *von* Paul Gerhardt; used by permission of the Verlagskontor des Evangelischen Gesangbuchs in Stuttgart.

197

Come, O Creator Spirit, Come

Veni Creator Spiritus, 9th century
Tr. Robert Bridges, 1844-1930

VENI CREATOR L.M.
Sarum plainsong, Mode VIII
Harm. Winfred Douglas, 1867-1944

Lord God, the Holy Ghost

198

James Montgomery, 1771-1854

PLATTEN S.M.
Lee Hastings Bristol, Jr., 1923-

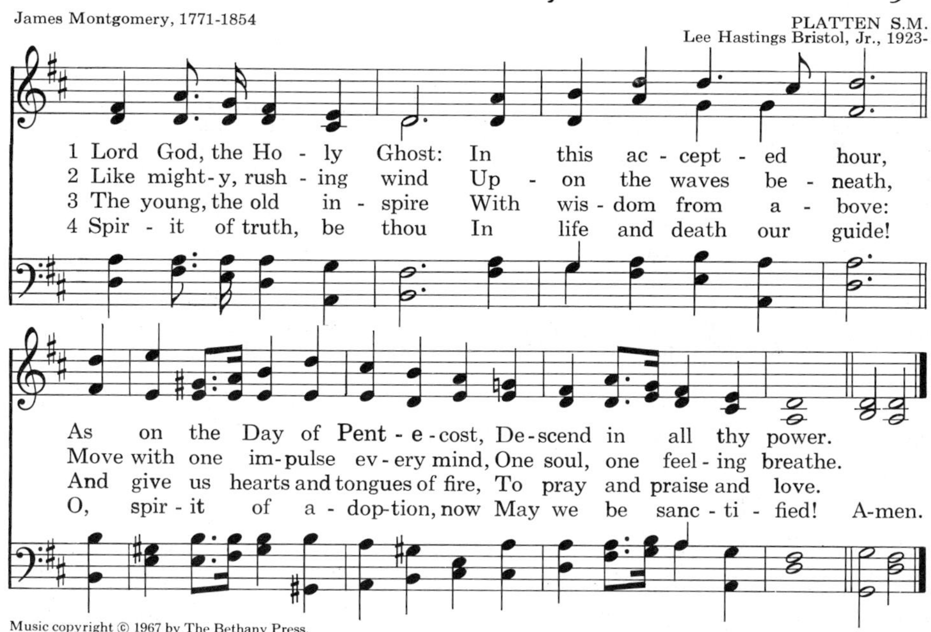

Holy Spirit, Hear Us

199

William Henry Parker, 1845-1929

GLENFINLAS 6.5.6.5.
Kenneth G. Finlay, 1882-

1 Ho - ly Spir - it, hear us; Help us while we sing;
2 Ho - ly Spir - it, prompt us When we kneel to pray;
3 Ho - ly Spir - it, shine thou On the book we read;
4 Ho - ly Spir - it, help us Dai - ly by thy might,

Breathe in - to the mu - sic Of the praise we bring.
Near - er come and teach us What we ought to say.
Gild its ho - ly pag - es With the light we need.
What is wrong to con - quer, And to choose the right. A - men.

Breathe on Me, Breath of God

Edwin Hatch, 1835-1889, alt.

TRENTHAM S.M.
Robert Jackson, 1840-1914

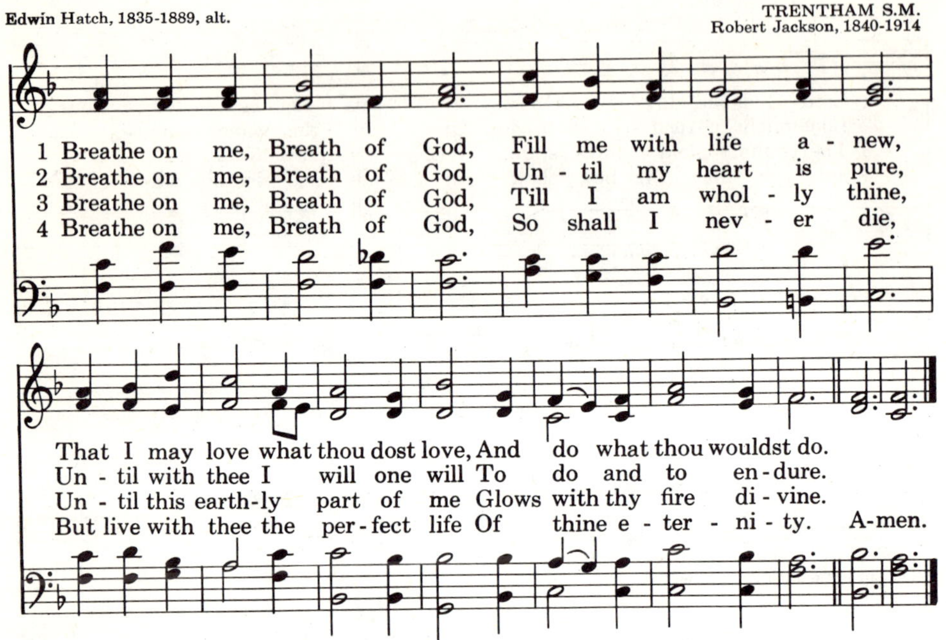

201

Spirit of God, Descend Upon My Heart

Attr. to George Croly, 1780-1860

MORECAMBE 10.10.10.10.
Frederick C. Atkinson, 1841-1897

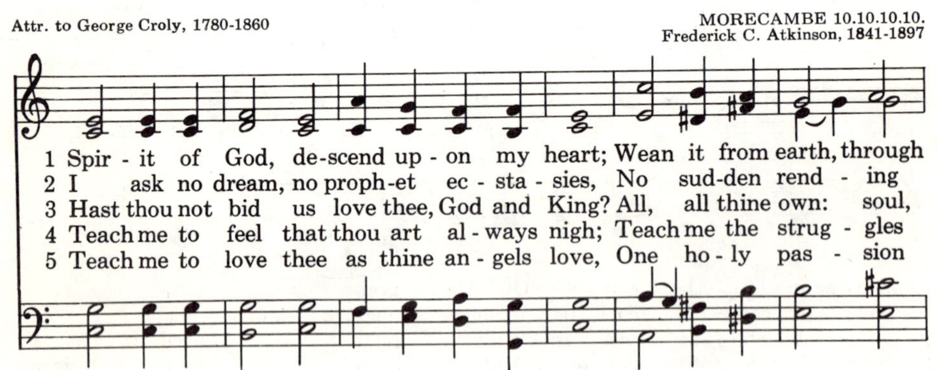

all its puls - es move; Stoop to my weak - ness, might - y as thou art,
of the veil of clay, No an - gel vis - it - ant, no o-pening skies,
heart, and strength, and mind; I see thy cross—there teach my heart to cling;
of the soul to bear: To check the ris - ing doubt, the reb - el sigh;
fill - ing all my frame; The bap-tism of the heaven-de-scend-ed Dove.
And make me love thee as I ought to love.
But take the dim - ness of my soul a - way.
O let me seek thee, and O let me find!
Teach me the pa - tience of un - an - swered prayer.
My heart an al - tar, and thy love the flame. A - men.
Spirit, Strength of All the Weak
202
Thomas Benson Pollock, 1836-1896
TON-MÂN 7.7.7.6.
David Evans, 1874-1948
1 Spir - it, strength of all the weak, Giv - ing cour - age to the meek,
2 Spir - it, aid - ing all who yearn More of truth di - vine to learn.
3 Spir - it, fount of faith and joy, Giv - ing peace with - out al - loy,
4 Source of love and light di - vine, With that hal - lowing grace of thine,
Teach - ing fal - tering tongues to speak; Hear us, Ho - ly Spir - it.
And with deep - er love to burn; Hear us, Ho - ly Spir - it.
Hope that noth - ing can de - stroy; Hear us, Ho - ly Spir - it.
More and more up - on us shine; Hear us, Ho - ly Spir - it. A - men.

203 God Almighty, God Eternal

Mary Jackson Cathey, 1926-

GENEVA 8.7.8.7.D.
George Henry Day, 1883-

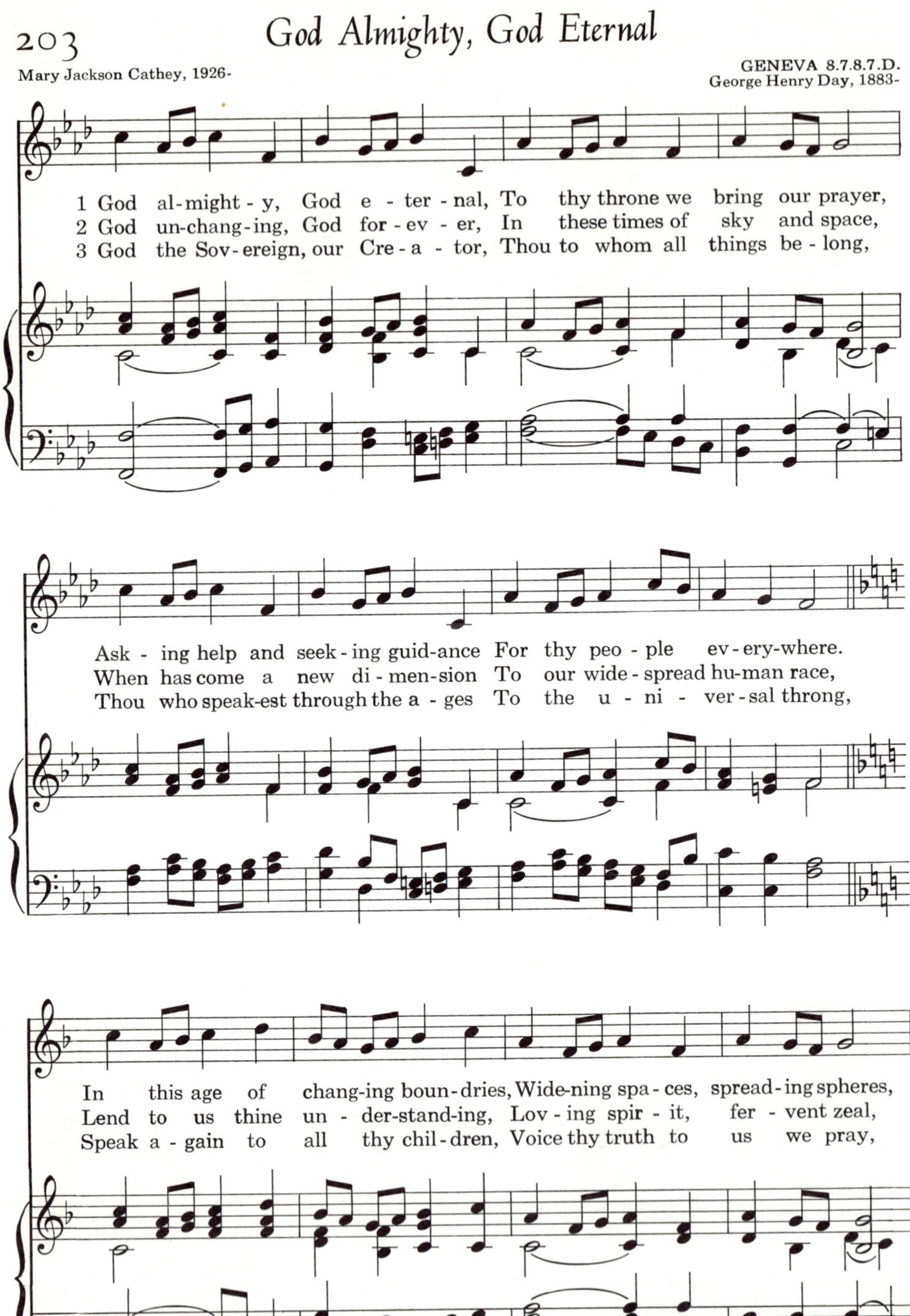

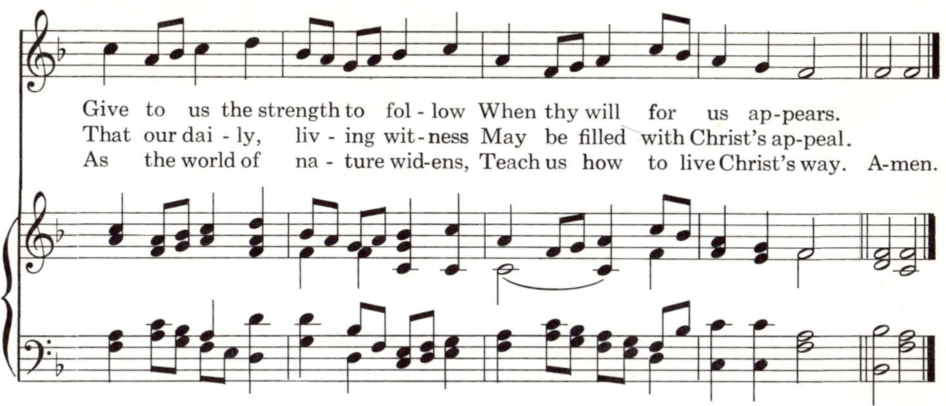

Jesus Calls Us O'er the Tumult 204

Cecil F. Alexander, 1818-1895

REGENSBURG 8.7.8.7.
Mel. Johann Crüger, 1598-1662

1 Je - sus calls us o'er the tu-mult Of our life's wild rest - less sea,
2 As of old a - pos-tles heard it By the Ga - li - le - an lake,
3 Je - sus calls us from the wor-ship Of the vain world's gold - en store,
4 In our joys and in our sor-rows, Days of toil and hours of ease,
5 Je - sus calls us! By thy mer-cies, Sav-ior, may we hear thy call,

Day by day his voice is sound-ing, Say-ing,"Chris-tian, fol - low me";
Turned from home, and toil, and kin-dred, Leav-ing all for his dear sake,
From each i - dol that would keep us, Say-ing,"Chris-tian, love me more."
Still he calls, in cares and plea-sures, "Chris-tian, love me more than these."
Give our hearts to thine o - be-dience, Serve and love thee best of all. A-men.

205

Jesus, Lover of My Soul

Charles Wesley, 1707-1788

ABERYSTWYTH 7.7.7.7.D.
Joseph Parry, 1841-1903

1 Je - sus, lov - er of my soul, Let me to thy bos - om fly,
2 Oth - er ref - uge have I none; Hangs my help - less soul on thee;
3 Plen - teous grace with thee is found, Grace to cov - er all my sin;

While the near - er wa - ters roll, While the tem - pest still is high;
Leave, ah! leave me not a - lone, Still sup - port and com - fort me.
Let the heal - ing streams a - bound, Make and keep me pure with - in.

Hide me, O my Sav - ior, hide, Till the storm of life is past;
All my trust on thee is stayed, All my help from thee I bring;
Thou of life the foun - tain art, Free - ly let me take of thee;

Safe in - to the ha - ven guide, O re - ceive my soul at last!
Cov - er my de - fense - less head With the shad - ow of thy wing.
Spring thou up with - in my heart, Rise to all e - ter - ni - ty. A - men.

More About Jesus Would I Know 206

Eliza E. Hewitt, 1851-1920

MORE ABOUT JESUS 8.8.8.8. with Refrain
John R. Sweney, 1837-1899

207 O Christ, We Climb the Hill with Thee

Kenneth Morse, 1913-

WINCHESTER NEW L.M.
Adapted from
Musicalisch Hand-Buch, Hamburg, 1690

1 O Christ, we climb the hill with thee, thou Master of the up-ward way. We scale the heights that we may see thy vis-ion of the com-ing day.

2 Show us thy king-dom, thou our King, point out the paths of peace and right; Though feet are wea-ry, hearts will sing, we climb in-to thy glo-rious light.

3 Give us the cour-age of thy cross to dare to live and die for thee; To walk through fire, to suf-fer loss in faith that keeps us strong and free.

4 New worlds of beau-ty greet our eyes as far hor-i-zons now we see; O Mas-ter of the hills that rise, to un-known heights we climb with thee. A-men.

208 In the Cross of Christ I Glory

John Bowring, 1792-1872

RATHBUN 8.7.8.7.
Ithamar Conkey, 1815-1867

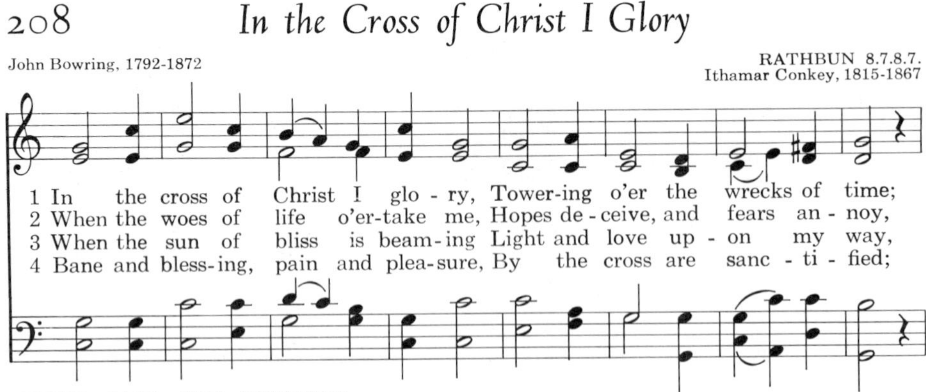

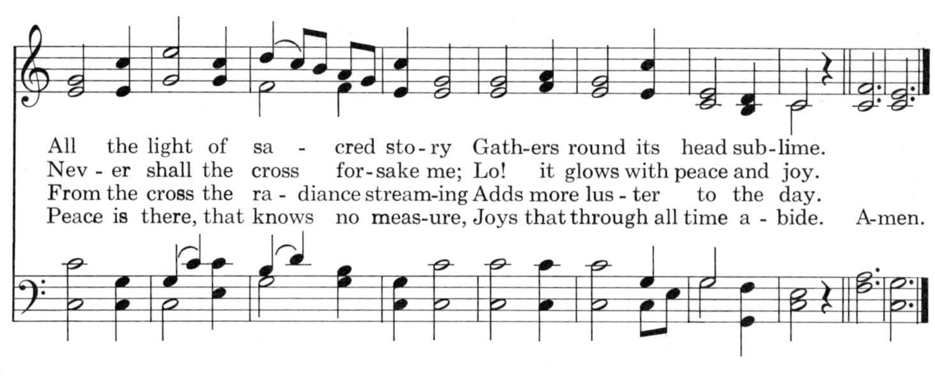

Art Thou Weary, Heavy Laden? 209

John Mason Neale, 1818-1866
Based on Stephen the Sabaite, 725-794

STEPHANOS 8.5.8.3.
Henry W. Baker, 1821-1877

1 Art thou wear - y, heav - y lad - en, Art thou sore dis - tressed?
"Come to me," saith One, "and, com - ing, Be at rest."

2 Hath he marks to lead me to him If he be my Guide?
"In his feet and hands are wound-prints, And his side!"

3 If I find him, if I fol - low, What his guer - don here?
"Man - y a sor - row, man - y a la - bor, Man - y a tear!"

4 Find - ing, fol-lowing, keep - ing, strug-gling, Is he sure to bless?
"Saints, a - pos - tles, proph - ets, mar - tyrs, An - swer, Yes!" A-men.

210 *O Master of the Waking World*

Frank Mason North, 1850-1935

MELITA 8.8.8.8.8.8.
John B. Dykes, 1823-1876

Father, Long Before Creation 211

212 Blessed Jesus, at Thy Word

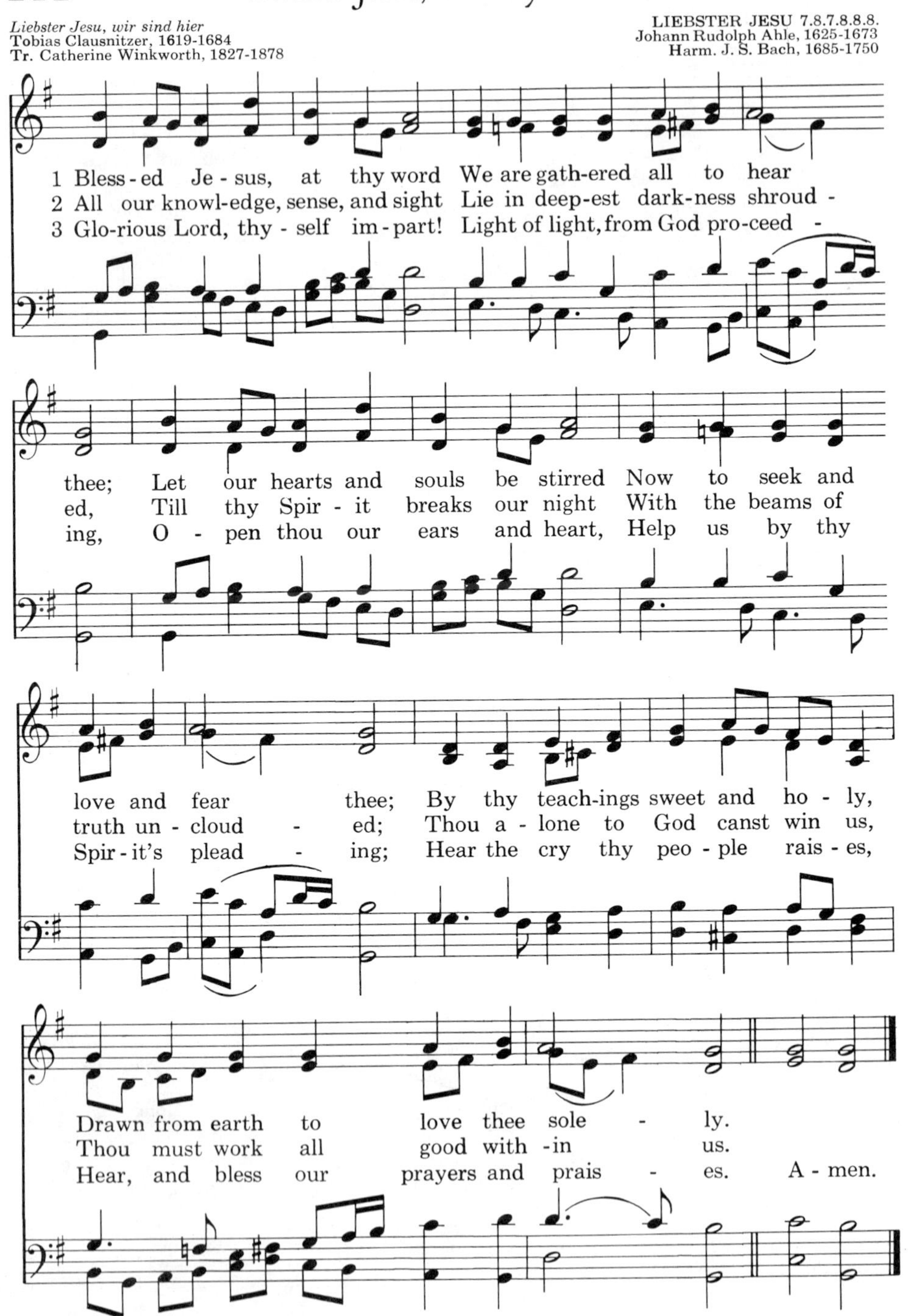

GOSPEL CALL AND RESPONSE

A simpler version of this tune is No. 329

O Jesus, I Have Promised

213

John E. Bode, 1816-1874

ANGEL'S STORY 7.6.7.6.D.
Arthur H. Mann, 1850-1929

Music used by permission of E. R. Goodliffe.

214 Go, Make of All Disciples

Matthew 28:19-20
Leon M. Adkins, 1896-

LANCASHIRE 7.6.7.6.D.
Henry Smart, 1813-1879

1 "Go, make of all dis - ci - ples." We hear the call, O Lord,
2 "Go, make of all dis - ci - ples." Bap - tiz - ing in the name
3 "Go, make of all dis - ci - ples." We at thy feet would stay

That comes from thee, our Fa - ther, In thy e - ter - nal Word.
Of Fa - ther, Son, and Spir - it From age to age the same,
Un - til each life's vo - ca - tion Ac - cents thy ho - ly way.

In - spire our ways of learn - ing Through ear - nest, fer - vent prayer,
We call each new dis - ci - ple To fol - low thee, O Lord,
We cul - ti - vate the na - ture God plants in ev - ery heart,

And let our dai - ly liv - ing Re - veal thee ev - ery - where.
Re - deem-ing soul and bod - y By wa - ter and the Word.
Re - veal-ing in our wit - ness The mas - ter teach-er's art. A-men.

Make Me a Captive, Lord 215

George Matheson, 1842-1906

LLANLLYFNI S.M.D.
John Jones, 1797-1857
Adapt. David Jenkins, 1849-1915

1 Make me a cap - tive, Lord, And then I shall be free;
2 My heart is weak and poor Un - til it mas - ter find;
3 My will is not my own Till thou hast made it thine;

Force me to ren - der up my sword, And I shall con - queror be.
It has no spring of ac - tion sure, It va - ries with the wind.
If it would reach a mon-arch's throne It must its crown re - sign;

I sink in life's a - larms When by my - self I stand;
It can - not free - ly move Till thou hast wrought its chain;
It on - ly stands un - bent A - mid the clash - ing strife,

Im - pris-on me with - in thine arms, And strong shall be my hand.
En - slave it with thy match-less love, And death - less it shall reign.
When on thy bos - om it has leant And found in thee its life. A - men.

216 Just as I Am, Without One Plea

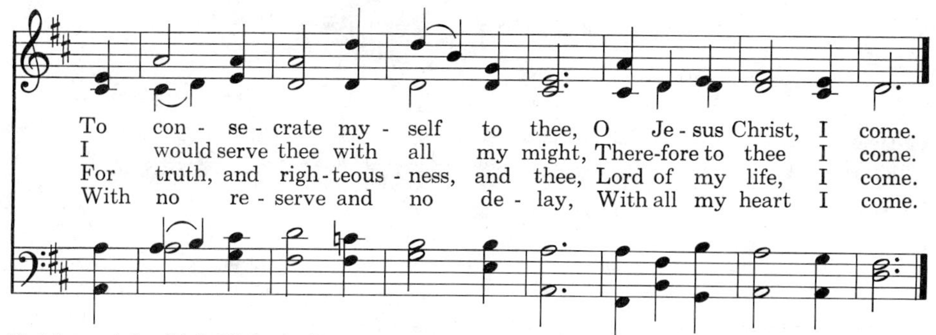

Music by permission of Oxford University Press.

O Master, Let Me Walk with Thee 218

Washington Gladden, 1836-1918

MARYTON L. M.
H. Percy Smith, 1825-1898

1 O Mas - ter, let me walk with thee In low - ly
2 Help me the slow of heart to move By some clear,
3 Teach me thy pa - tience; still with thee In clos - er,
4 In hope that sends a shin - ing ray Far down the

paths of serv - ice free; Tell me thy se - cret, help me
win - ning word of love; Teach me the way - ward feet to
dear - er com - pa - ny, In work that keeps faith sweet and
fu - ture's broad-ening way, In peace that on - ly thou canst

bear The strain of toil, the fret of care.
stay, And guide them in the home - ward way.
strong, In trust that tri - umphs o - ver wrong.
give, With thee, O Mas - ter, let me live. A - men.

219 I Bind My Heart This Tide

Savior, Like a Shepherd Lead Us

O Jesus, Thou Art Standing

William W. How, 1823-1897

ST. HILDA 7.6.7.6.D.
Justin H. Knecht, 1752-1817, and
Edward Husband, 1843-1908

Lord Christ, When First Thou Cam'st

222

I Heard the Voice of Jesus Say

Horatius Bonar, 1808-1889

KINGSFOLD C.M.D.
Traditional English Melody
Arr. and harm. R. Vaughan Williams, 1872-1958

1 I heard the voice of Jesus say, "Come unto me and rest;
Lay down, thou weary one, lay down Thy head upon my breast."
I came to Jesus as I was, Weary and worn and sad,
I found in him a resting place, And he has made me glad.

2 I heard the voice of Jesus say, "Behold, I freely give
The living water; thirsty one, Stoop down and drink, and live."
I came to Jesus, and I drank Of that life-giving stream;
My thirst was quenched, my soul revived, And now I live in him.

3 I heard the voice of Jesus say, "I am this dark world's Light;
Look unto me, thy morn shall rise, And all thy day be bright."
I looked to Jesus, and I found In him my Star, my Sun;
And in that Light of life I'll walk, Till traveling days are done. Amen.

GOSPEL CALL AND RESPONSE

What a Friend We Have in Jesus

Joseph Scriven, 1819-1886

ERIE 8.7.8.7.D
Charles C. Converse, 1832-1918

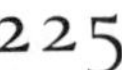

Father, in Thy Mysterious Presence

Samuel Johnson, 1822-1882

DONNE SECOURS 11.10.11.10.
Genevan Psalter, 1551

1 Father, in thy mysterious presence kneeling,
2 Lord, we have wandered forth through doubt and sorrow,
3 Now, Father, now, in thy dear presence kneeling,

Fain would our souls feel all thy kindling
And thou hast made each step an onward
Our spirits yearn to feel thy kindling

love, For we are weak, and need some deep revealing
one, And we will ever trust each unknown morrow;
love; Now make us strong, we need thy deep revealing

PRAYER

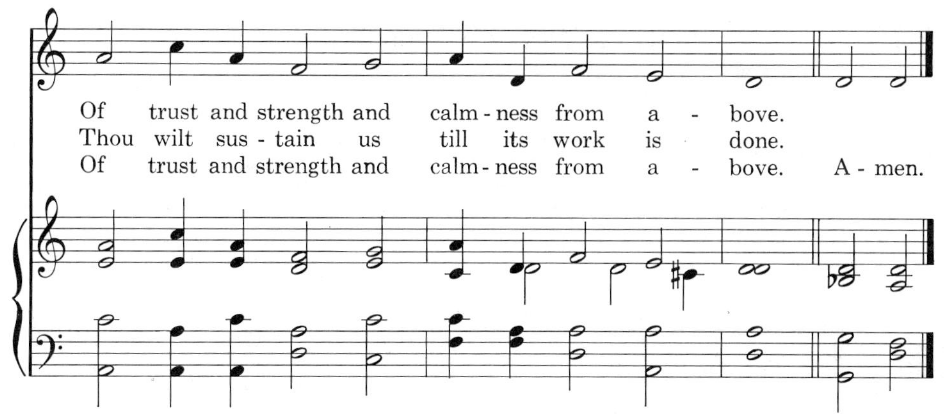

Father, Hear

226

L. M. Willis, 1824-1908

FATHER, HEAR 8.7.8.7.
Jacob Singer, 1883-1964
Adapted from folk-melody of *Eliyahu Hanavi*

1 Fa-ther, hear the prayer we of - fer! Not for ease that prayer shall be,
2 Not for-ev - er by still wa - ters Would we i - dly qui-et stay,
3 Be our strength in hours of weak-ness, In our wander-ings be our guide;

227 *Have Thine Own Way, Lord!*

Adelaide A. Pollard, 1860-1934

ADELAIDE 5.4.5.4.D.
George C. Stebbins, 1846-1945

1 Have thine own way, Lord! Have thine own way! Thou art the Potter; I am the clay. Mould me and make me After thy will, While I am waiting, Yielded and still.

2 Have thine own way, Lord! Have thine own way! Search me and try me, Master, today! Whiter than snow, Lord, Wash me just now, As in thy presence Humbly I bow.

3 Have thine own way, Lord! Have thine own way! Wounded and weary, Help me, I pray! Power, all power Surely is thine! Touch me and heal me, Savior divine!

4 Have thine own way, Lord! Have thine own way! Hold o'er my being Absolute sway! Fill with thy Spirit Till all shall see Christ only, always, Living in me! A-men.

228 *Lord Jesus Christ, Be Present Now*

J. Niedling's *Lutherisch Handbüchlein*, 1638
Tr. Catherine Winkworth, 1827-1878, alt.

HERR JESU CHRIST L.M.
Pensum Sacrum, 1648
Harm. from *Cantionale Sacrum*, 1651

Father Almighty, Bless Us with Thy Blessing 229

Berwick Hymnal, 1886

FLEMMING 11.11.11.5.
Friedrich F. Flemming, 1778-1813

230 *Take Time to Be Holy*

W. D. Longstaff, 1822-1894

HOLINESS 6.5.6.5.D.
George C. Stebbins, 1846-1945

PRAYER

Behold Us, Lord, a Little Space 231

John Ellerton, 1826-1893

WINCHESTER OLD C.M.
Thomas Este's *Whole Book of Psalms*, 1592

1 Be - hold us, Lord, a lit - tle space From dai - ly tasks set free,
2 A - round us rolls the cease-less tide Of busi-ness, toil, and care,
3 Yet these are not the on - ly walls Where-in thou mayst be sought;
4 Thine are the loom, the forge, the mart, The wealth of land and sea,
5 Work shall be prayer, if all be wrought As thou wouldst have it done;

And met with-in thy ho - ly place To rest a - while with thee.
And scarce - ly can we turn a - side For one brief hour of prayer.
On home-liest work thy bless-ing falls, In truth and pa-tience wrought.
The worlds of sci - ence and of art, Re-vealed and ruled by thee.
And prayer, by thee in-spired and taught, It - self with work be one. A-men.

232

John Oxenham, 1852-1941

ST. AGNES C.M.
John B. Dykes, 1823-1876

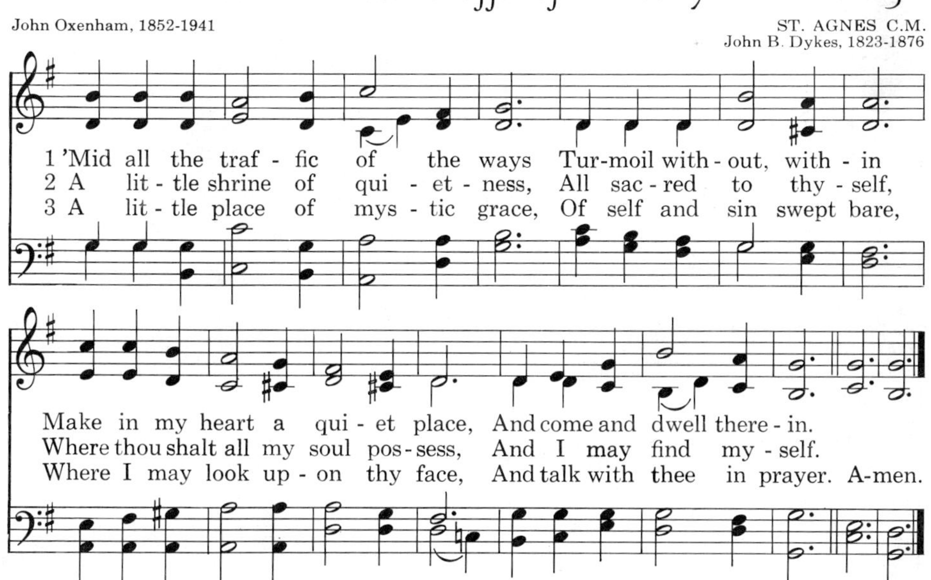

Words used by permission of Theo Oxenham.

233 Talk with Us, Lord

Charles Wesley, 1707-1788

NUN DANKET ALL' (Gräfenberg) C.M.
Johann Crüger, 1598-1662

Harmonization from *Gesangbuchs* No. 231 *von* Paul Gerhardt; used by permission of the Verlagskontor des Evangelischen Gesangbuchs in Stuttgart.

234 Have Faith in God

Bryn A. Rees, 1911-

SOUTHWELL S.M.
Adapted from Damon's *Psalmes*, 1579

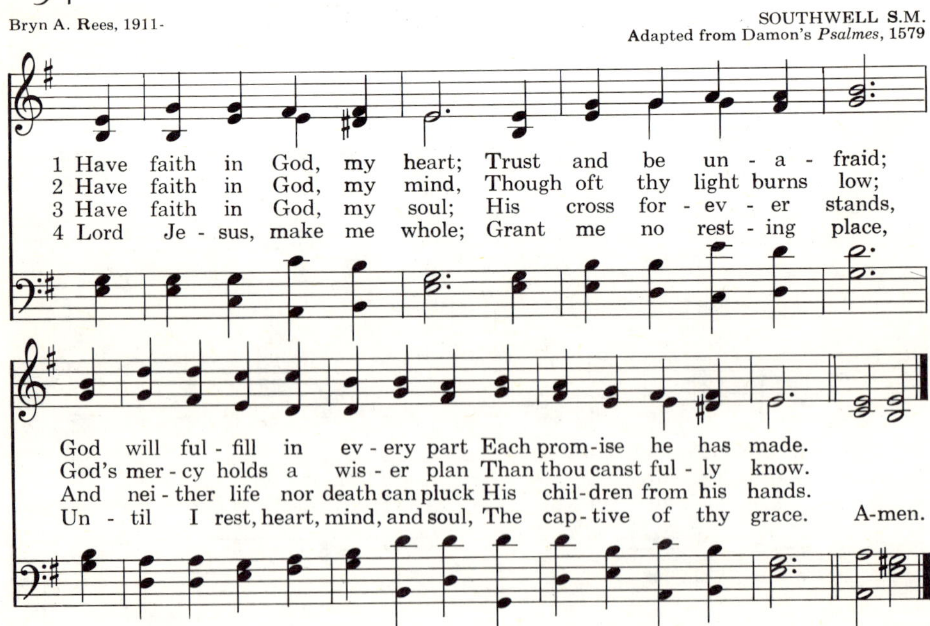

Father of Heaven

235

Music used by permission of A. Gregory Murray.

236

Hope of the World

Georgia Harkness, 1891-

DONNE SECOURS 11.10.11.10.
Genevan Psalter, 1551

FAITH, HOPE, LOVE

O Lord, We Do Adore Thee

238 *Jesus, My Lord, My God, My All*

Henry Collins, 1830-1919

ST. CHRYSOSTOM 8.8.8.8.8.8.
Joseph Barnby, 1838-1896

1 Je - sus, my Lord, my God, my all, Hear me, blest Sa - vior,
2 Je - sus, too late I thee have sought; How can I love thee
3 Je - sus, what didst thou find in me That thou hast dealt so

when I call; Hear me, and from thy dwell - ing place Pour
as I ought, And how ex - tol thy match - less fame, The
lov - ing - ly? How great the joy that thou hast brought! O

down the rich - es of thy grace. Je - sus, my Lord, I
glo - rious beau - ty of thy Name? Je - sus, my Lord, I
far ex - ceed - ing hope or thought! Je - sus, my Lord, I

thee a - dore; O make me love thee more and more!
thee a - dore; O make me love thee more and more!
thee a - dore; O make me love thee more and more! A - men.

I Look to Thee in Every Need

Samuel Longfellow, 1819-1892, alt.

O JESU 8.6.8.6.8.8.
Melody from *Hirschberg Gesangbuch*, 1741

240 I Need Thee Every Hour

Annie S. Hawks, 1835-1918
Robert Lowry, 1826-1899, Refrain

NEED 6.4.6.4. with Refrain
Robert Lowry, 1826-1899

And Can It Be

Charles Wesley, 1707-1788

SAGINA 8.8.8.8.8.8.
Thomas Campbell, 1825-1876

242 Jesus, Still Lead On

Jesu, geh' voran
Nicolaus L. Von Zinzendorf, 1700-1760
Tr. Jane L. Borthwick, 1813-1897

ROCHELLE 5.5.8.8.5.5.
Adam Drese, 1620-1701

243 We Walk by Faith, and Not by Sight

Henry Alford. 1810-1871

AZMON C.M.
Carl G. Gläser, 1784-1829
Mason's *Modern Psalmody*, 1839

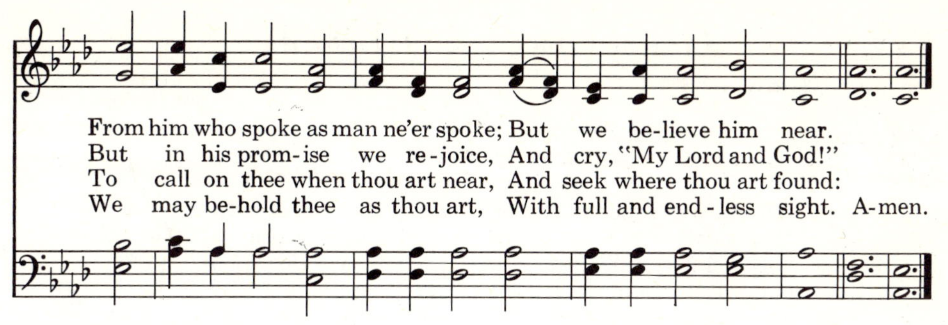

My Faith Looks Up to Thee 244

Ray Palmer, 1808-1887, alt.

OLIVET 6.6.4.6.6.6.4.
Lowell Mason, 1792-1872

1 My faith looks up to thee, Thou Lamb of Cal - va - ry,
2 May thy rich grace im - part Strength to my faint - ing heart,
3 While life's dark maze I tread, And griefs a - round me spread,

Sav - ior di - vine! Now hear me while I pray; Take all my
My zeal in - spire; As thou hast died for me, Oh, may my
Be thou my guide; Bid dark-ness turn to day; Wipe sor-row's

guilt a - way; Oh, let me from this day Be whol - ly thine.
love to thee Pure, warm, and change-less be, A liv - ing fire.
tears a - way; Nor let me ev - er stray From thee a - side. A-men.

245 God of Grace and God of Glory

Harry Emerson Fosdick, 1878-1969

CWM RHONDDA 8.7.8.7.8.7.7.
John Hughes, 1873-1932

Alternate tune No. 144

Lead On, O King Eternal

Ernest W. Shurtleff, 1862-1917

LANCASHIRE 7.6.7.6.D.
Henry Smart, 1813-1879

247 Once to Every Man and Nation

James Russell Lowell, 1819-1891
Adapt. W. Garrett Horder, 1814-1922

EBENEZER 8.7.8.7.D.
Thomas John Williams, 1869-1944

1 Once to ev - ery man and na - tion Comes the mo - ment
2 By the light of burn - ing mar - tyrs, Je - sus' bleed - ing
3 Though the cause of e - vil pros - per, Yet 'tis truth a -

to de - cide, In the strife of truth with false - hood,
feet I track, Toil - ing up new Cal - varies ev - er
lone is strong, Truth for - ev - er on the scaf - fold,

For the good or e - vil side;
With the cross that turns not back;
Wrong for - ev - er on the throne.

Some great cause, God's new mes - si - ah, Of - fering each the
New oc - ca - sions teach new du - ties, Time makes an - cient
Yet that scaf - fold sways the fu - ture, And, be - hind the
bloom or blight, And the choice goes by for - ev - er
good un - couth; They must up - ward still and on - ward,
dim un - known, Stand - eth God with - in the shad - ow
'Twixt that dark - ness and that light.
Who would keep a - breast of truth.
Keep - ing watch a - bove his own. A - men.

248 Christian, Dost Thou See Them

Attr. to St. Andrew of Crete, c. 660-c. 732
Tr. John M. Neale, 1818-1866, alt.

KING'S WESTON 6.5.6.5.D.
R. Vaughan Williams, 1872-1958

1 Chris-tian, dost thou see them On the ho - ly ground,
2 Chris-tian, dost thou feel them, How they work with - in,
3 Chris-tian, dost thou hear them, How they speak thee fair,
4 "Well I know thy trou - ble, O my serv - ant true;

How the powers of dark - ness Com-pass thee a - round?
Striv-ing, tempt - ing, lur - ing, Goad-ing in - to sin?
"Al-ways fast and vig - il, Al - ways watch and prayer"?
Thou art ver - y wea - ry; I was wea - ry, too.

Chris-tian, up and smite them, Count-ing gain but loss,
Chris-tian, nev - er trem - ble, Nev - er be down - cast;
Chris-tian, an - swer bold - ly, "While I breathe I pray!"
But that toil shall make thee Some day all mine own,

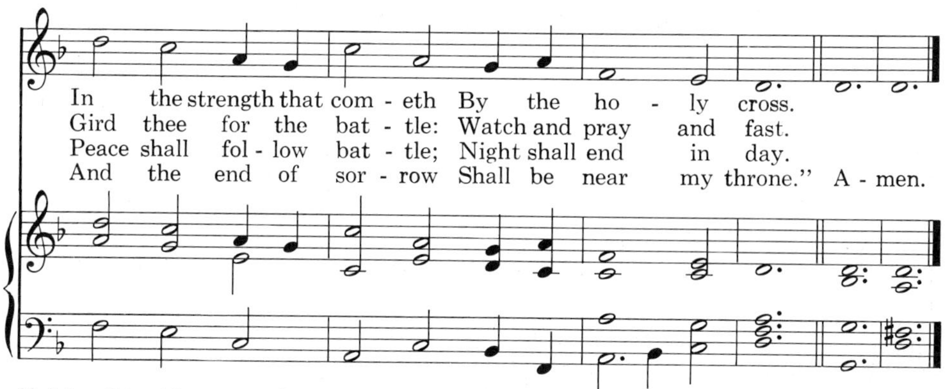

Music from *Enlarged Songs of Praise* by permission of Oxford University Press.

That Cause Can Neither Be Lost nor Stayed 249

Kristian Ostergaard, 1855-1931
Tr. Jens Christian Aaberg, 1877-

OSTERGAARD 9.9.10.10.
Danish folk tune
Arr. Ellwood S. Wolf, 1903-

1 That cause can nei - ther be lost nor stayed Which takes the course of what God has made, And is not trust - ing in walls and tow - ers But slow - ly grow - ing from seeds to flow - ers.

2 Each no - ble serv - ice that men have wrought Was first con - ceived as a fruit - ful thought; Each wor - thy cause with a fu - ture glo-rious By qui - et grow - ing be - comes vic - to - rious.

3 There - by it - self like a tree it shows; That high it reach - es as deep it grows; And, when the storms are its branch-es shak-ing, It deep - er root in the soil is tak - ing.

4 Be then no more by a storm dis - mayed, For by it the full-grown seeds are laid; And though the tree by its might it shat-ters, What then, if thou-sands of seeds it scat-ters!

250 God Is My Strong Salvation

James Montgomery, 1771-1854

WEDLOCK 7.6.7.6.D.
Melody *The Sacred Harp*, 1844
Harm. C. H. Heaton, 1928-

Unison

1 God is my strong sal - va - tion: What foe have I to fear?
In dark-ness and temp - ta - tion, My light, my help is near:
Though hosts en-camp a - round me, Firm in the fight I stand;
What ter-ror can con-found me, With God at my right hand?

2 Place on the Lord re - li - ance; My soul, with cour-age wait;
His truth be thine af - fi - ance, When faint and des - o - late.
His might thy heart shall strength-en, His love thy joy in - crease;
Mer - cy thy days shall length - en; The Lord will give thee peace. A-men.

Guide Me, O Thou Great Jehovah

William Williams, 1717-1791
Tr. Peter Williams, 1727-1796, and others

CWM RHONDDA 8.7.8.7.8.7.7.
John Hughes, 1873-1932

1 Guide me, O thou great Jehovah,
Pilgrim through this barren land;
I am weak, but thou art mighty;
Hold me with thy powerful hand;
Bread of heaven, bread of heaven,
Feed me till I want no more,
Feed me till I want no more.

2 Open now the crystal fountain,
Whence the healing stream doth flow;
Let the fire and cloudy pillar
Lead me all my journey through;
Strong Deliverer, strong Deliverer,
Be thou still my strength and shield,
Be thou still my strength and shield.

3 When I tread the verge of Jordan,
Bid my anxious fears subside;
Death of death, and hell's destruction,
Land me safe on Canaan's side;
Songs of praises, songs of praises,
I will ever give to thee,
I will ever give to thee. Amen.

252 He Who Would Valiant Be

Faith of Our Fathers! Living Still

253

Frederick W. Faber, 1814-1863, alt.

ST. CATHERINE 8.8.8.8.8.8.
Henri F. Hemy, 1818-1888
Adapt. James G. Walton, 1821-1905

1 Faith of our fa - thers! liv - ing still In spite of dun - geon,
2 Faith of our fa - thers! we will strive To win all na - tions
3 Faith of our fa - thers! we will love Both friend and foe in

fire, and sword, O how our hearts beat high with joy
un - to thee, And through the truth that comes from God
all our strife, And preach thee, too, as love knows how

When-e'er we hear that glo - rious word! Faith of our fa - thers,
Man - kind shall then be tru - ly free. Faith of our fa - thers,
By kind - ly words and vir - tuous life: Faith of our fa - thers,

ho - ly faith! We will be true to thee till death.
ho - ly faith! We will be true to thee till death.
ho - ly faith! We will be true to thee till death. A - men.

Soldiers of Christ, Arise

Charles Wesley, 1707-1788

SILVER STREET S.M.
Isaac Smith, 1725-1800

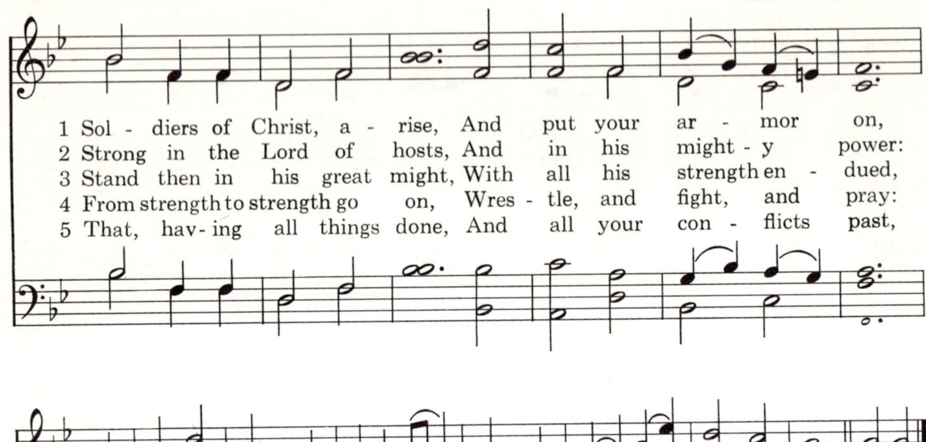

Strong in the strength which God sup - plies Thro' his e - ter - nal Son;
Who in the strength of Je - sus trusts Is more than con - quer - or.
And take, to arm you for the fight, The pan - o - ply of God.
Tread all the powers of dark-ness down, And win the well-fought day.
Ye may o'er-come, through Christ a - lone, And stand com - plete at last. A-men.

255 Lord Jesus, Think on Me

Synesius of Cyrene, *c.* 375-430
Tr. Allen W. Chatfield, 1808-1896, alt.

SOUTHWELL S.M.
Adapted from Damon's *Psalmes*, 1579

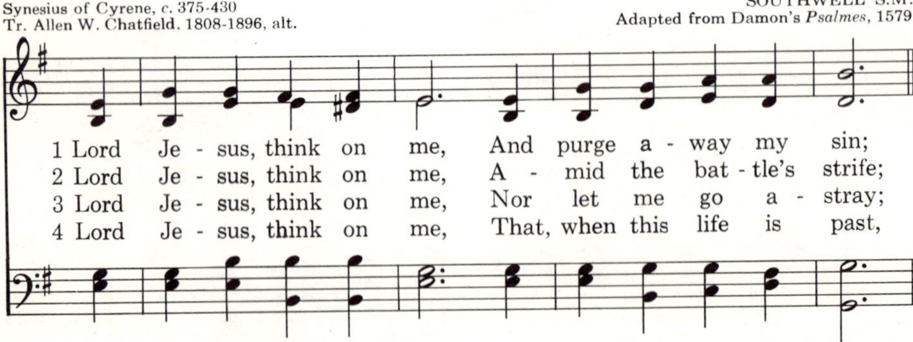

From earth-born pas-sions set me free, And make me pure with - in.
In all my pain and mis - er - y Be thou my health and life.
Through dark-ness and per - plex - i - ty Point thou the heaven-ly way.
I may the e - ter - nal bright-ness see, And share thy joy at last. A-men.
Fight the Good Fight
256
John Samuel Bewley Monsell, 1811-1875, alt.
DEUS TUORUM MILITUM L.M.
Grenoble Antiphoner, 1753
1 Fight the good fight with all thy might, Christ is thy strength and Christ thy right; Lay hold on life, and it shall be Thy joy and crown e - ter - nal - ly.
2 Run the straight race through God's good grace, Lift up thine eyes and seek his face; Life with its way be - fore us lies, Christ is the path and Christ the prize.
3 Cast care a - side, lean on thy Guide; His bound - less mer - cy will pro - vide; Trust, and thy trust - ing soul shall prove Christ is its life and Christ its love.
4 Faint not nor fear, his arms are near; He chang - eth not, and thou art dear; On - ly be - lieve, and thou shalt see That Christ is all in all to thee. A - men.

257 Now in the Days of Youth

Walter J. Mathams, 1853-1932

DIADEMATA S.M.D.
George J. Elvey, 1816-1893

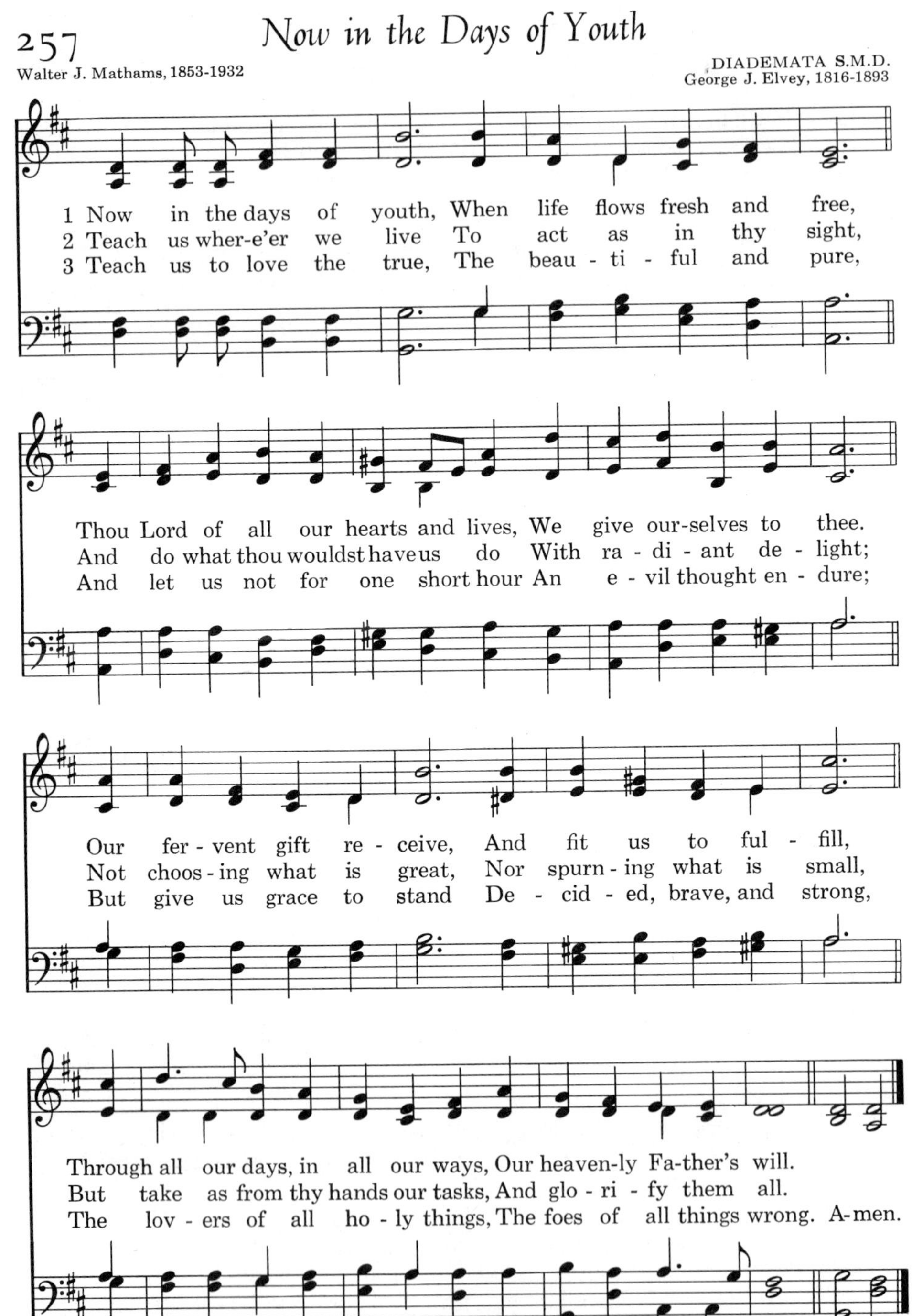

Lord, as to Thy Dear Cross We Flee 258

John H. Gurney, 1802-1862

ST. COLUMBA 8.7.8.7.
Ancient Irish Melody

Give to the Winds Thy Fears 259

Paul Gerhardt, 1607-1676
Tr. John Wesley, 1703-1791, alt.

ST. BRIDE S.M.
Samuel Howard, 1710-1782
Harm. David Evans, 1874-1948

260 Savior, Thy Dying Love

S. Dryden Phelps, 1816-1895, alt.

SOMETHING FOR JESUS 6.4.6.4.6.6.6.4.
Robert Lowry, 1826-1899

261 We Give Thee But Thine Own

William Walsham How, 1823-1897

SCHUMANN S.M.
Mason and Webb's *Cantica Laudis*
Boston, 1850

Alternate tune No. 400

All Things Are Thine; No Gift Have We 262

John G. Whittier, 1807-1892

GERMANY L.M.
Gardiner's *Sacred Melodies*, 1815

1 All things are thine; no gift have we, Lord of all
2 Thy will was in the build - er's thought; Thy hand un -
3 In weak - ness and in want we call On thee for
4 O Fa - ther, deign these walls to bless; Fill with thy

gifts, to of - fer thee, And hence with grate - ful hearts to-
seen a - midst us wrought; Through mor-tal mo - tive, scheme and
whom the heavens are small; Thy glo - ry is thy chil - dren's
love their emp - ti - ness; And let their door a gate - way

day Thine own be - fore thy feet we lay.
plan, Thy wise e - ter - nal pur - pose ran.
good, Thy joy thy ten - der Fa - ther - hood.
be To lead us from our - selves to thee. A - men.

STEWARDSHIP

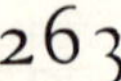

The Wise May Bring Their Learning

Anonymous
From *The Book of Praise for Children*, 1881

FOREST GREEN C.M.D.
English traditional melody
Arr. R. Vaughan Williams, 1872-1958

1 The wise may bring their learn - ing, The rich may bring their wealth,
2 We'll bring him hearts that love him; We'll bring him thank-ful praise,

And some may bring their great - ness, And some bring strength and health;
And young souls meek-ly striv - ing To walk in ho - ly ways:

We, too, would bring our treas - ures To of - fer to the King;
And these shall be the treas - ures We of - fer to the King,

We have no wealth or learn - ing: What shall we chil-dren bring?
And these are gifts that ev - en The poor - est child may bring. A-men.

STEWARDSHIP

O Brother Man, Fold to Thy Heart

John Greenleaf Whittier, 1807-1892

WELWYN 11.10.11.10.
Alfred Scott-Gatty, 1847-1918

1 O brother man, fold to thy heart thy brother;
Where pity dwells, the peace of God is there;
To worship rightly is to love each other,
Each smile a hymn, each kindly deed a prayer.

2 Follow with reverent steps the great example
Of him whose holy work was doing good;
So shall the wide earth seem our Father's temple,
Each loving life a psalm of gratitude.

3 Then shall all shackles fall; the stormy clangor
Of wild war music o'er the earth shall cease;
Love shall tread out the baleful fire of anger,
And in its ashes plant the tree of peace. Amen.

BROTHERHOOD

265 *Father Eternal, Ruler of Creation*

Laurence Housman, 1865-1959

LANGHAM 11.10.11.10.10.
Geoffrey Shaw, 1879-1943

1 Fa - ther e - ter - nal, Rul - er of cre - a - tion, Spir - it of
2 Ra - ces and peo - ples, lo, we stand di - vid - ed, And shar - ing
3 En - vious of heart, blind-eyed, with tongues con-found-ed, Na - tion by
4 How shall we love thee, ho - ly, hid - den Be - ing, If we love

life, which moved ere form was made, Through the thick dark - ness
not our griefs, no joy can share; By wars and tu - mults
na - tion still goes un - for - given; In wrath and fear, by
not the world which thou hast made? O give us broth - er -

cov - ering ev - ery na - tion, Light to man's blind-ness, O be thou our
love is mocked, de - rid - ed, His con-quering cross no king - dom wills to
jeal - ous-ies sur-round - ed, Build - ing proud towers which shall not reach to
love for bet - ter see - ing Thy Word made flesh, and in a man - ger

BROTHERHOOD

Words used by permission of Oxford University Press. Music used by permission of the League of Nations Union.

O Day of God, Draw Nigh 266

R. B. Y. Scott, 1899-, alt.

ST. MICHAEL S.M.
Adapted from *Genevan Psalter*, 1551

1 O Day of God, draw nigh
In beauty and in power,
Come with thy timeless judgment now
To match our present hour.

2 Bring to our troubled minds,
Uncertain and afraid,
The quiet of a steadfast faith,
Calm of a call obeyed.

3 Bring justice to our land,
That all may dwell secure,
And finely build for days to come
Foundations that endure.

4 Bring to our world of strife
Thy sovereign word of peace,
That war may haunt the earth no more
And desolation cease.

5 O Day of God, draw nigh
As at creation's birth;
Let there be light again, and set
Thy judgments in the earth. Amen.

Words used by permission of R. B. Y. Scott

BROTHERHOOD

267 The Savior's Wondrous Love

Korean
Tr. William Scott and
Yung Oon Kim, 1950

TAI JUN PARK S.M.
Korean

1 The Sav-ior's won-drous love, Hath made all na-tions one.
2 In this vast world of men, A world so filled with pain,
3 In this sad world of war Can peace be ev-er found?
4 The Mas-ter's new com-mand Was love each oth-er well.

U-nit-ed let us praise this deed The Fa-ther's love hath done.
No oth-er theme can be our prayer Than this: thy king-dom come.
Un-less the love of Christ pre-vail True peace will not a-bound.
O broth-ers, let us all u-nite To do his ho-ly will. A-men.

268 Where Cross the Crowded Ways of Life

Frank Mason North, 1850-1935

GERMANY L.M.
Gardiner's *Sacred Melodies,* 1815

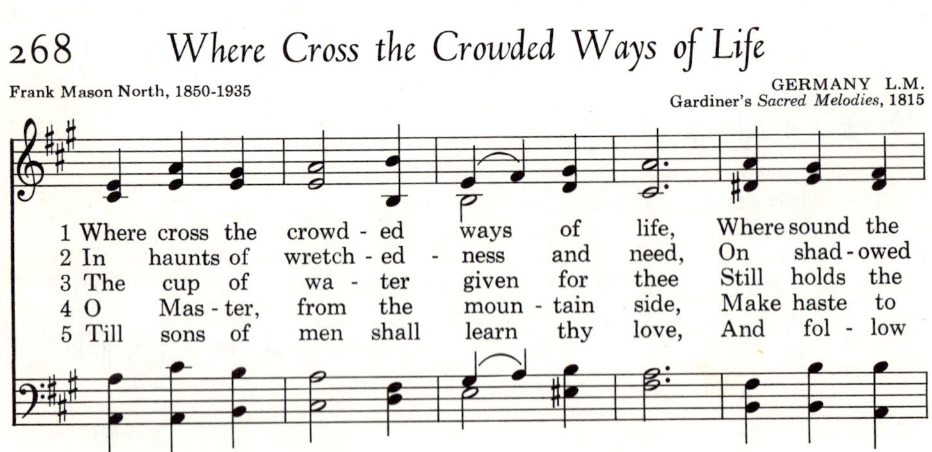

cries of race and clan, A - bove the noise of self - ish
thresh-olds dark with fears, From paths where hide the lures of
fresh - ness of thy grace; Yet long these mul - ti - tudes to
heal these hearts of pain; A - mong these rest - less throngs a -
where thy feet have trod, Till glo - rious from thy heaven a -
strife, We hear thy voice, O Son of man.
greed, We catch the vi - sion of thy tears.
see The sweet com - pas - sion of thy face.
bide, O tread the cit - y's streets a - gain.
bove, Shall come the cit - y of our God. A - men.
In Christ There Is No East or West
269
John Oxenham, 1852-1941
ST. PETER C.M.
Alexander R. Reinagle, 1799-1877
1 In Christ there is no East or West, In him no South or North;
2 In him shall true hearts ev - ery-where Their high com-mun - ion find;
3 Join hands, then, broth-ers of the faith, What-e'er your race may be!
4 In Christ now meet both East and West, In him meet South and North;
But one great fel - low - ship of love Through-out the whole wide earth.
His serv - ice is the gold - en cord Close-bind - ing all man - kind.
Who serves my Fa - ther as a son Is sure - ly kin to me.
All Christ-ly souls are one in him Through-out the whole wide earth. A-men.
Words reprinted by permission of the American Tract Society; Oradell, New Jersey.
BROTHERHOOD

270 *From Thee All Skill and Science Flow*

Charles Kingsley, 1819-1875

ST. MARIA C.M.D.
William Gawler, *c.* 1750-1809

1 From thee all skill and sci - ence flow, All pit - y, care, and love.
2 And has - ten, Lord, that per - fect day When pain and death shall cease,

All calm and cour - age, faith and hope: O pour them from a - bove.
And thy just rule shall fill the earth With health and light and peace.

And part them, Lord, to each and all, As each and all shall need,
When ev - er blue the sky shall gleam, And ev - er green the sod,

To rise, like in - cense, each to thee, In no - ble thought and deed.
And man's rude work de - face no more the par - a - dise of God. A-men.

The Voice of God Is Calling 271

John Haynes Holmes, 1879-1964

MEIRIONYDD 7.6.7.6.D.
William Lloyd, 1786-1852

1 The voice of God is call - ing Its sum-mons un - to men;
2 I hear my peo - ple cry - ing In cot and mine and slum;
3 We heed, O Lord, thy sum - mons, And an - swer: Here are we!
4 From ease and plen - ty save us; From pride of place ab - solve;

As once he spake in Zi - on, So now he speaks a - gain:
No field or mart is si - lent, No cit - y street is dumb.
Send us up - on thine er - rand; Let us thy serv - ants be.
Purge us of low de - sire; Lift us to high re - solve;

Whom shall I send to suc - cor My peo - ple in their need?
I see my peo - ple fall - ing In dark - ness and de - spair.
Our strength is dust and ash - es, Our years a pass - ing hour,
Take us, and make us ho - ly; Teach us thy will and way.

Whom shall I send to loos - en The bonds of shame and greed?
Whom shall I send to shat - ter The fet-ters which they bear?
But thou canst use our weak - ness To mag - ni - fy thy power.
Speak, and, be - hold! we an - swer; Command, and we o - bey! A-men.

BROTHERHOOD

272 Where Restless Crowds Are Thronging

Thomas Curtis Clark, 1877-1953

MEIRIONYDD 7.6.7.6.D.
William Lloyd, 1786-1852

1 Where rest - less crowds are throng-ing A - long the cit - y ways,
2 In scenes of want and sor - row And haunts of fla - grant wrong,
3 O Christ, be - hold thy peo - ple They press on ev - ery hand!

Where pride and greed and tur - moil Con - sume the fe - vered days,
In homes where kind-ness fal - ters, And strife and fear are strong,
Bring light to all the cit - ies Of our be - lov - ed land.

Where vain am - bi - tions ban - ish All thoughts of praise and prayer,
In bus - y street of bar - ter, In lone - ly thor - ough - fare,
May all our bit - ter striv - ing Give way to vi - sions fair

The peo - ple's spir - its wav - er: But thou, O Christ, art there.
The peo - ple's spir - its lan-guish: But thou, O Christ, art there.
Of right-eous-ness and jus - tice: For thou, O Christ, art there. A-men.

BROTHERHOOD

Blest Be the Tie that Binds 273

John Fawcett, 1740-1817

DENNIS S.M.
Johann G. Nägeli, 1768-1836
Arr. Lowell Mason, 1792-1872

275 Our Father, by Whose Name

F. Bland Tucker, 1895-

RHOSYMEDRE 6.6.6.6.8.8.8.
John D. Edwards, 1806-1885

Blest Is the Home When God Is There

Henry Ware, 1794-1843

ABBEY C.M.
Scottish Psalter, 1615

277

O God, Who to a Loyal Home

Harry Emerson Fosdick, 1878-1969

KINGSFOLD C.M.D.
Traditional English Melody
Arr. and harm. R. Vaughan Williams, 1872-1958

O Happy Home, Where Thou Art Loved

O selig Haus
Karl Johann Philipp Spitta, 1801-1859
Tr. Sarah Borthwick Findlater, 1823-1907

WELWYN 11.10.11.10.
Alfred Scott-Gatty, 1847-1918

279 For All the Saints

William Walsham How, 1823-1897

SINE NOMINE 10.10.10.4.
R. Vaughan Williams, 1872-1958

1 For all the saints, who from their la - bors rest, Who
2 Thou wast their rock, their for - tress, and their might:
3 O may thy sol - diers, faith - ful, true, and bold,
6 From earth's wide bounds, from o - cean's far - thest coast, Through

thee by faith be - fore the world con - fessed, Thy
Thou, Lord, their Cap - tain in the well-fought fight;
Fight as the saints who no - bly fought of old, And
gates of pearl streams in the count - less host,

Name, O Je - sus, be for - ev - er blest.
Thou, in the dark - ness drear, the one true light.
win, with them, the vic - tor's crown of gold.
Sing - ing to Fa - ther, Son, and Ho - ly Ghost,

VICTORY OVER DEATH

Al - le - lu - ia, al - le - lu - ia! A-men.
4 O blest com-mun - ion, fel - low-ship di - vine! We fee - bly strug - gle,
5 And when the strife is fierce, the war-fare long, Steals on the ear the
they in glo - ry shine; Yet all are one in thee, for all are thine.
dis-tant tri-umph song, And hearts are brave a - gain, and arms are strong.
D.C. for stanza 6
Al - le - lu - ia, al - le - lu - ia!

VICTORY OVER DEATH

Softly Now the Light of Day

George W. Doane, 1799-1859

SEYMOUR 7.7.7.7.
Arr. from Carl M. von Weber, 1786-1826

1 Soft - ly now the light of day Fades up - on my sight a - way;
2 Thou, whose all - per - vad - ing eye Naught es - capes, with - out, with - in,
3 Soon for me the light of day Shall for - ev - er pass a - way;
4 Thou who, sin - less, yet hast known All of man's in - firm - i - ty,

Free from care, from la - bor free, Lord, I would com-mune with thee.
Par - don each in - firm - i - ty, O - pen fault, and se - cret sin.
Then, from sin and sor - row free, Take me, Lord, to dwell with thee.
Then, from thine e - ter - nal throne, Je - sus, look with pity - ing eye. A-men.

Jesus, the Very Thought of Thee

Jesu dulcis memoria
Latin: 12th century
Tr. Edward Caswall, 1814-1878, alt.

ST. AGNES C.M.
John B. Dykes, 1823-1876

1 Je - sus, the ver - y thought of thee, With sweet-ness fills my breast;
2 No voice can sing, no heart can frame, Nor can the mem - ory find
3 O hope of ev - ery con - trite heart, O joy of all the meek,
4 Je - sus, our on - ly joy be thou, As thou our prize wilt be;

But sweet-er far thy face to see, And in thy pres-ence rest.
A sweet-er sound than thy blest name, O Sav-ior of man-kind.
To those who fall, how kind thou art! How good to those who seek!
Je - sus, be thou our glo - ry now, And through e-ter - ni - ty. A - men.

283 O Splendor of God's Glory Bright

PRAISE TO CHRIST

Music from *Hymnal for Colleges and Schools;* used by permission of Yale University Press.

All Hail the Power of Jesus' Name

284

Edward Perronet, 1726-1792
Alt. John Rippon, 1751-1836

CORONATION C.M.
Oliver Holden, 1765-1844

1 All hail the power of Je - sus' name! Let an - gels pros - trate
2 Ye seed of Is - rael's cho - sen race, Ye ran-somed of the
3 Sin - ners, whose love can ne'er for - get The worm-wood and the
4 Let ev - ery kin - dred, ev - ery tribe, On this ter - res - trial
5 O that with yon - der sac - red throng We at his feet may

fall; Bring forth the roy - al di - a - dem, And
fall, Hail him who saves you by his grace, And
gall, Go spread your tro - phies at his feet, And
ball, To him all maj - es - ty as - cribe, And
fall! We'll join the ev - er - last - ing song, And

crown him Lord of all; Bring forth the roy - al
crown him Lord of all; Hail him who saves you
crown him Lord of all; Go spread your tro - phies
crown him Lord of all; To him all maj - es -
crown him Lord of all; We'll join the ev - er -

di - a - dem, And crown him Lord of all.
by his grace, And crown him Lord of all.
at his feet And crown him Lord of all.
ty as - cribe, And crown him Lord of all.
last - ing song, And crown him Lord of all. A - men.

285 Christ, Whose Glory Fills the Skies

Charles Wesley, 1707-1788

LUX PRIMA 7.7.7.7.7.7.
Charles F. Gounod, 1818-1893

Fairest Lord Jesus

Anonymous in *Münster Gesangbuch*, 1677

ST. ELIZABETH 5.6.8.5.5.8.
Silesian Melody

PRAISE TO CHRIST

287 How Brightly Beams the Morning Star

Philipp Nicolai, 1556-1608
Tr. Hymnal Version, 1955

WIE SCHÖN LEUCHTET DER MORGENSTERN 8.8.7.8.8.7.4.8.4.8.
Philipp Nicolai?, 1556-1608
Harm. by J. S. Bach, 1685-1750

PRAISE TO CHRIST

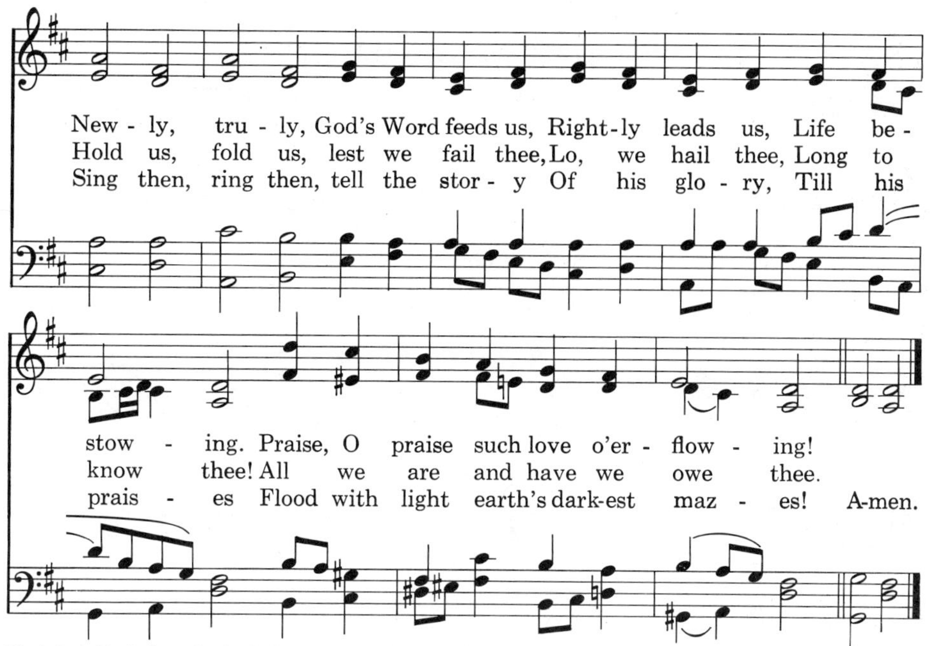

Words from *The Lutheran Service Book and Hymnal* by permission of the Commission on the Liturgy and Hymnal.

Jesus Shall Reign Where'er the Sun 288

Isaac Watts, 1674-1748

DUKE STREET L.M.
John Hatton, 1793

1 Je - sus shall reign wher-e'er the sun Doth his suc - ces - sive jour - neys run;
His king-dom stretch from shore to shore Till moons shall wax and wane no more.

2 For him shall end - less prayer be made, And prais-es throng to crown his head;
His name like sweet per - fume shall rise With ev - ery morn - ing sac - ri - fice.

3 Peo - ple and realms of ev - ery tongue Dwell on his love with sweet-est song,
And in - fant voic - es shall pro-claim Their ear - ly bless - ings on his name.

4 Bless-ings a - bound wher-e'er he reigns; The pris-oner leaps to lose his chains,
The wea - ry find e - ter - nal rest, And all the sons of want are blest.

5 Let ev - ery crea - ture rise and bring Pe - cul - iar hon - ors to our King;
An - gels de - scend with songs a - gain, And earth re - peat the loud A - men.

289 Jesus, Priceless Treasure

Jesu, meine Freude
Johann Franck, 1618-1677
Tr. Catherine Winkworth, 1827-1878 alt.

JESU, MEINE FREUDE 6.6.5.6.6.5.7.8.6.
German Traditional Melody
Adapt. and harm. Johann Crüger, 1598-1662

The Church's One Foundation

Samuel John Stone, 1839-1900

AURELIA 7.6.7.6.D.
Samuel Sebastian Wesley, 1810-1876

291 At the Name of Jesus

Caroline Maria Noel, 1817-1877

KING'S WESTON 6.5.6.5.D.
Ralph Vaughan Williams, 1872-1958

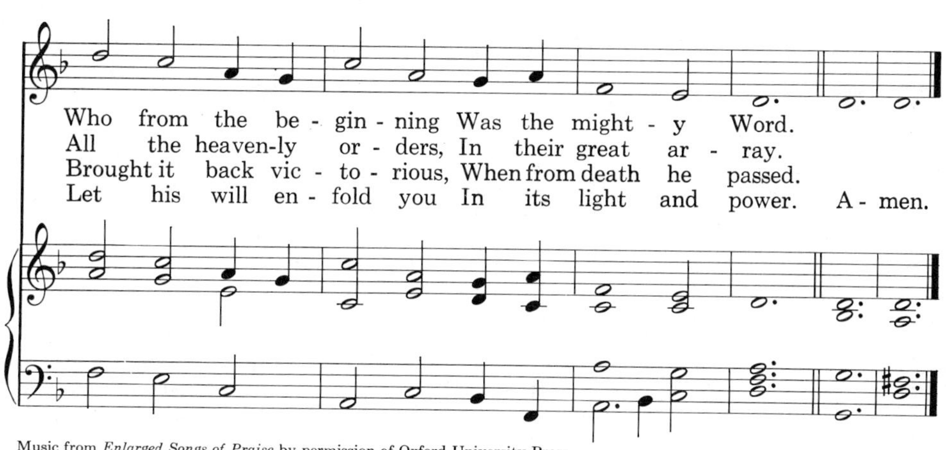

Music from *Enlarged Songs of Praise* by permission of Oxford University Press.

O Gladsome Light 292

Greek: φῶς ἱλαρόν 3rd century?
Tr. Robert S. Bridges, 1844-1930

NUNC DIMITTIS 6.6.7.6.6.7.
Attr. to Louis Bourgeois, c. 1510-c. 1561
Harm. adapted from Claude Goudimel, d. 1572

1 O glad-some light, O grace Of God the Fa-ther's face, Th'e-
2 Now, ere day fad - eth quite, We see the eve-ning light, Our
3 To thee of right be - longs All praise of ho - ly songs, O

ter - nal splen-dor wear - ing; Ce - les - tial, ho - ly, blest, Our
wont - ed hymn out - pour - ing; Fa - ther of might un - known, Thee,
Son of God, life - giv - er; Thee, there-fore, O Most High, The

Sav - ior Je - sus Christ, Joy - ful in thine ap - pear - ing.
his in - car-nate Son, And Ho - ly Spirit a - dor - ing.
world doth glo - ri - fy, And shall ex - alt for - ev - er. A - men.

Words from *The Yattendon Hymnal* by permission of Oxford University Press.

293 Master of Eager Youth

St. Clement of Alexandria, *c.* 170-220
Para. F. Bland Tucker, 1895-

ST. DUNSTAN'S 6.5.6.5.6.6.6.5.
Winfred Douglas, 1867-1944

PRAISE TO CHRIST

Alleluia! Sing to Jesus

William Chatterton Dix, 1837-1898

HYFRYDOL 8.7.8.7.D.
Melody by Rowland H. Prichard, 1811-1887

295 Come, Christians, Join to Sing

PRAISE TO CHRIST

When Morning Gilds the Skies

296

Beim frühen Morgenlicht
German: anon., 1828
Tr. Edward Caswall, 1814-1878, alt.

LAUDES DOMINI 6.6.6.6.6.6.
Joseph Barnby, 1838-1896

1 When morn - ing gilds the skies, My heart a - wak - ing
2 Be this, while life is mine, My can - ti - cle di -
3 Ye na - tions of man - kind, In this your con - cord
4 Sing, suns and stars of space, Sing, ye that see his

cries, May Je - sus Christ be praised! A -
vine, May Je - sus Christ be praised! Be
find: May Je - sus Christ be praised! Let
face, Sing, Je - sus Christ be praised! God's

like at work and prayer To Je - sus I re -
this the e - ter - nal song, Through all the a - ges
all the earth a - round Ring joy - ous with the
whole cre - a - tion o'er, For aye and ev - er -

pair; May Je - sus Christ be praised!
long, May Je - sus Christ be praised!
sound: May Je - sus Christ be praised!
more Shall Je - sus Christ be praised! A - men.

297 Love Divine, All Loves Excelling

Charles Wesley, 1707-1788, alt.

BEECHER 8.7.8.7.D.
John Zundel, 1815-1882

1 Love di - vine, all loves ex - cel - ling, Joy of heaven, to earth come down;
2 Breathe, O breathe thy lov - ing Spir - it In - to ev - ery trou - bled breast;
3 Come, al-might - y to de - liv - er, Let us all thy life re - ceive;
4 Fin - ish, then, thy new cre - a - tion; Pure and spot - less let us be,

Fix in us thy hum - ble dwell-ing, All thy faith-ful mer - cies crown;
Let us all in thee in - her - it, Let us find thy prom - ised rest;
Sud - den - ly re - turn and nev - er, Nev - er - more thy tem - ples leave.
Let us see thy great sal - va - tion Per - fect - ly re - stored in thee;

Je - sus, thou art all com-pas - sion, Pure, un-bound-ed love thou art;
Take a - way our love of sin - ning; Al - pha and O - me - ga be;
Thee we would be al - ways bless-ing, Serve thee as thy hosts a - bove,
Changed from glo-ry in - to glo - ry, Till in heaven we take our place,

Vis - it us with thy sal - va - tion, En - ter ev - ery trem - bling heart.
End of faith, as its be - gin-ning, Set our hearts at lib - er - ty.
Pray, and praise thee with-out ceas-ing, Glo - ry in thy per - fect love.
Till we cast our crowns be - fore thee, Lost in won-der, love, and praise. A-men.

Alternate tune No. 294

Jesus, Our Lord and King

300 Come, Holy Spirit, Dove Divine

A. Judson, 1788-1850

WILTON L.M.
S. Stanley, 1767-1822

BAPTISM

Dear Master, in Thy Way
301
J. Thomas, 1859- ?
ST. AUGUSTINE S.M.
Choralgesänge, 1769
1 Dear Mas - ter, in thy way Our will - ing feet shall tread;
2 The clos - ing wa - ters hid Our form - er world, and we,
3 And as we rise a - gain, Be this con - fes - sion given,
4 So would we die to live, And live no more to die;
What joy thy man-date to o - bey, Our great and glo-rious Head:
Seek-ing through death our Sav-ior's side, Re - joice to die with thee.
That we have risen with Christ to reign The Lord of earth and heaven.
Our ris - en lives, O Christ, re-ceive, And seal them in the sky. A-men.
A Parting Hymn We Sing
302
Aaron R. Wolfe, 1821-1902
FRANCONIA S.M.
Melody by J. B. König, 1691-1758
Arr. by William H. Havergal, 1793-1870
1 A part - ing hymn we sing A - round thy ta - ble, Lord;
2 Here have we seen thy face, And felt thy pres - ence here;
3 In self - for - get - ting love Be our com - mun - ion shown,
A - gain our grate-ful trib-ute bring, Our sol-emn vows re - cord.
So may the sav - or of thy grace In word and life ap - pear.
Un - til we join the church a - bove, And know as we are known. A-men.

303 Bread of the World, in Mercy Broken

First Tune

Reginald Heber, 1783-1826

RENDEZ À DIEU 9.8.9.8.D.
Genevan Psalter, 1543

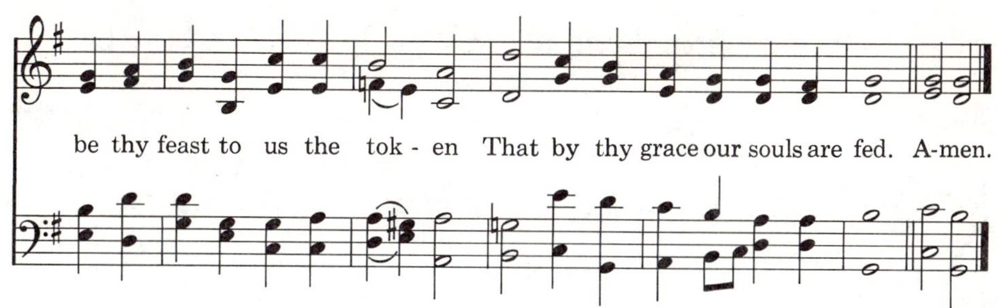

Bread of the World, in Mercy Broken 304

Second Tune

Reginald Heber, 1783-1826

EUCHARISTIC HYMN 9.8.9.8.
John S. B. Hodges, 1830-1915

1 Bread of the world, in mer - cy bro - ken, Wine of the
2 Look on the heart by sor - row bro - ken, Look on the

soul, in mer - cy shed, By whom the words of life were spo - ken,
tears by sin - ners shed, And be thy feast to us the to - ken

And in whose death our sins are dead,
That by thy grace our souls are fed. A - men.

305 Come, Risen Lord, and Deign to Be Our Guest

First Tune

George W. Briggs, 1875-1959

HOLBORN 10.10.10.10.
Eric H. Thiman, 1900-

Come, Risen Lord, and Deign to Be Our Guest

Second Tune

George W. Briggs, 1875-1959

BIRMINGHAM 10.10.10.10.
From F. Cunningham's *A Selection of Psalm Tunes*, 1834

307 Here at Thy Table, Lord
May P. Hoyt
BREAD OF LIFE 6.4.6.4.D.
William F. Sherwin, 1826-1888
1 Here at thy ta - ble, Lord, This sa - cred hour, O let us
2 Sit at the feast, dear Lord, Break thou the bread; Fill thou the
3 So shall our life of faith Be full, be sweet; And we shall
4 Come then, O ho - ly Christ, Feed us, we pray; Touch with thy
feel thee near, In lov - ing power; Call - ing our thoughts a - way
cup that brings Life to the dead; That we may find in thee,
find our strength For each day meet; Fed by thy liv - ing bread,
pierc - ed hand Each com - mon day; Mak - ing this earth - ly life
From self and sin. As to thy ban-quet hall We en - ter in.
Par - don and peace; And from all bond-age win A full re - lease.
All hun-ger past, We shall be sat - is - fied, And saved at last.
Full of thy grace, Till in the home of heaven We find our place. A-men.
308 Jesus, to Thy Table Led
Robert Hall Baynes, 1831-1895, alt.
TYHOLLAND 7.7.7.
German Carol Melody
Adapt. D. F. R. Wilson, 1871-1957
1 Je - sus, to thy ta - ble led, Now let ev - ery
2 When we taste the mys - tic wine, Of thine out - poured
3 From the bonds of sin re - lease; Cold and wav - ering

For the Bread, Which Thou Hast Broken 309

Louis F. Benson, 1855-1930

KINGDOM 8.7.8.7.
V. Earle Copes, 1921-

1 For the bread, which thou hast bro - ken, For the
2 By this pledge that thou dost love us, By thy
3 With our saint - ed ones in glo - ry Seat - ed
4 In thy ser - vice, Lord, de - fend us; In our

wine, which thou hast poured, For the words, which thou hast
gift of peace re - stored, By thy call to heaven a -
at our Fa - ther's board, May the Church that wait - eth
hearts keep watch and ward; In the world where thou dost

spo - ken, Now we give thee thanks, O Lord.
bove us, Hal - low all our lives, O Lord.
for thee Keep love's tie un - bro - ken, Lord.
send us Let thy king - dom come, O Lord. A - men.

310 Deck Thyself, My Soul, with Gladness

Schmücke dich, O liebe Seele
Johann Franck, 1618-1677
Tr. Catherine Winkworth, 1827-1878

SCHMÜCKE DICH 8.8.8.8.D.
Johann Crüger, 1598-1662

1 Deck thy - self, my soul, with glad - ness, Leave the gloom - y haunts of
2 Sun, who all my life dost bright - en; Light, who dost my soul en -
3 Je - sus, bread of life, I pray thee, Let me glad - ly here o -

sad - ness, Come in - to the day-light's splen - dor, There with
light - en; Joy, the sweet-est man e'er know - eth; Fount, whence
bey thee; Nev - er to my hurt in - vit - ed; Be thy

joy thy prais-es ren - der Un - to him whose grace un - bound - ed
all my be - ing flow - eth At thy feet I cry, my Mak - er,
love with love re - quit - ed; From this ban-quet let me meas - ure,

Hath this won-drous ban-quet found - ed; High o'er all the heavens he
Let me be a fit par - tak - er Of this bless-ed food from
Lord, how vast and deep its trea - sure; Through the gifts thou here dost

Be Known to Us in Breaking Bread 311

James Montgomery, 1771-1854

DUNFERMLINE C.M.
Scottish Psalter, 1615

1 Be known to us in breaking bread,
But do not then depart;
Savior, abide with us, and spread
Thy table in our heart.

2 There sup with us in love divine;
Thy body and thy blood,
That living bread, that heavenly wine,
Be our immortal food. Amen.

312 O Lord and Savior, as We Kneel Before Thee

George MacLaren Brydon, 1875-

DONNE SECOURS 11.10.11.10.
Genevan Psalter, 1551

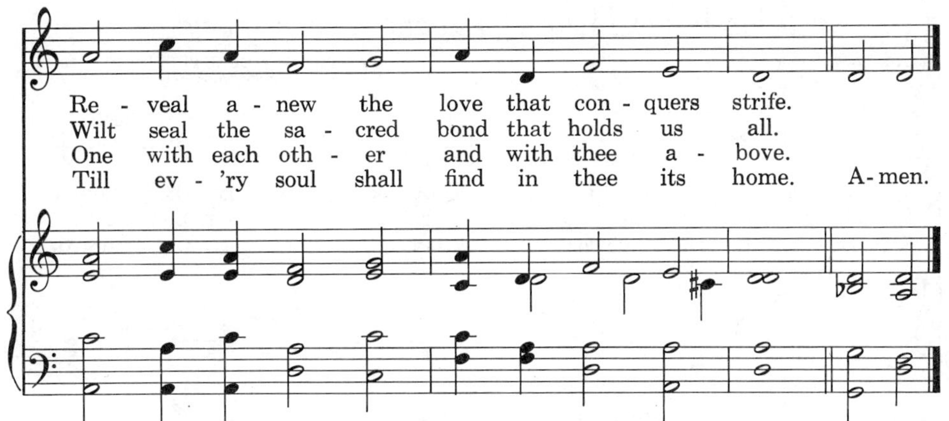

From Every Race, from Every Clime 313

Thomas B. McDormand, 1904-

BLACKBOURNE C.M.
Harrison's *Sacred Harmony,* 1784

1 From ev - ery race, from ev - ery clime Thy peo - ple gath - ered 'round
2 Par - tak - ing of the bread, we know Our strength from thee de - rives,
3 Through-out the world thy ta - ble's set, Dear Lord, our Sav - ior, Guide,
4 From north to south, from east to west Men ga - ther to re - call

The em-blems of thy grace sub-lime With grat - i - tude a - bound.
And as we take the cup, we go To wit-ness with our lives.
In hope we know that men shall yet In broth-er - hood a - bide.
In rev-erent mem - o - ry thy blest Re - demp-tive love for all. A-men.

314 This Is the Hour of Banquet and of Song

Horatius Bonar, 1808-1889, alt.

CANTICUM REFECTIONIS 10.10.10.10.
David McKinley Williams, 1887-

Let Us Break Bread Together

Negro Spiritual

LET US BREAK BREAD 7.3.7.3. with Refrain
Negro Melody

316 *Draw Us in the Spirit's Tether*

Percy Dearmer, 1867-1936

UNION SEMINARY 8.7.8.7.4.4.7.
Harold Friedell, 1905-1958
Adapt. Jet Turner, 1928-

Unison

1 Draw us in the Spir - it's te - ther, For when hum - bly
2 As the breth - ren used to gath - er In the name of
3 All our meals and all our liv - ing Make as sac - ra -

in thy name, Two or three are met to - geth - er, Thou art
Christ to sup, Then with thanks to God the Fa - ther Break the
ments of thee, That by car - ing, help-ing, giv - ing, We may

in the midst of them; Al - le - lu - ya! Al - le -
bread and bless the cup, Al - le - lu - ya, Al - le -
true dis - ci - ples be. Al - le - lu - ya, Al - le -

lu - ya! Touch we now thy gar - ment's hem.
lu - ya, So knit thou our friend - ship up.
lu - ya, We will serve thee faith - ful - ly. A-men.

Beneath the Forms of Outward Rite 317

First Tune

James A. Blaisdell, 1867-1957

BELMONT C.M.
William Gardiner's *Sacred Melodies* 1815

319 Humbly I Adore Thee

Thomas Aquinas, 1227-1274
Tr. J. R. Woodford, 1820-1885 (vss. 2, 3)

ADORO TE DEVOTE 11.11.11.11.
Solesmes version of the plainsong melody; adapted

The words for verse 1 are used by permission of The Church Pension Fund. Music from *Hymns for the Celebration of Life*, copyright © 1964 by The Unitarian Universalist Association. Reprinted by permission of the Beacon Press.

Jesus, Thou Joy of Loving Hearts 320

Anonymous, Latin, 12th century
Tr. and arr. by Ray Palmer, 1808-1887

HESPERUS L.M.
Henry Baker, 1835-1910

321 Jesus Christ, Our Blessed Savior

Jesus Christus nostra salus
?Jan Hus, 1369?-1415
German version, Martin Luther, 1483-1546
Tr. from *Hymnal for Colleges and Schools*, 1956

JESUS CHRISTUS, UNSER HEILAND 8.8.9.8.
Enchiridion, Erfurt, 1524
Harm. from *Songs of Syon*, 1904

1 Je - sus Christ, our bless - ed Sav - ior,
2 As his pledge of love un - dy - ing
3 Praise the Fa - ther, who from heav - en
4 If thy heart this truth pro - fess - es,

Shows his Fa - ther's love for - ev - er;
He, this pre - cious food sup - ply - ing,
Un - to us such food hath giv - en,
And thy mouth thy sin con - fess - es,

By his bit - ter grief and cru - el pain
Gives his sa - cred bod - y with the bread,
And, to mend the wrong that we have done,
As his wel - come guest thou here shalt be,

He purg - es us from ev - ery stain.
And with the wine the blood he shed.
Gave un - to death his on - ly Son.
And Christ him - self shall ban - quet thee. A - men.

Father, We Thank Thee Who Hast Planted

Greek, from the Didache, *c.* 110
Tr. F. Bland Tucker, 1895-

WEISSE 9.8.9.8.
Source unknown
Harm. J. S. Bach, 1685-1750

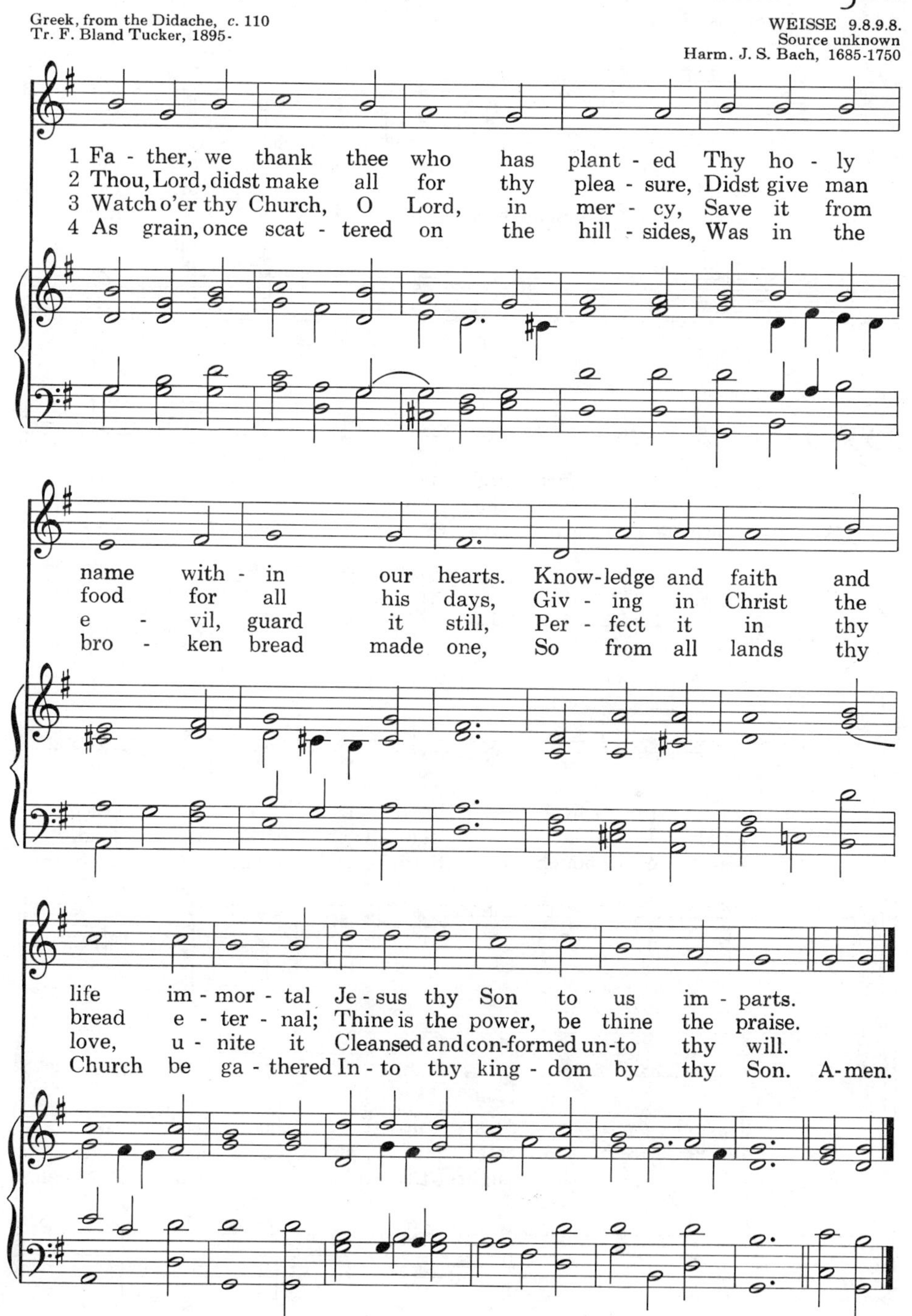

323 Here, O My Lord, I See Thee Face to Face

Horatius Bonar, 1808-1889

HOLBORN 10.10.10.10.
Eric H. Thiman, 1900-

According to Thy Gracious Word 324

James Montgomery, 1771-1854

DUNDEE C.M.
Scottish Psalter, 1615

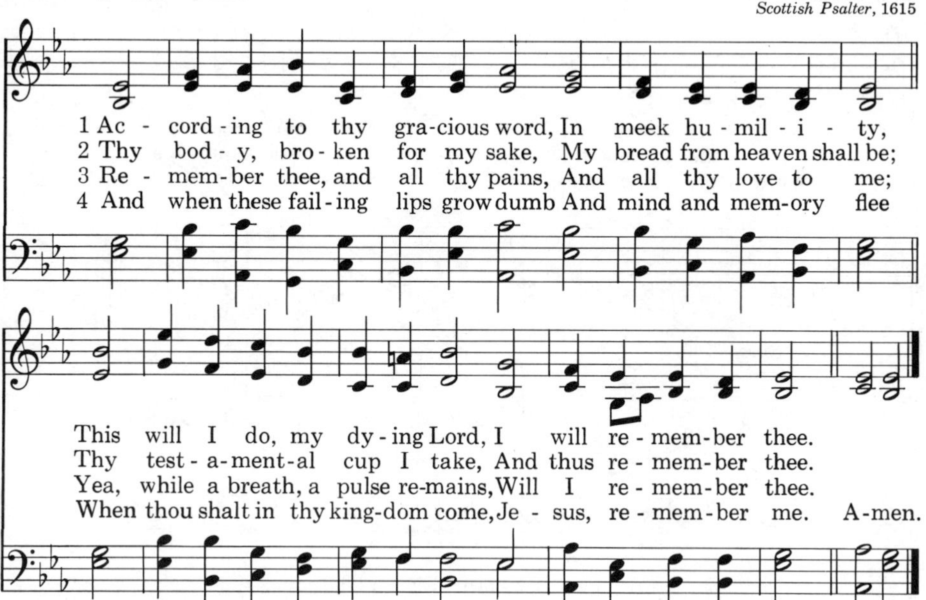

The Heavens Declare Thy Glory, Lord 325

Based on Psalm 19
Isaac Watts, 1674-1748

UXBRIDGE L.M.
Lowell Mason, 1792-1872

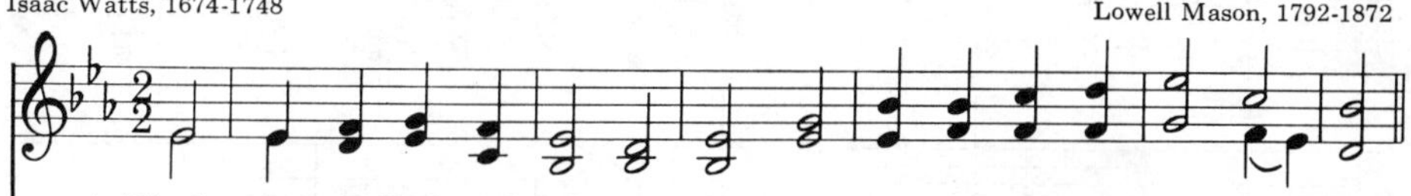

1 The heavens de-clare thy glo - ry, Lord; In ev - ery star thy wis-dom shines;
2 The roll - ing sun, the chang-ing light, And nights and days, thy power con-fess;
3 Sun, moon, and stars con-vey thy praise Round the whole earth and nev-er stand,
4 Nor shall thy spread-ing gos-pel rest Till through the world thy truth has run,

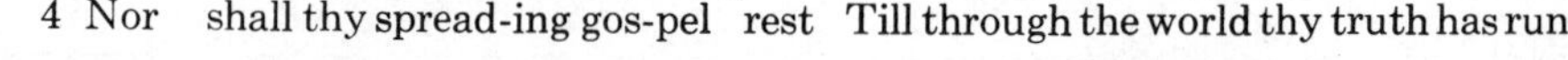

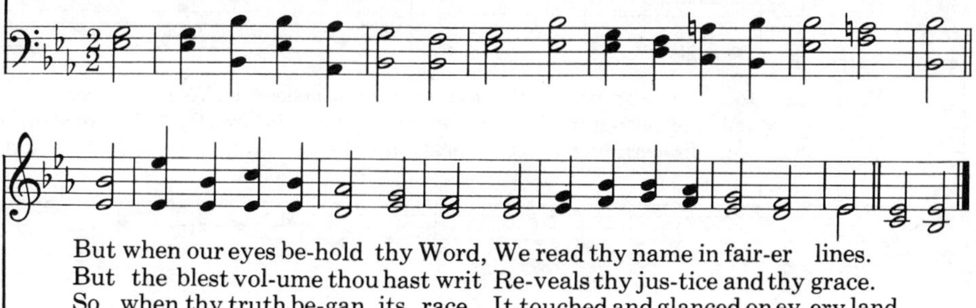

But when our eyes be-hold thy Word, We read thy name in fair-er lines.
But the blest vol-ume thou hast writ Re-veals thy jus-tice and thy grace.
So when thy truth be-gan its race, It touched and glanced on ev-ery land.
Till Christ has all the na-tions blest That see the light or feel the sun. A-men.

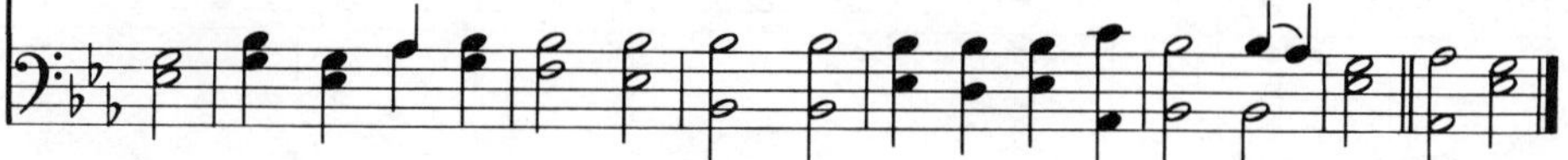

326 Lord, Thy Word Abideth

H. W. Baker, 1821-1877

CHESTERTON 6.6.6.6.D.
Geoffrey Beaumont, 1903-

Music taken from *Three Hymn Tunes from 20th-Century Folk Mass* by permission of the publishers, W. Paxton & Co. Ltd., London, W.1., England.

Break Thou the Bread of Life 327

Mary A. Lathbury, 1841-1913

BREAD OF LIFE 6.4.6.4.D.
William F. Sherwin, 1826-1888

1 Break thou the bread of life, Dear Lord, to me, As thou didst
2 Bless thou the truth, dear Lord, To me, to me, As thou didst
3 O send thy Spir - it, Lord, Now un - to me, That he may

break the loaves Be - side the sea; Be - yond the sa - cred page
bless the bread By Gal - i - lee; Then shall all bon-dage cease,
touch my eyes, And make me see: Show me the truth made known

I seek thee, Lord; My spir - it pants for thee, O liv - ing Word.
All fet - ters fall; And I shall find my peace, My all in all.
With-in thy Word, And in thy Book re-vealed I see the Lord. A-men.

Words and music used by permission of Chautauqua Institute.

SCRIPTURES

328 O Word of God Incarnate

SCRIPTURES

Book of Books, Our People's Strength 329

Percy Dearmer, 1867-1936

LIEBSTER JESU 7.8.7.8.8.8.
Melody by Johann R. Ahle, 1625-1673

Alternate version No. 212

Words from *Enlarged Songs of Praise* by permission of Oxford University Press.

330 O Zion, Haste, Thy Mission High Fulfilling

Mary A. Thomson, 1834-1923

TIDINGS 11.10.11.10. with Refrain
James Walch, 1837-1901

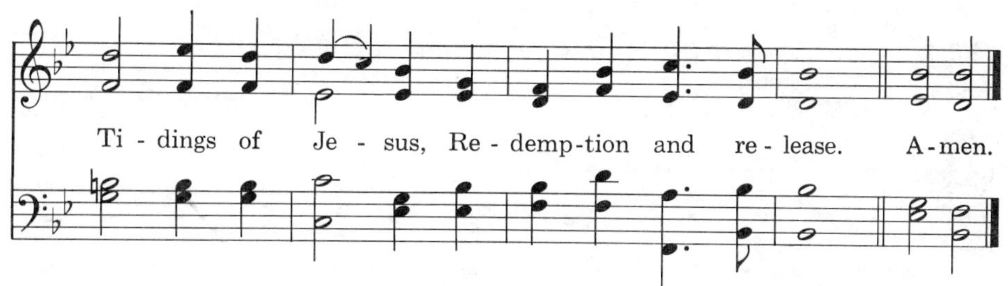

Let There Be Light, Lord God of Hosts 331

William M. Vories, 1880-1964, alt.

ELTON L.M.
Lowell Mason, 1792-1872

1 Let there be light, Lord God of hosts! Let there be
2 With - in our pas - sioned hearts in - still The calm that
3 Give us the peace of vi - sion clear To see our
4 Let woe and waste of war - fare cease, That use - ful

wis - dom on the earth! Let broad hu - man - i - ty have birth!
end - eth strain and strife; Make us thy min - is - ters of life;
broth-ers' good our own, To joy and suf - fer not a - lone:
la - bor yet may build Its homes with love and laugh - ter filled!

Let there be deeds, in - stead of boasts!
Purge us from lusts that curse and kill!
The love that cast - eth out all fear!
God, give thy way - ward chil - dren peace! A - men.

Words used by permission of the American Peace Society.

332 Draw Thou My Soul, O Christ
Lucy Larcom, 1826-1893
ST. EDMUND 6.4.6.4.6.6.6.4.
Arthur S. Sullivan, 1842-1900
1 Draw thou my soul, O Christ, Clos - er to thine; Breathe in - to ev - ery wish Thy will di - vine; Raised my low self a - bove, Won by thy death-less love, Ev - er, O Christ, through mine Let thy life shine.
2 Lead forth my soul, O Christ, One with thine own, Joy - ful to fol-low thee Through paths unknown; In thee my strength renew; Give me thy work to do; Through me thy truth be shown, Thy love made known.
3 Not for my-self a - lone May my prayer be; Lift thou thy world, O Christ, Clos - er to thee; Cleanse it from guilt and wrong; Teach it sal-va - tion's song, Till earth, as heaven, ful - fill God's ho - ly will. A-men.
333 Not Always on the Mount
Frederick Lucian Hosmer, 1840-1929
DANIEL L.M.
Irish Traditional Melody
1 Not al-ways on the mount may we Rapt in the heaven-ly vi - sion be:
2 "Lord, it is good a - bid-ing here," We cry, the heaven-ly pres-ence near:
3 Yet hath one such ex - alt - ed hour Up - on the soul re - deem-ing power,
4 The mount for vi - sion: but be - low The paths of dai - ly dut - y go,

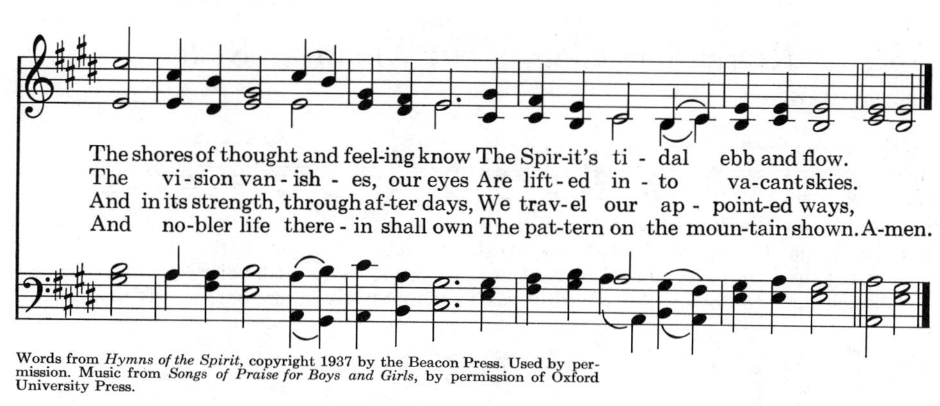

Words from *Hymns of the Spirit,* copyright 1937 by the Beacon Press. Used by permission. Music from *Songs of Praise for Boys and Girls,* by permission of Oxford University Press.

God of the Prophets! Bless the Prophets' Sons 334

Denis Wortman, 1835-1922

TOULON 10.10.10.10.
Genevan Psalter, 1551

1 God of the proph-ets! Bless the proph-ets' sons; E - li - jah's man - tle o'er E - li - sha cast; Each age its sol - emn task may claim but once; Make each one no-bler, strong-er than the last.

2 A - noint them proph-ets! Make their ears at - tent To thy di - vin - est speech; their hearts a-wake To hu-man need; their lips make el - o - quent To as-sure the right, and ev - ery e - vil break.

3 A - noint them priests! Strong in - ter - ces - sors they For par - don, and for char - i - ty and peace! O that with them might pass the world, a - stray, In - to the dear Christ's life of sac - ri - fice.

4 Make them a - pos - tles! Her - alds of the cross, Forth may they go to tell all realms thy grace, In - spired of thee, may they count all but loss, And stand at last with joy be - fore thy face. A-men.

335 Renew Thy Church, Her Ministries Restore

Mid Blackness of the City's Night

336

Sarah E. Taylor, 1883-1954

ST. PETERSBURG 8.8.8.8.8.8.
Arr. from Dmitri S. Bortniansky, 1751-1825

1 Mid blackness of the city's night
Beyond its cheering warmth and light,
The sons of want and misery
Send forth their anguished prayers to thee;
With weary eyes they seek thy face,
O God of mercy and of grace.

2 We see thee in the starry height,
A God of mystery and might;
But from the crowded city street,
Its turmoil, conflict and defeat,
The children of thine erring race
Entreat thy mercy and thy grace.

3 Forgive thy servants, Lord, we pray,
Who name thy name from day to day,
Yet hide thee from the soul in need
By careless word and selfish deed;
While love of gold and pride of race
Hinder thy mercy and thy grace.

4 As our Redeemer, sent of thee,
Through busy towns of Galilee
Revealed thy goodness and thy love,
Inspire thy servants, Lord to prove
To every son of every race
Thy way of universal grace. Amen.

337 Give Me the Eyes to See This Child

Miriam Dewey Ross, 1927-

SALVATION 8.6.8.8.6.
Ananias Davisson's *Kentucky Harmony*, c. 1815, adapted

Come, Labor On

Jane L. Borthwick, 1813-1897, alt.

ORA LABORA 4.10.10.10.4.
T. Tertius Noble, 1867-1953

339 Turn Back, O Man, Forswear Thy Foolish Ways

Clifford Bax, 1886-1962

OLD 124th 10.10.10.10.10.
Genevan Psalter, 1551

Word of Life, Most Pure, Most Strong 340

J. F. Bahnmaier, 1774-1841
Tr. Catherine Winkworth, 1827-1878, alt.

PLEYEL'S HYMN 7.7.7.7.
Ignace Pleyel, 1757-1831

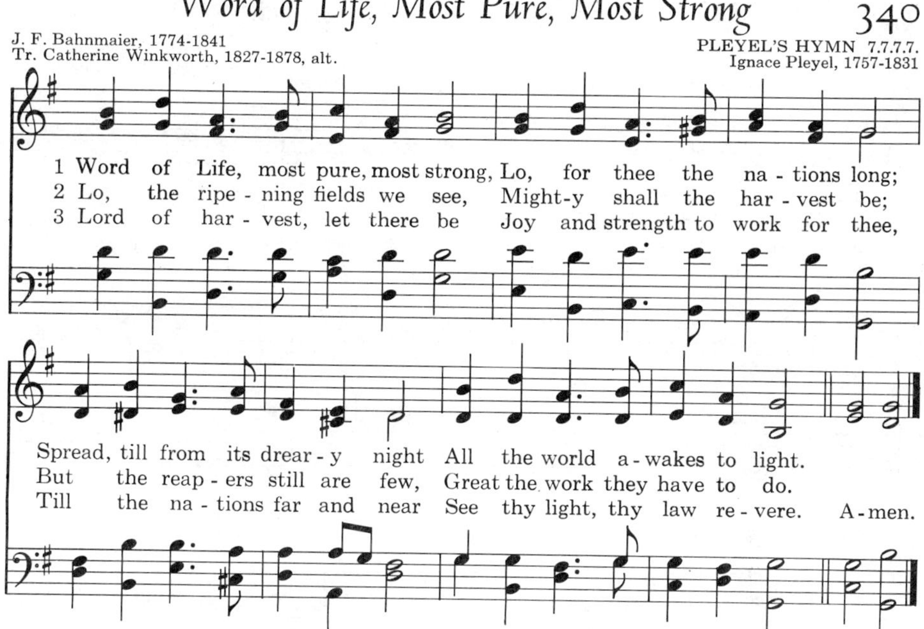

Teach Me, My God and King 341

George Herbert, 1593-1632
Adapt. John Wesley, 1703-1791

MORNINGTON S.M.
Garret Wellesley, 1735-1781

1 Teach me, my God and King, In all things thee to see;
2 To scorn the sens - es sway, While still to thee I tend,
3 All may of thee par - take; Noth - ing so small can be,
4 If done be - neath thy laws, E'en ser - vile la - bors shine;

And what I do in an - y - thing, To do it as for thee.
In all I do, be thou the way, In all, be thou the end.
But draws, when act - ed for thy sake, Great-ness and worth from thee.
Hal-lowed is toil if this the cause; The mean-est work di - vine. A-men.

342 We Are Living, We Are Dwelling

Arthur C. Coxe, 1818-1896, alt.

EBENEZER 8.7.8.7.D.
Thomas John Williams, 1869-1944

Hark! the waking up of nations, Hosts advancing
Worlds are charging, heaven beholding; Thou hast but an
O let all the soul within you For the truth's sake
to the fray, Hark! what soundeth is creation's
hour to fight; Now, the blazoned cross unfolding,
go abroad! Strike! let every nerve and sinew
Groaning for the latter day.
On, right onward for the right!
Tell on ages, tell for God. Amen.

343 *Break Forth, O Living Light of God*

Frank von Christierson, 1900-

ST. PETER C.M.
Alexander R. Reinagle, 1799-1877

344 *Lord, Speak to Me, that I May Speak*

Frances R. Havergal, 1836-1879

HOLLEY L.M.
George Hews, 1806-1873

1 Lord, speak to me, that I may speak In liv-ing ech - oes of thy tone;
2 O teach me, Lord, that I may teach The pre-cious things thou dost im - part;
3 O fill me with thy ful - ness, Lord, Un - til my ver - y heart o'er - flow
4 O use me, Lord, use e - ven me, Just as thou wilt, and when, and where;

As thou hast sought, so let me seek Thy err-ing chil-dren lost and lone.
And wing my words, that they may reach The hid-den depths of man-y a heart.
In kind-ling thought and glow-ing word, Thy love to tell, thy praise to show.
Un - til thy bless-ed face I see, Thy rest, thy joy, thy glo - ry share. A-men.

O God of Might, O Son of Light

Ross Coggins, 1927-

Indonesian Folk Tune
Arr. James Bigelow, 1956

1 O God of might, O Son of light, O Ho - ly Spir - it sweet,
2 With ho - ly fire my heart in - spire Thy Spir - it's sword to wield;

Thy church ex - pand till all shall stand At Je - sus' pierc - ed feet.
With bor-rowed might I'll take thy light, Till dark-ness' doom be sealed.

Let all who once thy Son dis-owned Re - joice to see him now en-throned;
If oth - ers stop to count the cost, For fear of earth - ly treas - ures lost,

Yet while one stray - ing soul there be, Send me, O Lord, send me.
I'll count it gain to die for thee; Send me, O Lord, send me.

346 O Church of God in Every Land
Wilbur C. Christians, 1912-
WINDHAM L.M.
Daniel Read, 1757-1836
1 O Church of God in ev - ery land, O force for right from God's own hand, Through thee God's love is shown to all, To na - tions great, and chil - dren small.
2 O Lord of time and space and power, We seek thee in this ho - ly hour. O grant us cour - age to be free, In mind, in soul, in all, in thee.
3 O Lord, our God, whose pres - ence now, We sense in song and sa - cred vow. Grant us for - give - ness, in - ner peace, And then from sin a sure re - lease.
Words used by permission of the author.
347 Lord Christ, the Father's Mighty Son
Brian A. Wren, 1936-
HAMPTON POYLE 8.8.5.8.6.
Peter Warwick Cutts, 1937-
1 Lord Christ, the Fa - ther's might - y Son, Whose
2 To make us one your prayers were said, To
3 Lord Christ, for - give us, make us new! What
4 We will not ques - tion or re - fuse The

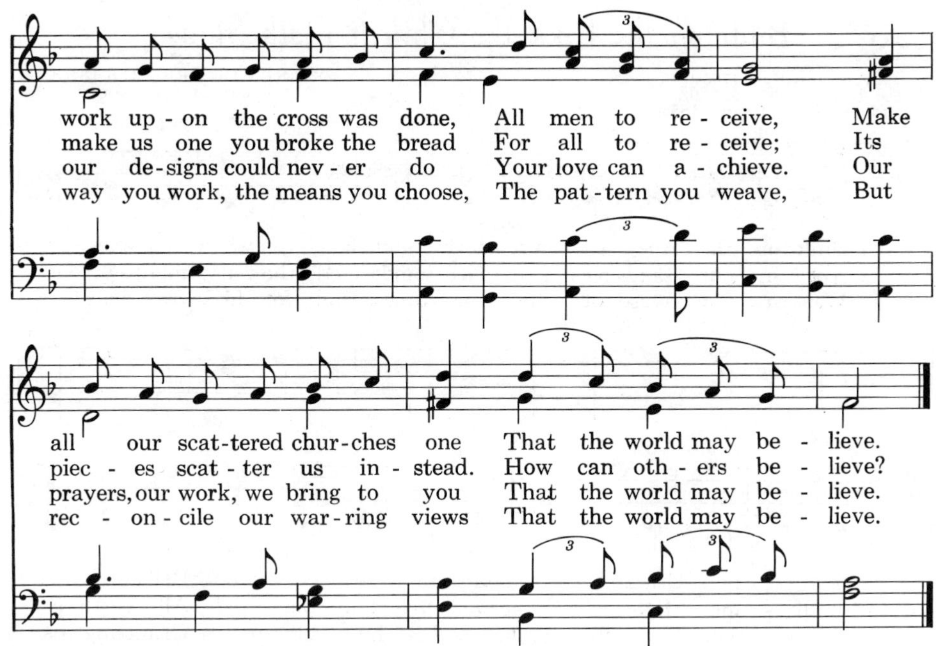

I Love Thy Kingdom, Lord 348

Timothy Dwight, 1752-1817

ST. THOMAS S.M.
Williams' *New Universal Psalmodist,* 1770

1 I love thy king - dom, Lord, The house of thine a - bode,
2 I love thy Church, O God! Her walls be - fore thee stand,
3 For her my tears shall fall, For her my prayers as - cend,
4 Be - yond my high - est joy I prize her heaven-ly ways,
5 Sure as thy truth shall last, To Zi - on shall be given

The Church our blest Re - deem - er saved With his own pre-cious blood.
Dear as the ap - ple of thine eye, And grav - en on thy hand.
To her my cares and toils be given, Till toils and cares shall end.
Her sweet com-mun-ion, sol - emn vows, Her hymns of love and praise.
The bright-est glo - ries earth can yield, And bright-er bliss of heaven. A - men.

UNITY

349 Built on the Rock the Church Doth Stand

Nicolai F. S. Grundtvig, 1783-1872
Tr. Carl Doving, 1867- 1937, alt.
Revised, Fred C. M. Hansen, 1888-

KIRKEN DEN ER ET 8.8.8.8.8.8.8.
Ludwig M. Lindeman, 1812-1887

1 Built on the Rock the church doth stand, E - ven when stee-ples are
2 Not in our tem-ples made with hands God, the al-might-y, is
3 We are God's house of liv-ing stones, Built for his own hab-i-

fall - ing; Crum-bled have spires in ev-ery land, Bells still are
dwell - ing; High in the heavens his tem-ple stands, All earth-ly
ta - tion; He fills our hearts, his hum-ble thrones, Grant-ing us

chim-ing and call - ing; Call-ing the young and old to rest, Call-ing the
tem-ples ex-cell - ing; Yet he who dwells in heaven a-bove Deigns to a-
life and sal-va - tion; Were two or three to seek his face, He in their

souls of men dis-tressed, Long-ing for life ev-er-last - ing.
bide with us in love, Mak-ing our bod-ies his tem - ple.
midst would show his grace, Bless-ings up-on them be-stow - ing. A-men.

UNITY

Forgive, O Lord, Our Severing Ways 350

John Greenleaf Whittier, 1807-1892, and others

EISENACH L.M.
Johann Hermann Schein, 1586-1630
Harm. J. S. Bach, 1685-1750

1 For - give, O Lord, our sev-ering ways, The ri - val al - tars
2 A sweet - er song shall then be heard, Con - fess - ing, in a

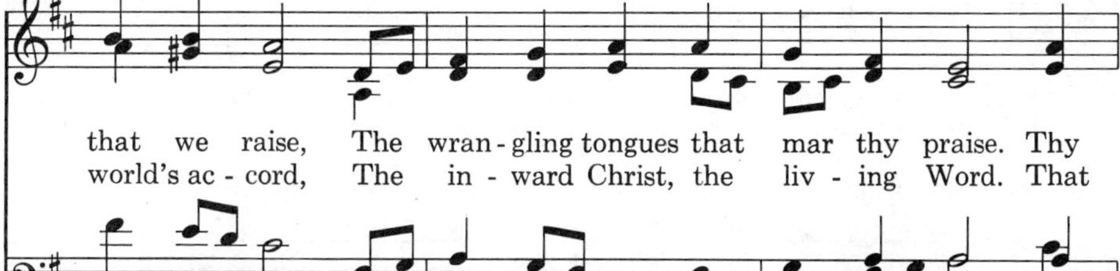

that we raise, The wran - gling tongues that mar thy praise. Thy
world's ac - cord, The in - ward Christ, the liv - ing Word. That

grace im - part; in time to be Shall one great tem - ple
song shall swell from shore to shore, One hope, one faith, one

rise to thee— One church for all hu - man - i - ty.
love re - store, The seam - less robe that Je - sus wore. A - men.

UNITY

351 Our Father, Thou Almighty God

Russell F. Harrison, 1918-

ALL SAINTS NEW C.M.D.
Henry S. Cutler, 1824-1902

UNITY

Lord, We Thank Thee for Our Brothers

Roger K. Powell, 1914-

AUSTRIAN HYMN 8.7.8.7.D.
Franz Joseph Haydn, 1732-1809

1 Lord, we thank thee for our broth-ers Keep-ing faith with us and thee,
Join-ing heart to heart with oth-ers, Mak-ing strong our com-pa-ny,
With the cross our on-ly stand-ard Let us sing with one great voice,
Glo-ry, glo-ry, thine the king-dom; Church-es in thy Church re-joice.

2 God be praised for con-gre-ga-tions Com-ing side by side to thee;
Man-y tongues of man-y na-tions Sing the great-er u-ni-ty.
Sweet the psalm and sweet the car-ol When our song is raised as one.
Glo-ry, glo-ry, thine the pow-er, As in heaven thy will be done.

3 Hal-lowed be thy name for-ev-er! Heal our dif-feren-ces of old;
Bless thy Church's new en-deav-or; For thy king-dom makes us bold.
One our Christ and one our gos-pel, Make us one we now im-plore.
Glo-ry, glo-ry, thine the glo-ry Through the a-ges ev-er-more. A-men.

Words used by permission of Roger K. Powell.

353
O Church of God, Divided
Marion Franklin Ham, 1867-1956
BLOMSTERTID 7.6.7.6.D.
Swedish Koralbok, 1697
1 O Church of God, di - vid - ed And rent by end - less strife!
2 The sub - tle powers of dark - ness, Like foe - men in the night,
3 Dis - perse thy war - ring fac - tions, And bid their con - flicts cease;
Thy war - ring sects ob - scur - ing The way, the truth, the life;
Ad - vance up - on the strong-holds Of jus - tice, truth and right;
Lift high the fall - en stand - ard Of Christ, the Prince of Peace;
A strick - en world, de - spair - ing, Is call - ing un - to thee;
The might - y sway of e - vil Pre - vails in ev - ery land;
One Lord, one faith, one Spir - it, One God of all pro - claim;
O Church of Christ's e - van - gel, What shall thine an - swer be?
O Church of God's a - noint - ing, A - rise, and take thy stand!
Go forth, O Church, u - nit - ed, To con-quer in his name! A-men.

UNITY

Glorious Things of Thee Are Spoken

John Newton, 1725-1807

AUSTRIAN HYMN 8.7.8.7.D.
Franz Joseph Haydn, 1732-1809

1 Glo - rious things of thee are spo - ken, Zi - on, cit - y of our God;
2 See, the streams of liv - ing wa - ters, Springing from e - ter - nal love,
3 Round each hab - i - ta - tion hov-ering, See the cloud and fire ap - pear

He whose word can-not be bro - ken Formed thee for his own a - bode.
Well sup-ply thy sons and daughters, And all fear of want re - move.
For a glo - ry and a covering, Show - ing that the Lord is near!

On the Rock of A - ges founded, What can shake thy sure re - pose?
Who can faint, while such a riv - er Ev - er flows their thirst to as-suage?
Thus de - riv - ing from their ban - ner Light by night and shade by day,

With sal-va-tion's walls surrounded, Thou may'st smile at all thy foes.
Grace, which like the Lord, the Giver, Nev - er fails from age to age.
Safe they feed up - on the man-na Which he gives them when they pray. A-men.

355 Christ Is the King!

George Kennedy Allen Bell, 1883-1958

SOUTH GORE 8.8.8.8.8.8.
Ronald Arnatt, 1930-

faith for - ev - er new Fol - lowed the
a - ges is the same: Place the same
will on earth be done, New lamps be
King, and round him drew Thou-sands of faith - ful men and
hope in his great Name, With the same faith his word pro -
lit, new tasks be - gun, And the whole Church at last be
1, 2
3.
true
claim.
one. A - men.
rall . . . en . . tan . . . . do . . . .

UNITY

356 *Thy Hand, O God, Has Guided*

E. H. Plumptre, 1821-1891

REX SUMMAE MAJESTATIS 7.6.7.6.D.
A. Gregory Murray, 1905-

1 Thy hand, O God, has guid - ed Thy flock from age to age;
2 Thy her-alds brought glad tid - ings To great-est, as to least;
3 Through man-y a day of dark - ness, Through man-y a scene of strife,
4 Thy mer - cy will not fail us, Nor leave thy work un - done;

The won-drous tale is writ - ten, Full clear, on ev - ery page;
They bade men rise, and hast - en To share the great King's feast;
The faith - ful few fought brave - ly To guard the na - tion's life.
With thy right hand to help us, The vic - tory shall be won;

Our fa - thers owned thy good - ness, And we their deeds re - cord;
And this was all their teach - ing, In ev - ery deed and word,
Their gos - pel of re - demp - tion, Sin par-doned, man re - stored,
And then, by men and an - gels, Thy name shall be a - dored,

And both of this bear wit - ness, One Church, one Faith, one Lord.
To all a - like pro - claim - ing One Church, one Faith, one Lord.
Was all in this en - fold - ed, One Church, one Faith, one Lord.
And this shall be their an - them, One Church, one Faith, one Lord.

UNITY

Father, Let Me Dedicate

Lawrence Tuttiett, 1825-1897

DEDICATION 7.5.7.5.D.
G. A. Macfarren, 1813-1887

1 Fa - ther, let me de - di-cate All this year to thee,
2 Can a child pre - sume to choose Where or how to live?
3 If in mer - cy thou wilt spare Joys that yet are mine;
4 If thou call - est to the cross, And its shad - ow come,

In what - ev - er world - ly state Thou wilt have me be.
Can a fa - ther's love re - fuse All the best to give?
If on life, se - rene and fair, Bright - er rays may shine,
Turn-ing all my gain to loss, Shroud - ing heart and home,

Not for sor - row, pain, or care, Free - dom dare I claim;
More thou giv - est ev - ery day Than the best can claim,
Let my glad heart, while it sings, Thee in all pro - claim,
Let me think how thy dear Son To his glo - ry came,

This a-lone shall be my prayer: "Glo - ri - fy thy name."
Nor with-hold-est aught that may "Glo - ri - fy thy name."
And what-e'er the fu - ture brings, "Glo - ri - fy thy name."
And in deep-est woe pray on: "Glo - ri - fy thy name." A - men.

358 God Is Working His Purpose Out

Arthur C. Ainger, 1841-1919

PURPOSE Irregular
Martin Shaw, 1875-1958

Music from *Enlarged Songs of Praise* by permission of Oxford University Press.

359 *Another Year Is Dawning*

Frances R. Havergal, 1836-1879

AURELIA 7.6.7.6.D.
Samuel Sebastian Wesley, 1810-1876

1 An - oth - er year is dawn - ing, Dear Fa - ther, let it be
2 An - oth - er year of mer - cies, Of faith - ful - ness and grace,
3 An - oth - er year of serv - ice, Of wit - ness for thy love,

In work - ing or in wait - ing An - oth - er year with thee;
An - oth - er year of glad - ness In the shin - ing of thy face,
An - oth - er year of train - ing For ho - lier work a - bove.

An - oth - er year of prog - ress, An - oth - er year of praise,
An - oth - er year of lean - ing Up - on thy lov - ing breast,
An - oth - er year is dawn - ing, Dear Fa - ther, let it be

An - oth - er year of prov - ing Thy pres - ence all the days;
An - oth - er year of trust - ing, Of qui - et, hap - py rest;
On earth, or else in heav - en, An - oth - er year for thee. A - men.

Lord, Thou Hast Set an Open Door 360

Roger K. Powell, 1914-

PARIS 8.10.10.10.
William Billings, 1746-1800

361 Sing to the Great Jehovah's Praise
Charles Wesley, 1707-1788
LOBT GOTT IHR CHRISTEN C.M.
Melody by Nikolaus Herman, c. 1485-1561
1 Sing to the great Je - ho - vah's praise! All praise to him be - longs; Who kind - ly length - ens out our days, In - spires our choic - est songs, In - spires our choic - est songs.
2 His prov - i - dence hath brought us through An - oth - er var - ious year; We all, with vows and an - thems new, Be - fore our God ap - pear, Be - fore our God ap - pear.
3 O God, thy mer - cies past we own, And thy con - tin - ued care; To thee pre - sent - ing through thy Son What - e'er we have and are, What - e'er we have and are.
A - men.

Praise to God, Your Praises Bring 362

William C. Gannett, 1840-1923, alt.

SAVANNAH 7.7.7.7.
The Foundery Collection, 1742

364 Great God, We Sing That Mighty Hand

Philip Doddridge, 1702-1751

WAREHAM L.M.
William Knapp, 1698-1768

1 Great God, we sing that mighty hand
By which supported still we stand;
The opening year thy mercy shows,
That mercy crowns it till it close.

2 By day, by night, at home, abroad,
Still are we guarded by our God:
By his incessant bounty fed,
By his unerring counsel led.

3 With grateful hearts the past we own;
The future, all to us unknown,
We to thy guardian care commit,
And, peaceful, leave before thy feet.

4 In scenes exalted or depressed,
Thou art our joy, and thou our rest;
Thy goodness all our hopes shall raise,
Adored through all our changing days. Amen.

Lord of the Church, We Humbly Pray

Charles Wesley, 1707-1788

CORNWALL 8.8.6.D.
Samuel Sebastian Wesley, 1810-1876

DEDICATION: MINISTER

366 In This House by Men Constructed

Herbert E. Hinton, 1890-

PLEADING SAVIOR 8.7.8.7.D.
Joshua Leavitt's *Christian Lyre*, 1830

DEDICATION: CHURCH

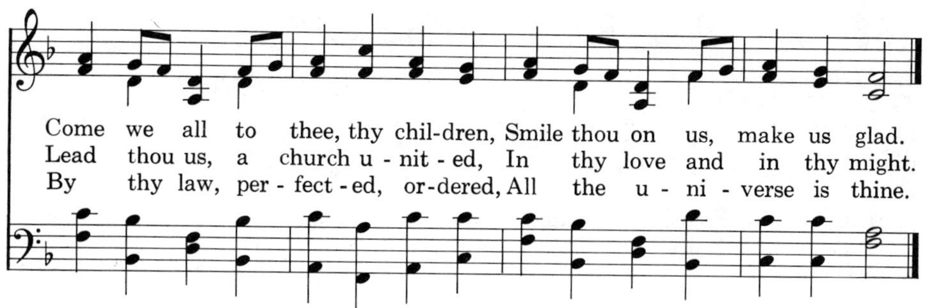

Words used by permission of Herbert Ernest Hinton; music from *Hymns for the Celebration of Life* by permission of Beacon Press.

367 O Thou, Whose Own Vast Temple Stands

William Cullen Bryant, 1794-1878

DUNDEE C.M.
Scottish Psalter; 1615

1 O thou, whose own vast temple stands
Built o - ver earth and sea,
Accept the walls that human hands
Have raised to worship thee.

2 Lord, from thine in - most glory send,
With - in these courts to a - bide,
The peace that dwell - eth without end
Se - rene - ly by thy side.

3 May err - ing minds that worship here
Be taught the better way;
And they who mourn and they who fear
Be strength - ened as they pray.

4 May faith grow firm and love grow warm,
And pure de - vo - tion rise,
While round these hal - lowed walls the storm
Of earth - born pas - sion dies. A - men.

368 *Jesus, Friend, So Kind and Gentle*

Philip E. Gregory, 1886-

DULCE CARMEN 8.7.8.7.8.7.
"An Essay on the Church Plain Chant," 1782

DEDICATION: CHILDREN

Words used by permission of Philip E. Gregory.

God of the Nations, Who from Dawn of Days

W. Russell Bowie, 1882-1969

TOULON 10.10.10.10.
Abridged from *Genevan Psalter*, 1551

370 Eternal Father, Strong to Save

My Country, 'Tis of Thee 371

4 Our father's God, to thee,
Author of liberty,
To thee we sing;
Long may our land be bright
With freedom's holy light;
Protect us by thy might,
Great God, our King.

372 Thou Judge by Whom Each Empire Fell

Percy Dearmer, 1867-1936

NUN FREUT EUCH 8.7.8.7.8.8.7.
Klug's *Geistliche Lieder*, Wittenberg, 1535

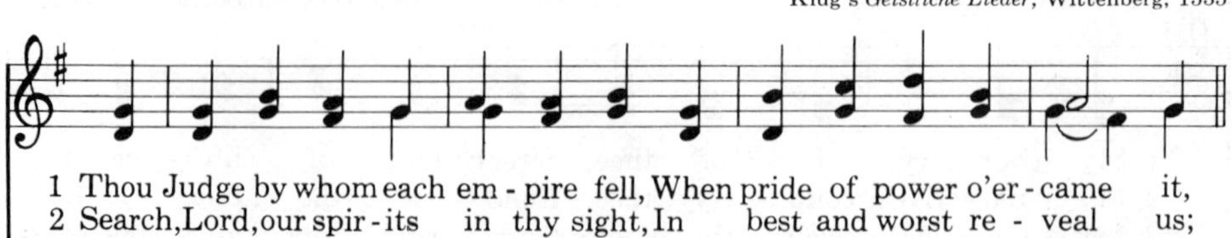

1 Thou Judge by whom each em - pire fell, When pride of power o'er - came it,
2 Search, Lord, our spir - its in thy sight, In best and worst re - veal us;
3 Lo, fear - ing nought we come to thee, Though by our fault con - found - ed;

Con - vict us now, if we re - bel, Our na - tion judge, and shame it.
Shed on our souls a blaze of light, And judge, that thou may'st heal us.
Though self - ish, mean, and base we be, Thy jus - tice is un - bound - ed:

In each sharp cri - sis, Lord, ap - pear, For - give, and show our
The pres - ent be our judg - ment day, When all our lack thou
So large, it nought but love re - quires, And, judg - ing, pard - ons,

du - ty clear: To serve thee by re - pent - ance.
dost sur - vey: Show us our - selves and save us.
frees, in - spires. De - liv - er us from e - vil! A - men.

O God of Earth and Altar

Gilbert K. Chesterton, 1874-1936

LLANGLOFFAN 7.6.7.6.D.
Traditional Welsh Melody

1 O God of earth and altar, Bow down and hear our cry;
Our earthly rulers falter, Our people drift and die;
The walls of gold entomb us, The swords of scorn divide;
Take not thy thunder from us, But take away our pride.

2 From all that terror teaches, From lies of tongue and pen,
From all the easy speeches That comfort cruel men,
From sale and profanation Of honor and the sword,
From sleep and from damnation, Deliver us, O Lord!

3 Tie in a living tether The prince and priest and thrall;
Bind all our lives together, Smite us and save us all;
In fire and exultation Aflame with faith, and free,
Lift up a living nation, A single sword to thee. Amen.

374 O Beautiful for Spacious Skies

Katharine Lee Bates, 1859-1929

MATERNA C.M.D.
Samuel A. Ward, 1847-1903

1 O beau - ti - ful for spa - cious skies, For am - ber waves of grain,
2 O beau - ti - ful for pil - grim feet, Whose stern, im - pas - sioned stress
3 O beau - ti - ful for he - roes proved In lib - er - at - ing strife,
4 O beau - ti - ful for pa - triot dream That sees be - yond the years

For pur - ple moun - tain maj - es - ties A - bove the fruit - ed plain!
A thor - ough - fare for free - dom beat A - cross the wil - der - ness!
Who more than self their coun - try loved, And mer - cy more than life!
Thine al - a - bas - ter cit - ies gleam, Un - dimmed by hu - man tears!

A - mer - i - ca! A - mer - i - ca! God shed his grace on thee,
A - mer - i - ca! A - mer - i - ca! God mend thine ev - ery flaw,
A - mer - i - ca! A - mer - i - ca! May God thy gold re - fine,
A - mer - i - ca! A - mer - i - ca! God shed his grace on thee,

And crown thy good with broth - er - hood From sea to shin - ing sea.
Con - firm thy soul in self - con - trol, Thy lib - er - ty in law.
Till all suc - cess be no - ble - ness, And ev - ery gain di - vine.
And crown thy good with broth - er - hood From sea to shin - ing sea. A - men.

Before Thee, Lord, We Join Our Hearts

Mildred Harner Foltz, 1910-

ROSEATE HUES C.M.D.
Joseph Barnby, 1838-1896

1 Be - fore thee, Lord, we join our hearts And hands in mar - riage now;
2 Then, help us find in com-mon tasks, With which each home is filled,
3 Though our own strength so of - ten fails We thank thee that we know

Be thou the guard-ian of this rite, And con - se - crate each vow.
The beau-ty and the lov - ing joy In which life's storms are stilled;
Thy prom-ise to a - bide with us Wher-ev - er we must go.

We would so build our home, O Lord, That it shall ev - er be
And give us gra - ti - tude to speak A word of thanks or praise
Be thou our glo-rious morn-ing song With ev - ery day be - gun:

A shel - ter from the stress of life, A ha-ven blest by thee.
To those who do the kind-ly things That glad-den all our days.
Be thou our clos-ing ves-per hymn When ev-ery day is done. A-men.

376 O Love Divine and Golden

John Samuel Bewley Monsell, 1811-1875

BLAIRGOWRIE (Dykes) 13.13.13.13.
John B. Dykes, 1823-1876

1 O Love di - vine and gold - en, Mys - ter - ious depth and height,

To thee the world be - hold - en, Looks up for life and light.

God bless these hands u - nit - ed; God bless these hearts made one!

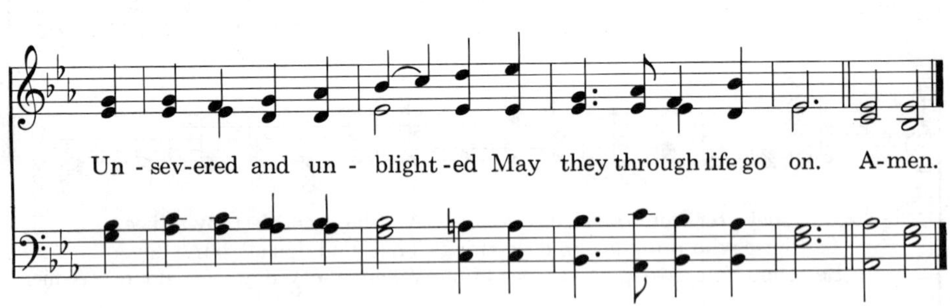

O Thou Whose Favor Hallows All Occasions 377

Miriam Drury, 1900-

THOMAS CIRCLE 11.10.11.10.11.10.
Lawrence P. Schreiber, 1933-

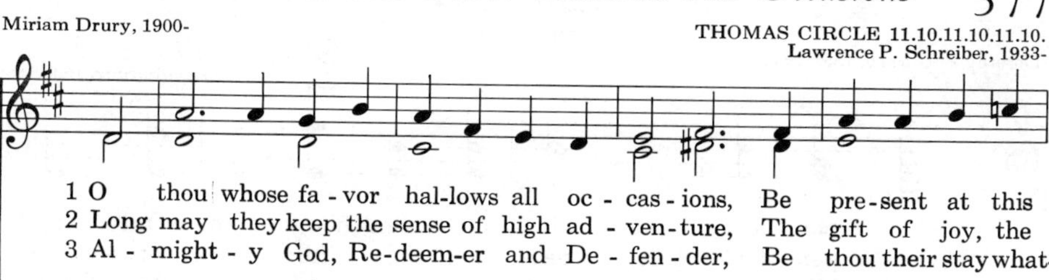

1 O thou whose fa - vor hal-lows all oc - cas - ions, Be pre - sent at this
2 Long may they keep the sense of high ad - ven - ture, The gift of joy, the
3 Al - might - y God, Re-deem-er and De - fen - der, Be thou their stay what-

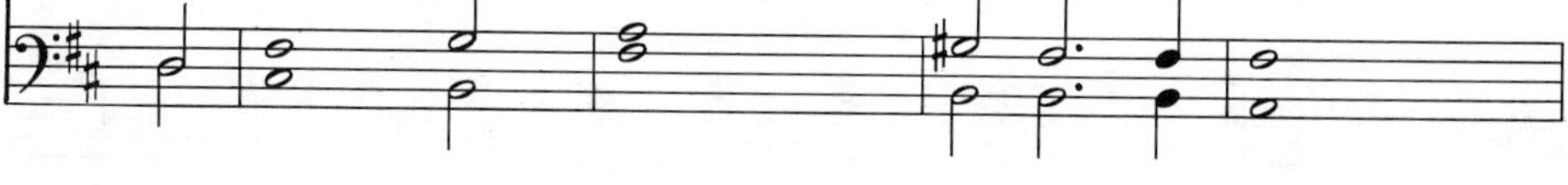

cov - e-nant-ing rite; May ev - ery pledge of true and last - ing pur - pose Be
mar-vel of a dream, Nor ev - er lose the vis - ion as they cher - ish Each
ev - er may be - tide; In - creas-ing - ly may each new year dis - cov - er Their

con - se - crat - ed in thy ho - ly sight; Con - fer on those be - fore thee
for the oth - er, hon - or and es - teem; En - rich them with the bless - ing
lives ma-tured, their mar-riage sanc-ti - fied, Their hearts firm fixed on this ex -

hea - ven - ly aid To keep the sol - emn vows that here are made.
of thy grace, And make their home thy con-stant dwell-ing place.
alt - ed goal: The praise of God whose name their vows ex - tol. A-men.

378 O Perfect Love

First Tune

MARRIAGE

O Perfect Love

Second Tune

Dorothy F. Gurney, 1858-1932

ZU MEINEM HERRN 11.10.11.10.
Johann G. Schicht, 1753-1823
Harm. David Evans, 1874-1948

380 As We Before Thine Altar Bow

Franklin P. Frye, 1903-

EMMANUEL L.M.
Carl C. N. Balle, 1806-1855

O Father, All Creating 381

John Ellerton, 1826-1893

NYLAND 7.6.7.6.D.
Finnish Melody
Adapt. David Evans, 1874-1948; arranged

1 O Fa - ther, all cre - a - ting, Whose wis-dom, love, and power
2 O Sav - ior, Guest most boun - teous Of old in Gal - i - lee,
3 Ex - cept thou build it, Fa - ther, The house is built in vain;

First bound two lives to - geth - er In E - den's pri - mal hour,
Vouch-safe to - day thy pres - ence With these who call on thee;
Ex - cept thou, Sav - ior, bless it, The joy will turn to pain;

To - day to these thy chil - dren Thine ear - liest gifts re - new,
Their store of earth - ly glad - ness Trans-form to heaven-ly wine,
But nought can break the u - nion Of hearts in thee made one;

A home by thee made hap - py, A love by thee kept true.
And teach them, in the tast - ing, To know the gift is thine.
And love thy Spir - it hal - lows Is end - less love be - gun. A-men.

Service Music

Come, Bless the Lord

382

Psalm 134:2

Austin C. Lovelace, 1919-

Enrich, Lord, Heart, Mouth, Hands in Me

383

George Herbert, 1593-1632, alt.

WULFRUN 8.8.8.
George W. Briggs, 1875-1959

384 I Was Glad

Psalm 122:1

Austin C. Lovelace, 1919-

385 Glory to Thee, O God Most High

Philip Gell's *Psalms and Hymns,* 1815

MAINZER L.M.
Joseph Mainzer, 1801-1851
Alt. and harm. Austin C. Lovelace, 1919-

Glo - ry to thee, O God most high! Fa - ther, we praise thy

maj - es - ty, The Son, the Spir - it, we a -

dore: One God - head, blest for - ev - er - more.

Praise to the Holiest in the Height 386

John H. Newman, 1801-1890

ST. MARY C.M.
Melody, *Prys' Psalter*, 1621

Lord, for the Mercies of the Night 387

John Mason, *c.* 1645-1694

FARRANT C.M.
Attr. to Richard Farrant, *c.* 1530-1580

1 Lord, for the mer-cies of the night Our hum-ble thanks we pay,
2 Let this day praise thee, O Lord God, And so let all our days;

And un - to thee we ded - i - cate The first fruits of the day.
And O let heaven's e - ter - nal day Be thine e - ter - nal praise!

Bless the Lord, O My Soul

Minister: O all ye works of the Lord; bless ye the Lord; praise him and magnify him forever.

Choir:

Minister: O ye servants of the Lord, bless ye the Lord; praise him, and magnify him forever.

Choir:

Minister: O ye holy and humble men of heart, bless ye the Lord; praise him, and magnify him forever.

Choir:

Glory Be to God the Father

Christopher Wordsworth, 1807-1885, alt.

REX GLORIAE 8.7.8.7.D.
Henry Smart, 1813-1879

This Is the Day the Lord Hath Made

Isaac Watts, 1674-1748

TWENTY-FOURTH C.M.
Probably by Lucius Chapin, 1760-1842

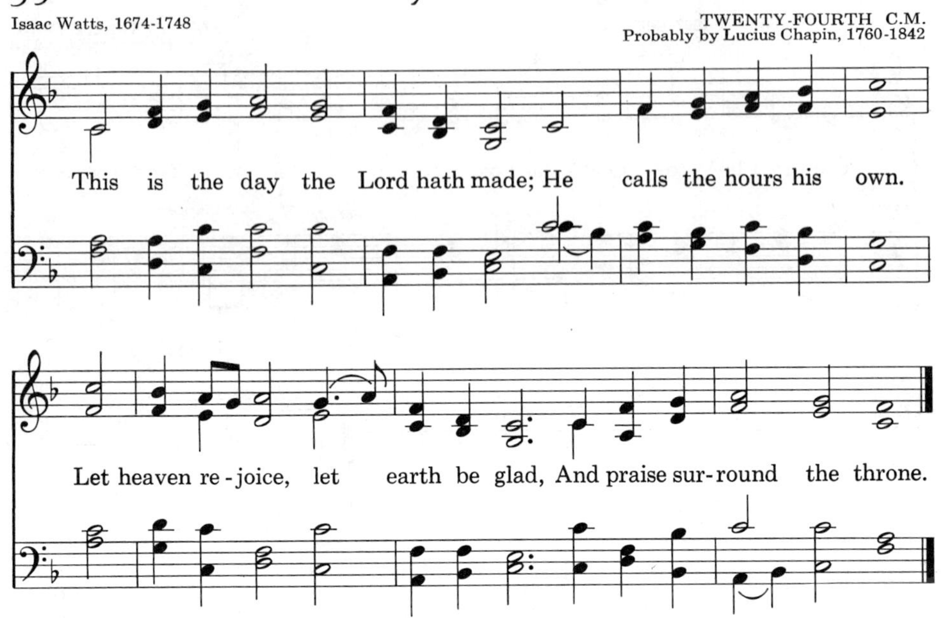

391 Jesus, Stand Among Us

William Pennefather, 1816-1873

GLENFINLAS 6.5.6.5.
Kenneth G. Finlay, 1882-

392

Benjamin Schmolck, 1672-1737
Tr. Catherine Winkworth, 1827-1878

UNSER HERRSCHER 8.7.8.7.7.7.
Melody by Joachim Neander, 1650-1680

1 O - pen now thy gates of beau - ty, Zi - on, let me en - ter there,
Where my soul in joy - ful du - ty, Waits for him who an - swers prayer.
O how bless - ed is this place, Filled with sol - ace, light, and grace!

2 Gra - cious God, I come be - fore thee, Come thou al - so un - to me;
Where we find thee and a - dore thee, There a heaven on earth must be.
To my heart O en - ter thou, Let it be thy tem - ple now.

INTROITS

OFFERTORY

394 All Things Are Thine

John Greenleaf Whittier, 1807-1892

HERR JESU CHRIST L.M.
Pensum Sacrum, Gorlitz, 1648
Arr. Johann Sebastian Bach, 1685-1750

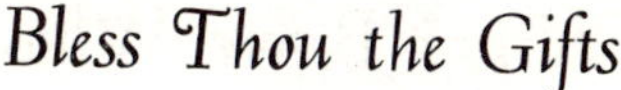

Bless Thou the Gifts

396

Second Tune

Samuel Longfellow, 1819-1892

EAST DALLAS L.M.
A. Eugene Ellsworth, 1910-

Bless thou the gifts our hands have brought, Bless thou the work our hearts have planned; Ours is the faith, the will, the thought, The rest, O God, is in Thy hand. A - men.

Bless Thou the Gifts

397

Third Tune

Samuel Longfellow, 1819-1892

BRESLAU L.M.
Melody, Leipzig, 1625

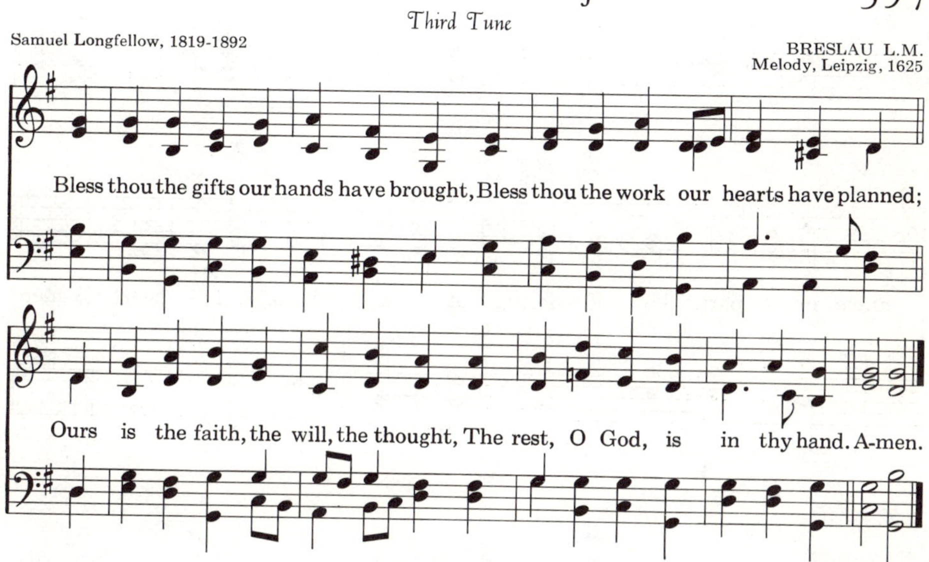

OFFERTORY

398 O King of Kings, Before Whose Throne

John Quarles, 1624-1665
Alt. Thomas Darling, 1816-1893

LEICESTER 8.8.8.8.8.8.
John Bishop, c. 1665-1737

O King of kings, be - fore whose throne The an - gels bow, no gift can we Pre - sent that is in - deed our own, Since heaven and earth be - long to thee; Yet this our souls through grace im - part, The of - fering of a thank - ful heart. A-men.

OFFERTORY

All Things Come of Thee 399

I Chronicles 29:14

Ludwig van Beethoven, 1770-1827

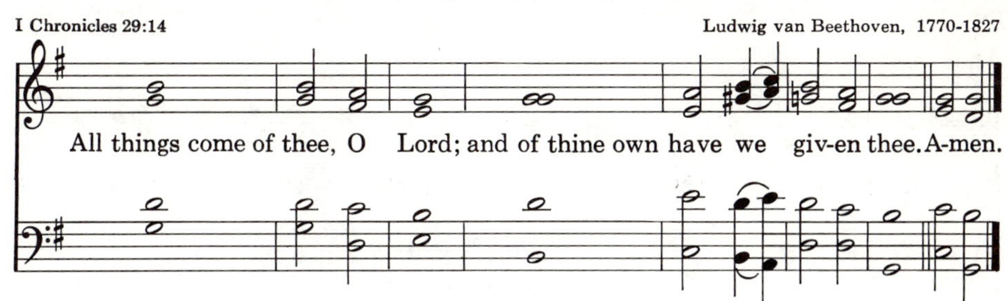

We Give Thee But Thine Own 400

William Walsham How, 1823-1897

ST. ANDREW S.M.
Joseph Barnby, 1838-1896

We give thee but thine own, What - e'er the gift may be; All that we have is thine a - lone, A trust, O Lord, from thee. A-men.

Alternate tune No. 261.

401 Thy Word Have I Hid

Psalm 119: 11,12

CHESHIRE TUNE 8.8.8.5.
Este's Psalter, 1592

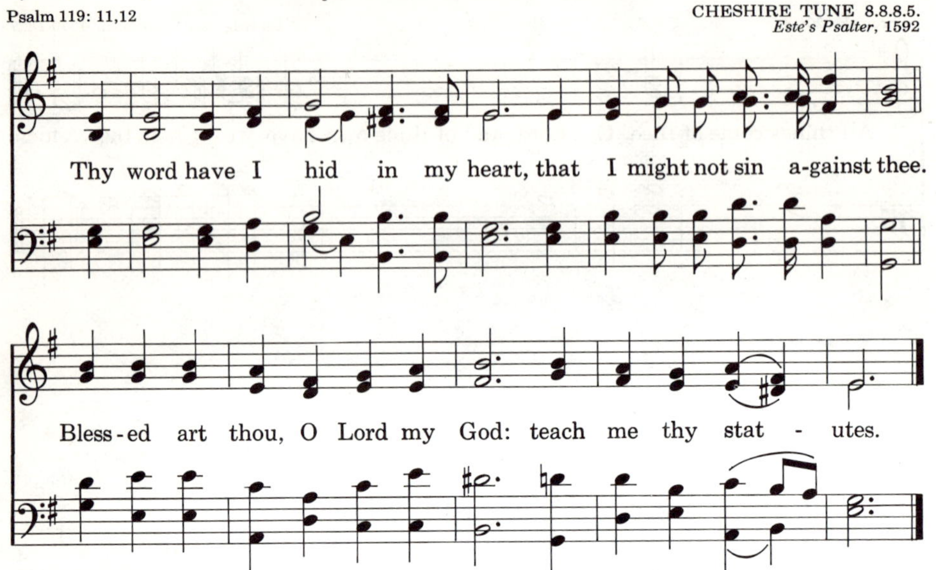

402 Divine Instructor, Gracious Lord

Anne Steele, 1716-1778

TALLIS' ORDINAL C.M.
Thomas Tallis, *c.* 1505-1585

Teach Me, O Lord
403
Psalm 119: 33
William Henry Hewlett, 1873-
Teach me, O Lord, the way of thy stat - utes, and
I will keep it un - to the end.
Music arrangement by permission of the United Church Publishing House, Toronto.
O Lord, Open Thou Our Eyes
404
Psalm 119:18
John Camidge, 1735-1803
V. O Lord, open thou our eyes
R. That we may behold
won - drous things out of thy law.
Thanks Be to Thee 405
Thomas Tallis, c. 1505-1585
Thanks be to thee, O Christ, for this thy ho - ly gos - pel.
Praise Be to Thee 406
John Playford, 1674-1730
Praise be to thee, O Christ.

407 Glory Be to Thee

Thomas Tallis, *c.* 1505-1585

Glo - ry be to thee, O Lord.

408 Glory Be to Thee

Thomas Tallis, *c.* 1505-1585

Glo - ry be to thee, O Lord.

409 Lord, Have Mercy Upon Us

John Merbecke, 1523-*c.* 1585

Lord, have mer-cy up-on us; Christ, have mer-cy up-on us; Lord, have mer-cy up-on us.

410 Lord, Have Mercy Upon Us

KYRIE
From a Lutheran Service of 1528

Lord, have mer-cy up-on us; Christ, have mer-cy up-on us; Lord, have mer-cy up-on us.

From *The Lutheran Service Book and Hymnal* by permission of the Commission on the Liturgy and Hymnal.

411 Write These Words

Ancient Chant

SCRIPTURE

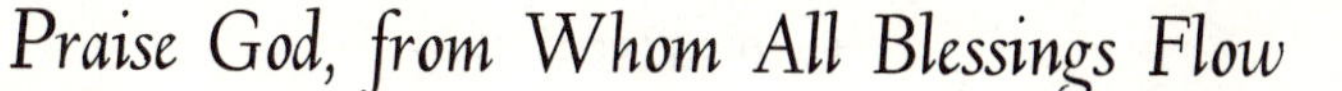

412

Thomas Ken, 1637-1711

OLD HUNDREDTH L.M.
Attr. to Louis Bourgeois, *c.* 1510-1561
Genevan Psalter, 1551

Praise God from whom all bless-ings flow; Praise him, all crea-tures here be - low;

Praise him a-bove, ye heaven-ly host: Praise Fa-ther, Son, and Ho - ly Ghost. A-men.

Praise God, from Whom All Blessings Flow 413

Thomas Ken, 1637-1711

OLD HUNDREDTH L.M. (altered rhythm)
Attr. to Louis Bourgeois, *c.* 1510-1561
Genevan Psalter, 1551

414 Gloria Patri

Henry W. Greatorex, 1813-1858

415 Gloria Patri

Charles Meineke, 1782-1850

Glo - ry be to the Fa - ther, and to the Son, and to the

Ho - ly Ghost; As it was in the be - gin - ning, is

now, and ev - er shall be, world with-out end. A - men. A - men.

GLORIA PATRIS

Gloria Patri

416

Old Scottish Chant

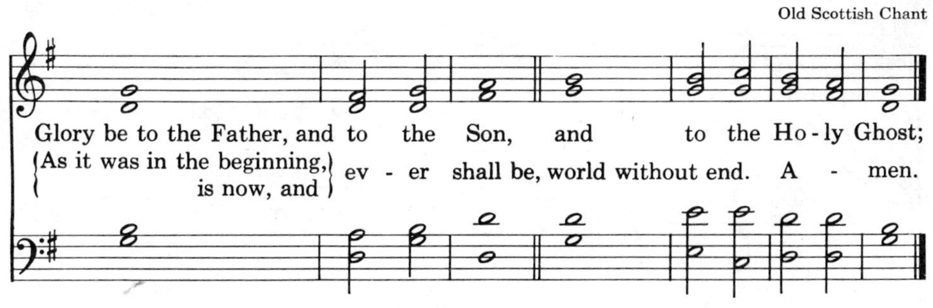

GLORIA PATRI

Holy, Holy, Holy

417

Peter C. Lutkin, 1858-1931

In unison

Ho - ly, ho - ly, ho - ly, Lord God of hosts, Heaven and earth are full of thy glo - ry: Glo - ry be to thee, O Lord most high. A - men.

Music by permission of The Parish Press; Fond du Lac, Wisconsin.

SANCTUS

418 Holy, Holy, Holy

Communion Service in E Minor
Philip R. Dietterich, 1931-

SANCTUS

Holy, Holy, Holy

419

John Merbecke, 1523-*c.* 1585

SANCTUS

The Lord Be with You

420

Thomas Tallis, *c.* 1505-1585

To be said or sung: *Choir and Congregation:*

The {Lord be with you,} And with thy spir - it. Let us pray.

{O Lord, show thy mercy up-} on us, And grant us thy sal - va - tion.

{O God, make clean our hearts with-} in us. And take not thy Ho - ly Spir - it from us.

CALL TO PRAYER

421 The Lord Be with You

Traditional

To be said or sung: *Choir and Congregation:*

The {Lord be with you,} And with thy spir - it. Let us pray.

{O Lord, show thy mercy up-} on us, And grant us thy sal - va - tion.

{O God, make clean our hearts with-} in us. And take not thy Holy Spirit from us.

CALL TO PRAYER

422 Hear Our Prayer

Psalm 143:1

George Whelpton, 1847-1930

PRAYER RESPONSES

Our Father, Who Art in Heaven

Anonymous

Harold W. Friedell, 1905-1958

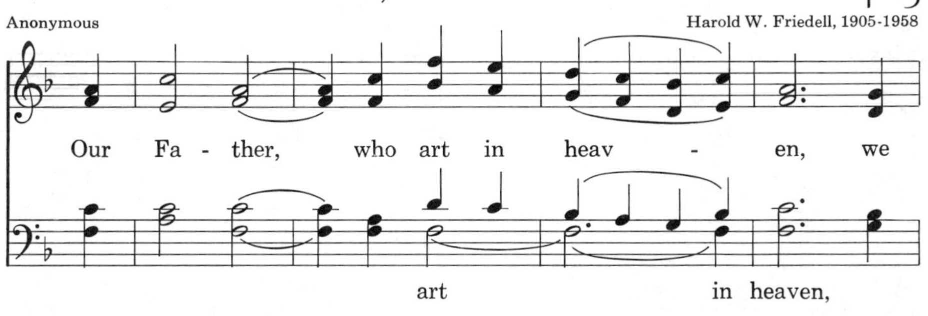

424 Day by Day, Dear Lord

St. Richard of Chichester, 1197-1253

Harold W. Friedell, 1905-1958

Day by day, Dear Lord, of thee three things I pray: To see thee more clear - ly, Love thee more dear - ly,

To see thee, Love thee,

Fol - low thee more near - ly, Day by day.

425 Father of All Grace

Arden D. Keen, 1930-

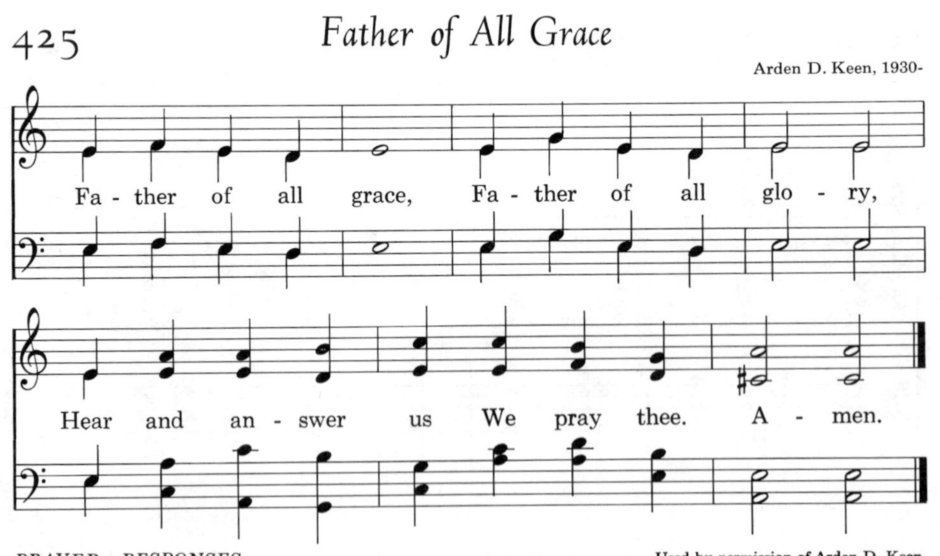

Lead Me, Lord 426

Based on Psalms 5:8 and 4:8

Samuel S. Wesley, 1810-1876

Lead me, Lord, lead me in thy right-eous-ness, make thy way plain be-fore my face. For it is thou, Lord, thou, Lord, on - ly, that mak - est me dwell in safe - ty.

May the Words of Our Mouths 427

Psalm 19:14, alt.

Alan Walker, 1927-

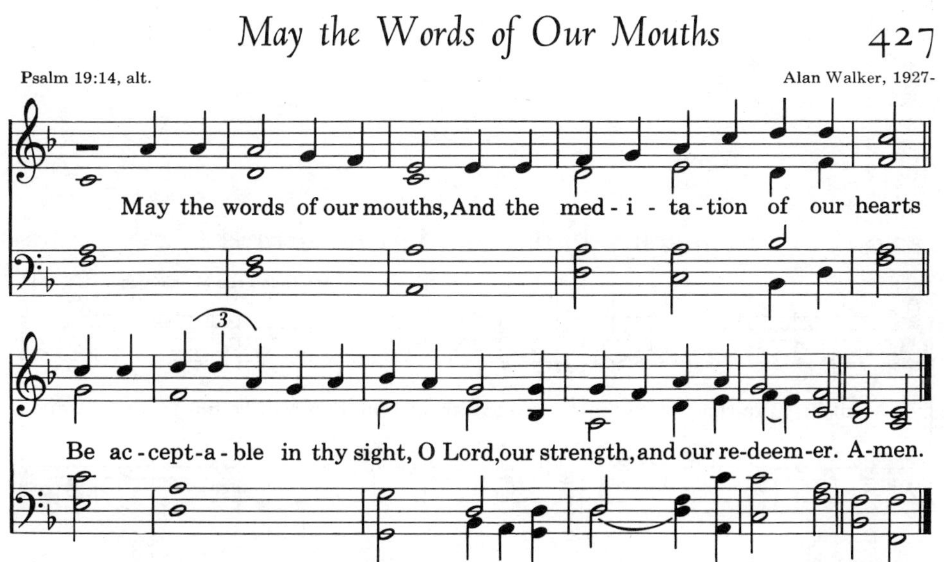

428 O Thou Who Hearest Prayer

Unknown

6.6.6.6.8.8.
Welsh Melody

O thou who hear - est prayer, Give ear un - to our cry;
O let thy chil - dren share thy bless - ing from on high.
We plead the prom-ise of thy word, O grant us peace, al - might-y Lord! A-men.

429 Almighty Father, Hear Our Prayer

Arr. from Felix Mendelssohn, 1809-1847

430

Joseph Bryan, *c.* 1610; alt., 1955

MON DIEU, PRÊTE-MOI L'OREILLE 8.8.7.7.
Genevan Psalter, 1543

1 To my hum-ble sup-pli - ca-tion, Lord, give ear and ac-cep - ta - tion
2 Heaven-ly Tu- tor, of thy kind-ness, Teach my dull-ness, guide my blind-ness

Save thy serv-ant, who doth own Help and hope in thee a - lone.
That my steps thy paths may tread, Which to end-less bliss do lead. A-men.

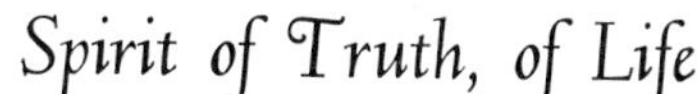

431

Horace Westwood, 1884-

MENDON L.M.
German melody
Arr. Samuel Dyer, 1785- 1835

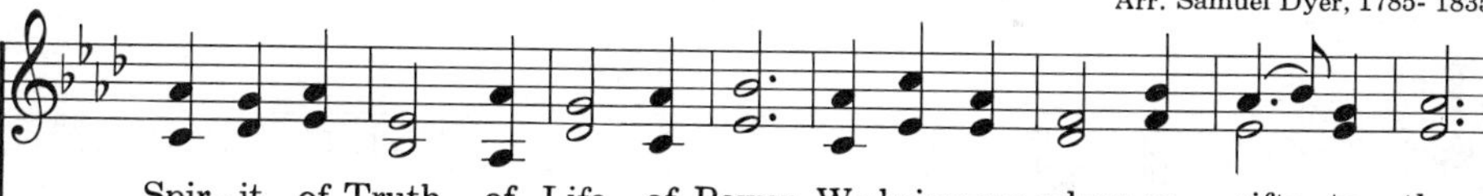

Spir - it of Truth, of Life, of Power, We bring our-selves as gifts to thee.

Oh, bind our hearts this sa - cred hour In faith and hope and char - i - ty. A-men.

432 God Be in My Head

Sarum Primer, 1558

LYTLINGTON Irregular
Sydney H. Nicholson, 1875-1947

BENEDICTION

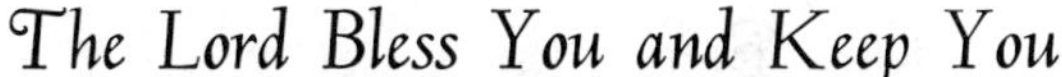

433

Numbers 6: 24-26

Peter C. Lutkin, 1858-1931

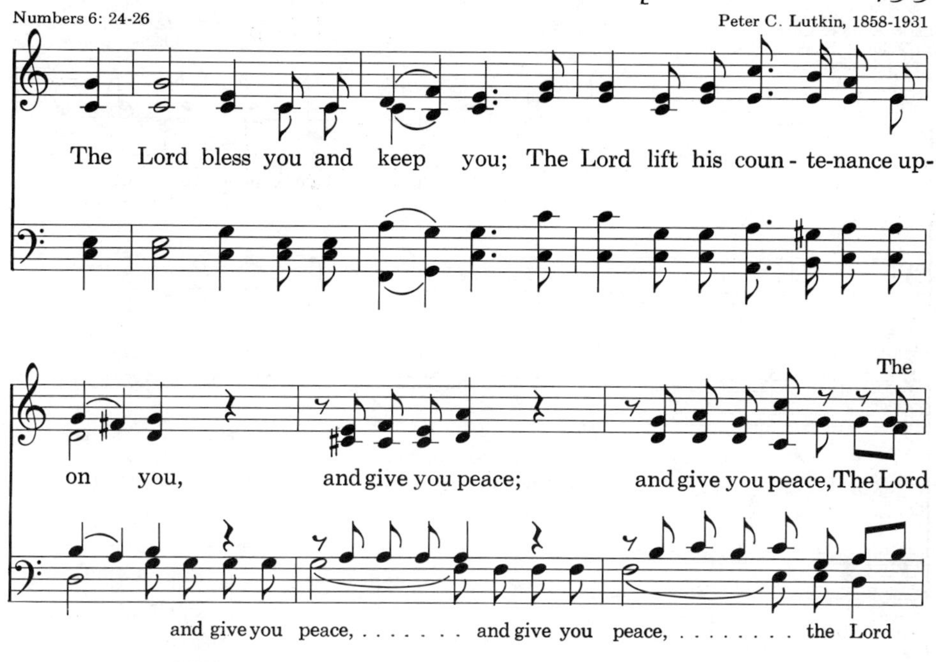

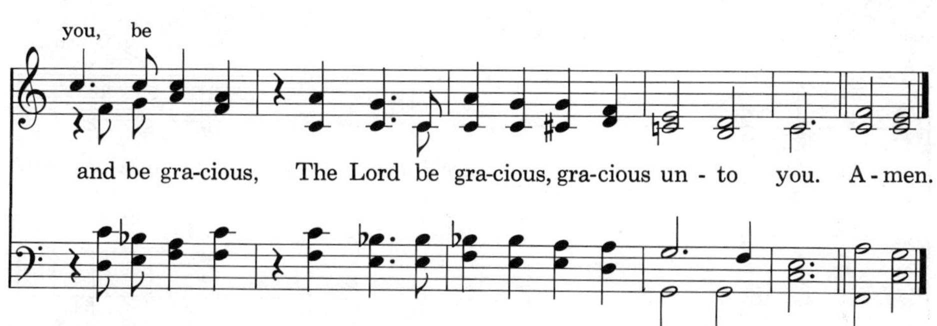

Music by permission of The Parish Press, Fond du Lac.

BENEDICTION

434 To Thee Before the Close of Day

Latin, *c.* 7th century
Tr. John M. Neale, 1818-1866

JAM LUCIS L.M.
Plainsong, Mode VI

435 Thou Wilt Keep Him in Perfect Peace

Isaiah 26:3

DUKE'S TUNE 8.6.
Scottish Psalter, 1615, abridged

Thou wilt keep him in per-fect peace Whose mind is stayed on thee. A-men.

BENEDICTION

May the Grace of Christ Our Savior 436

John Newton, 1725-1807

OMNI DEI 8.7.8.7.
Corner's *Gesangbuch*, 1631
Harm. Hubert Lamb, 1909-

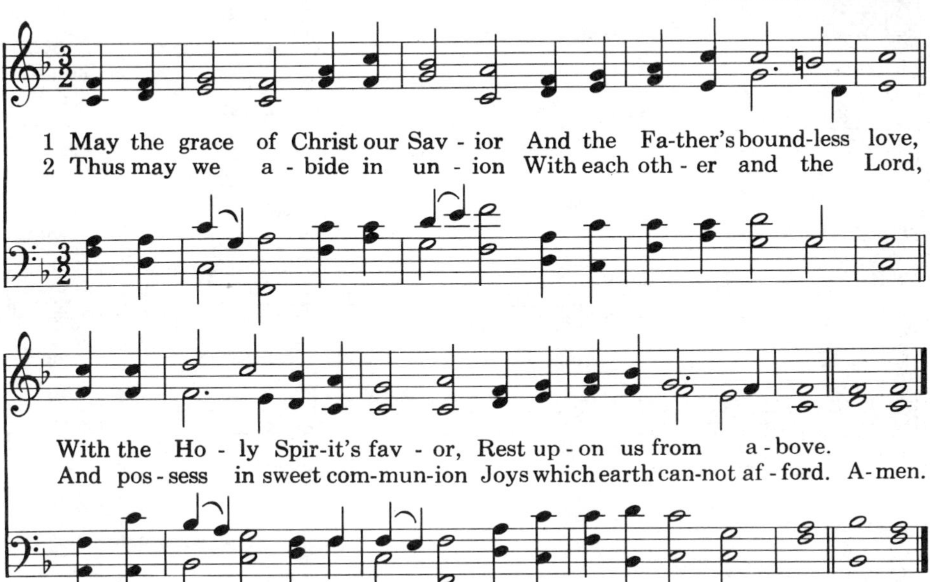

Music by permission of Milton Academy from *The Milton Hymnal* and Middlesex School from *The Middlesex Hymn Book.*

Father, Give Thy Benediction 437

Samuel Longfellow, 1819-1892

ALTA TRINITÀ BEATA 8.7.8.7.
Laudi Spirituali, 14th century

BENEDICTION

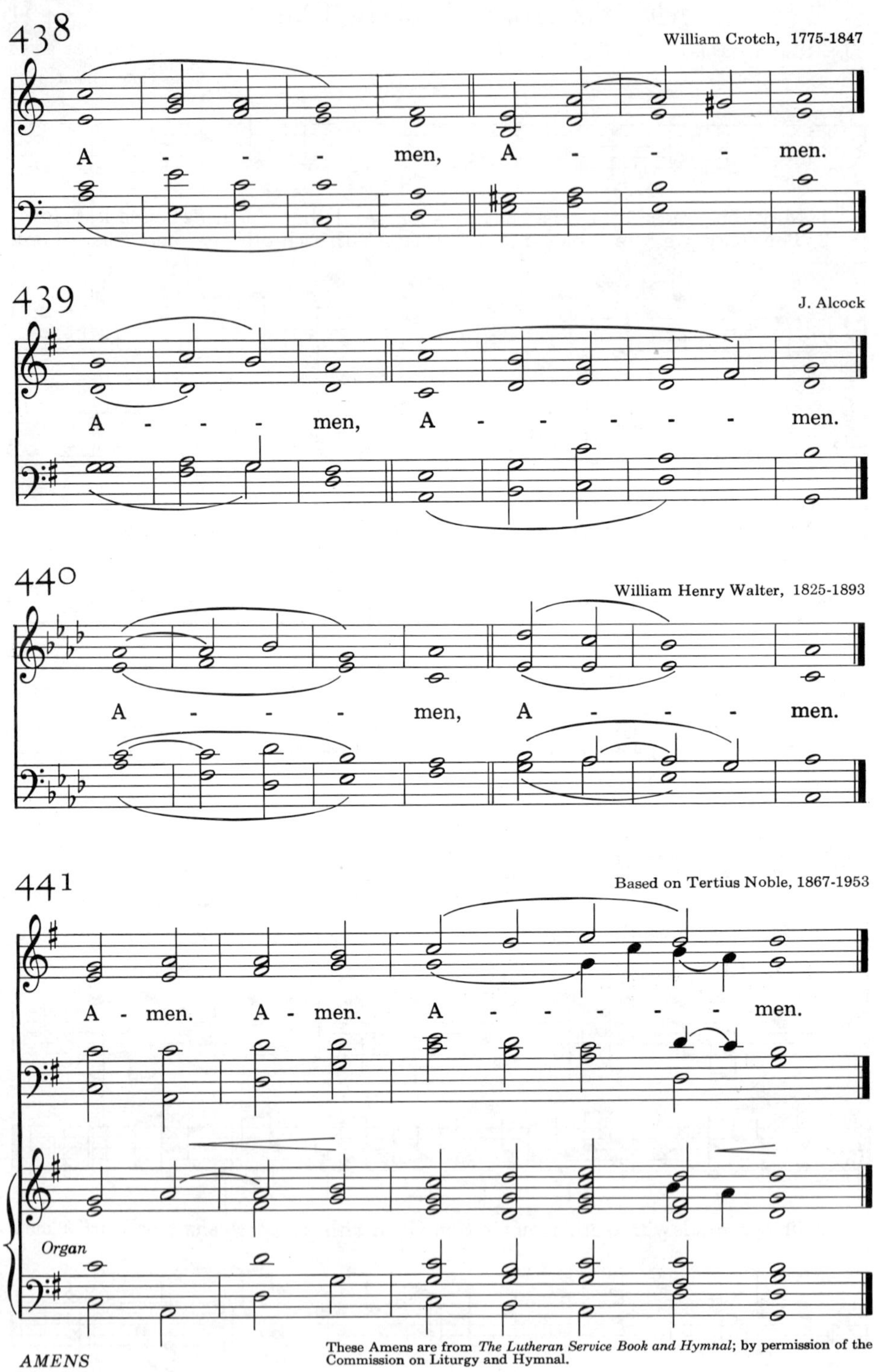

These Amens are from *The Lutheran Service Book and Hymnal*; by permission of the Commission on Liturgy and Hymnal.

442

A - - men, A - men.

443

A - men, A - - men.

444

A - - men, A-men, A - men.

445

A-men, A-men, A - - men.

446

Eric DeLamarter, 1880-1953

A - - - men, A - men.

447

Louis Bourgeois, *c.* 1510-*c.* 1561

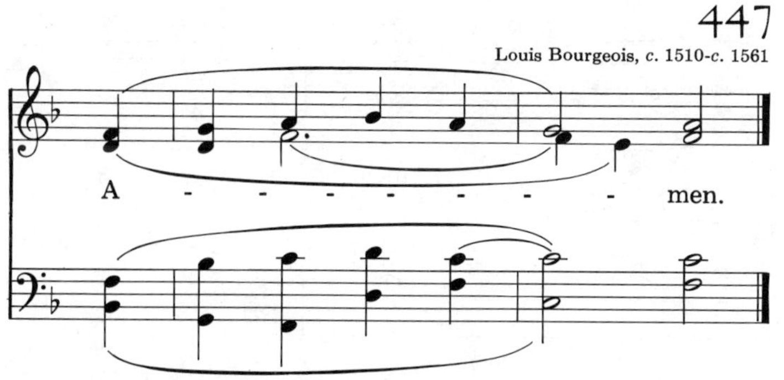

448

Franklin E. Perkins, 1929-

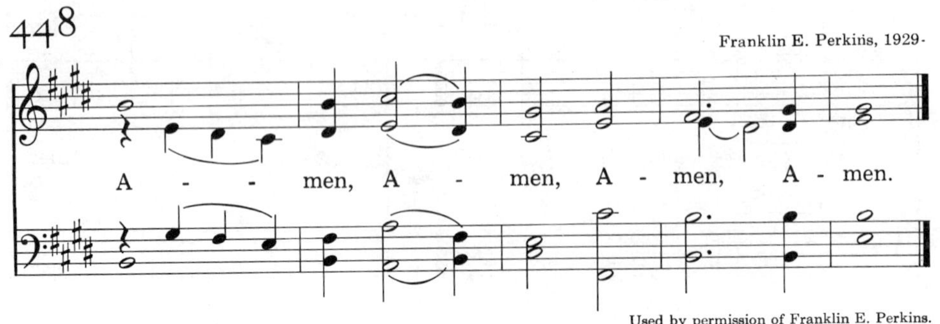

Used by permission of Franklin E. Perkins.

449

Arden D. Keen, 1930-

450

Franklin E. Perkins, 1929-

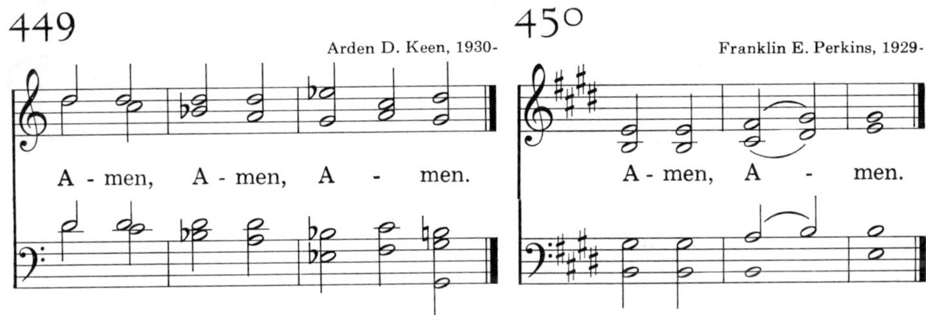

Used by permission of Arden D. Keen.

Used by permission of Franklin E. Perkins.

451

John Stainer, 1840-1901

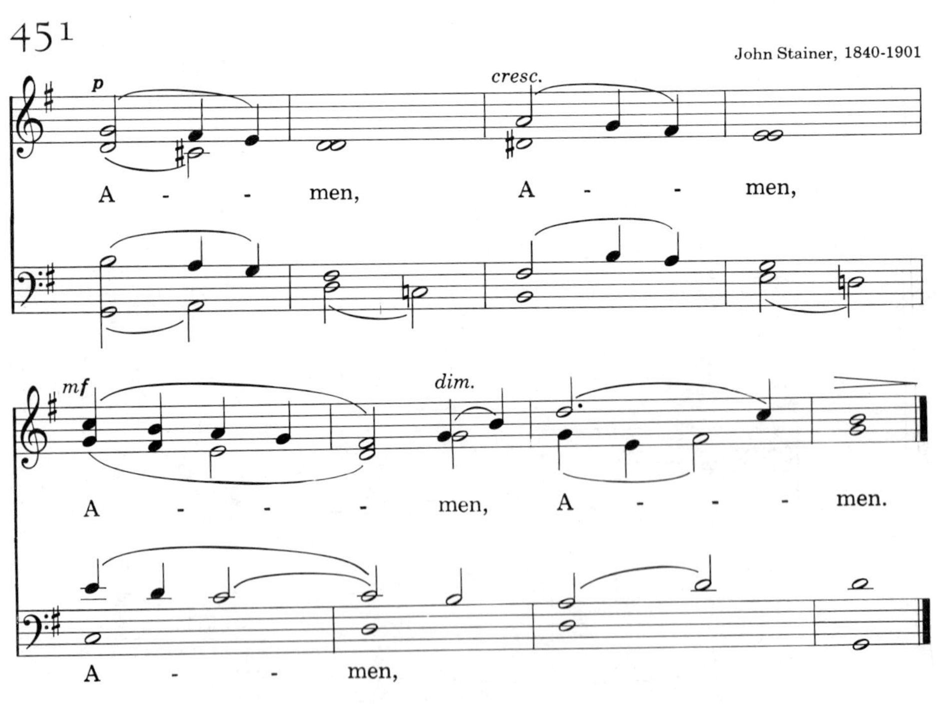

452

John Stainer, 1840-1901

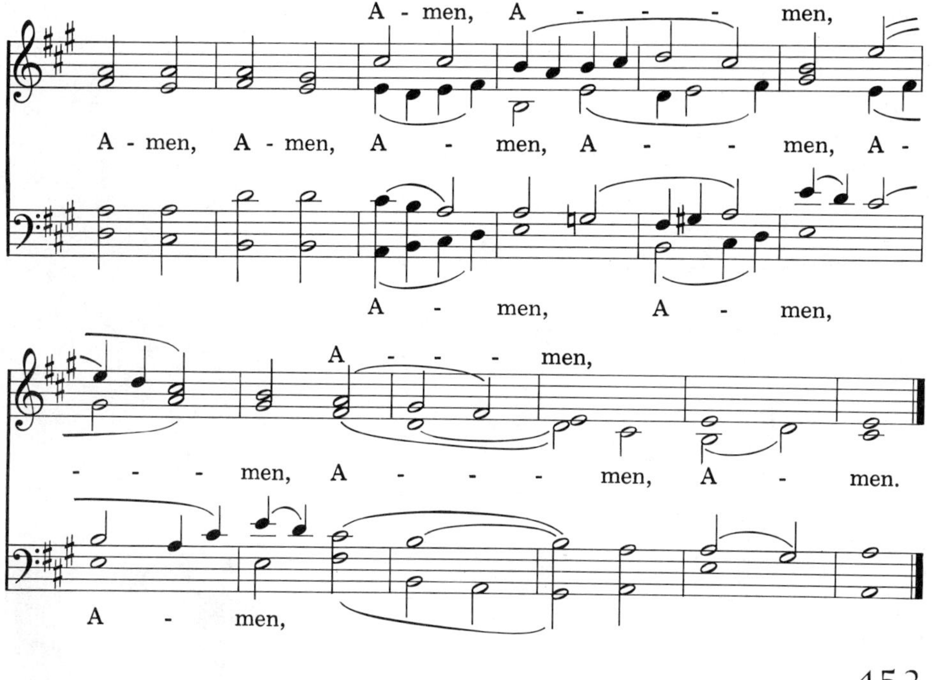

453

Vincent Persichetti, 1915-

454

Vincent Persichetti, 1915-

The Written Word

Adoration and Praise

Litanies

Affirmation of Faith

Scripture Readings

Psalms

Prayers of Worship

Offering

The Lord's Supper

- SCRIPTURES
- INVITATION
- PRAYERS

Baptism

Benedictions

Adoration and Praise

455

O God, thou source of all pure desires and holy affections, give me now a quiet mind and a reverent heart, that I may worthily worship thee at this time.

456

O Lord, enable me this day to worship thee in spirit and in truth. Keep me from vain affections and wandering thoughts. Help me to join heartily in the praises and prayers of thy people. Cause me to take heed how I hear thy Word. O teach me this day by the mouth of thy minister so that I may better know and do thy will. Give me understanding in spiritual things, and may I receive the message thou dost send with all humility and eagerness to be instructed and made better. Forgive all wherein I come amiss, and accept and bless me for Jesus' sake. *Amen.*

457

O God, who makest thyself known in the stillness, let me feel thy presence in this sacred place; make me to be of the company of earnest souls who have worshiped here in spirit and in truth; through the voices of men and the instruments of praise help me to lift my heart to thee; and so, O Lord, purify my life, that, going forth into the world, I may go in thy strength and in thy love; through Jesus Christ our Lord. *Amen.*

458

"But the hour is coming, and now is, when the true worshipers will worship the Father in spirit and truth, for such the Father seeks to worship him. God is spirit, and those who worship him must worship in spirit and truth."
John 4:23-24

459

For thus said the Lord GOD, the Holy One of Israel,
"In returning and rest you shall be saved;
in quietness and in trust shall be your strength."
Isaiah 30:15

460

As a hart longs
for flowing streams,
so longs my soul
for thee, O God.
My soul thirsts for God,
for the living God.
Psalm 42:1-2

461

For God alone my soul waits in silence;
from him comes my salvation.
He only is my rock and my salvation,
my fortress; I shall not be greatly moved.
Psalm 62:1-2

462

O God, thou art my God, I seek thee,
my soul thirsts for thee;
my flesh faints for thee,
as in a dry and weary land where no water is.
So I have looked upon thee in the sanctuary,
beholding thy power and glory.
Because thy steadfast love is better than life,
my lips will praise thee.
So I will bless thee as long as I live;
I will lift up my hands and call on thy name.
Psalm 63:1-4

463

My heart is steadfast, O God, my heart is steadfast!
I will sing, and make melody!
Awake, my soul!

I will give thanks to thee, O LORD, among the peoples,
  I will sing praises to thee among the nations.
For thy steadfast love is great above the heavens,
  thy faithfulness reaches to the clouds.

Psalm 108:1, 3, 4

464

"My soul magnifies the Lord,
and my spirit rejoices in God my Savior,
for he who is mighty has done great things for me,
and holy is his name."

Luke 1:46b, 47, 49

465

I will bless the LORD at all times;
  his praise shall continually be in my mouth.
My soul makes its boast in the LORD;
  let the afflicted hear and be glad.
O magnify the LORD with me,
  and let us exalt his name together!
The LORD redeems the life of his servants;
  none of those who take refuge in him will be condemned.

Psalm 34:1-3, 22

466

O come, let us sing to the LORD;
  let us make a joyful noise to the rock of our salvation!
Let us come into his presence with thanksgiving;
  let us make a joyful noise to him with songs of praise!
For the LORD is a great God,
  and a great King above all gods.
In his hand are the depths of the earth;
  the heights of the mountains are his also.
The sea is his, for he made it;
  for his hands formed the dry land.
O come, let us worship and bow down.

Psalm 95:1-6a

467

O come, let us worship and bow down,
 let us kneel before the LORD, our Maker!
For he is our God,
 and we are the people of his pasture,
 and the sheep of his hand.

Psalm 95:6-7

468

Have you not known? Have you not heard?
The LORD is the everlasting God,
 the Creator of the ends of the earth.
He does not faint or grow weary,
 his understanding is unsearchable.
He gives power to the faint,
 and to him who has no might he increases strength.
But they who wait for the LORD shall renew their strength,
 they shall mount up with wings like eagles,
they shall run and not be weary,
 they shall walk and not faint.

Isaiah 40:28-29, 31

469

Praise the LORD!
Praise, O servants of the LORD,
 praise the name of the LORD!
Blessed be the name of the LORD
 from this time forth and for evermore!
From the rising of the sun to its setting
 the name of the LORD is to be praised!
The LORD is high above all the nations,
 and his glory above the heavens!
Praise the LORD!

Psalm 113:1-4, 9b

470

Arise, shine; for your light has come,
and the glory of the LORD has risen upon you.
For behold, darkness shall cover the earth,

and thick darkness the peoples;
but the LORD will arise upon you,
and his glory will be seen upon you.
And nations shall come to your light,
and kings to the brightness of your rising.
Lift up your eyes round about, and see.
Then you shall see and be radiant,
your heart shall thrill and rejoice.
Isaiah 60:1-4a, 5a

471

O give thanks to the LORD, call on his name,
make known his deeds among the peoples!
Sing to him, sing praises to him,
tell of all his wonderful works!
Glory in his holy name;
let the hearts of those who seek the LORD rejoice!
Seek the LORD and his strength,
seek his presence continually!
Psalm 105:1-4

472

Praise the LORD!
For it is good to sing praises to our God;
for he is gracious, and a song of praise is seemly.
He heals the brokenhearted,
and binds up their wounds.

The Lord *is gracious and merciful,*
slow to anger and abounding in steadfast love.
The Lord *is good to all,*
and his compassion is over all that he has made.
Psalms 147:1, 3; 145:8-9

473

Blessed be the name of the LORD
from this time forth and for evermore!
From the rising of the sun to its setting
the name of the LORD is to be praised!

The LORD is high above all nations,
 and his glory above the heavens!

Praise the Lord!
Praise the Lord, *O my soul!*
 I will praise the Lord *as long as I live;*
  I will sing praises to my God while I have being.

Psalms 113:2-4; 146:1-2

474

"Seek the LORD while he may be found,
 call upon him while he is near;
let the wicked forsake his way,
 and the unrighteous man his thoughts;
let him return to the LORD, that he may have mercy on him,
 and to our God, for he will abundantly pardon."

Isaiah 55:6-7

475

"Come to me, all who labor and are heavy laden, and I will give you rest. Take my yoke upon you, and learn from me; for I am gentle and lowly in heart, and you will find rest for your souls. For my yoke is easy, and my burden is light."

Matthew 11:28-30

476

Therefore, if any one is in Christ, he is a new creation; the old has passed away, behold, the new has come. All this is from God, who through Christ reconciled us to himself and gave us the ministry of reconciliation; that is, God was in Christ reconciling the world to himself, not counting their trespasses against them. For our sake he made him to be sin who knew no sin, so that in him we might become the righteousness of God.

2 Corinthians 5:17-19a, 21

477

But God, who is rich in mercy, out of the great love with which he loved us, even when we were dead through our trespasses, made us alive together with Christ (by grace you have been saved), and raised us up with him, and

made us sit with him in the heavenly places in Christ Jesus, that in the coming ages he might show the immeasurable riches of his grace in kindness toward us in Christ Jesus. For by grace you have been saved through faith; and this is not your own doing, it is the gift of God.
Ephesians 2:4-8

478

While we were yet helpless, at the right time Christ died for the ungodly. God shows his love for us in that while we were yet sinners Christ died for us.
Romans 5:6, 8

479

The LORD is merciful and gracious,
slow to anger and abounding in steadfast love.
He will not always chide,
nor will he keep his anger for ever.
He does not deal with us according to our sins,
nor requite us according to our iniquities.
For as the heavens are high above the earth,
so great is his steadfast love toward those who fear him;
as far as the east is from the west,
so far does he remove our transgressions from us.
Psalm 103:8-12

480

When the righteous cry for help, the LORD hears,
and delivers them out of all their troubles.
The LORD is near to the brokenhearted,
and saves the crushed in spirit.
Psalm 34:17-18

Litanies

481

O Thou the Source of every good and perfect gift; from thee comes grace sufficient for all our strivings, our suffering, our sin. For all that thou art and for the unnumbered blessings received from thine outstretched hand,

Accept our heartfelt thanksgiving.

From that coldness of heart which does not acknowledge thy goodness; from the self-centeredness which denies our need of thy grace; from our preoccupation with things immediate which makes us forget our dependence upon thee for health of body, mind and spirit,

Deliver us, dear Lord.

That our eyes may behold thy glory revealed in the world, with its every living thing; that our minds may perceive thy truth about life and death; that our hearts, filled with thy love, may respond in thy name to every human need,

Be pleased to hear us, good Lord.

That our thanksgiving may be expressed by worship that is sincere and true, by service to others that is unselfish and gladhearted, by humility when confronted by our inestimable debt to thee for thy manifold mercies,

Hear us, O Lord.

Praise God from whom all blessings flow;
Praise him all creatures here below;
Praise him above, ye heavenly hosts;
Praise Father, Son, and Holy Ghost. *Amen.*

482

Heavenly Father, we wait upon thee now with trust and love, and in full devotion to thy holy will. By all thy works; by the remembrance of all thy mercies; by the revelation of thyself to the prophets of old:

Teach us and draw us ever nearer to thee.

By the memory of Jesus Christ our Lord; by his life and teaching; by his life laid down for our salvation, and by the work of his Spirit in the world:

Teach us and draw us ever nearer to thee.

By the noble example of all the saints and martyrs of the church; by all that we owe to Christian faith and devotion down the years:

Teach us and draw us ever nearer to thee.

By the joys of life; by human love; by the affection and fidelity of friends; by the capacity for pleasure, and the sense of humor; by the persistency in our hearts of optimism and hope:

Teach us and draw us ever nearer to thee.

By the sorrows of life; by our falls and failures; by our disappointments and disasters; by the stern discipline of loneliness, of unrealized dreams, and the heartache of unsatisfied desire:

Teach us and draw us ever nearer to thee.

By our want of thee; by the hunger within us for the eternal life; by our search for truth and by our hands outstretched in prayer:

Teach us and draw us ever nearer to thee.

483

In peace let us pray to the Lord.

Lord, have mercy.

For the peace that is from above, and for the salvation of our souls, let us pray to the Lord.

Lord, have mercy.

For the peace of the whole world, for the well-being of the churches of God, and for the unity of all, let us pray to the Lord.

Lord, have mercy.

For this holy house, and for them that in faith, piety, and fear of God offer here their worship and praise, let us pray to the Lord.

Lord, have mercy.

Help, save, pity, defend us, O God, by thy grace. *Amen.*

484

O Savior of the world, who by thy cross and precious blood hast redeemed us;

Save us and help us, we humbly beseech thee, O Lord.

From the impatience which prevents us from finding thy purpose in pain and sorrow,

Save us, good Lord.

From refusing to share the suffering of the world, from seeking only comfort and pleasure, from forgetting those in distress, from the selfishness which brings needless grief to others,

Save us, good Lord.

Almighty Father, who in the afflictions of thy people art thyself afflicted, and art full of compassion and tender mercy; as we pray for those who suffer, for the aged and the dying;

We beseech thee to hear us, good Lord.

For all who are hindered in the race of life through no fault of their own; for the defective and the delicate; and for those who have been maimed and disabled;

We beseech thee to hear us, good Lord.

For those whose livelihood is insecure; for the hungry, the homeless and the destitute; for those who are overworked, down-trodden and in despair;

We beseech thee to hear us, good Lord.

For those who have to bear their burdens alone; for those who are in doubt and anguish of soul; for those who are oversensitive, and for those who suffer through their own wrongdoing;

We beseech thee to hear us, good Lord.

For all who do not pray for themselves, for all who have not the consolation of the prayers of others, and for all whose anguish is unrelieved by the knowledge of thy love;

We beseech thee to hear us, good Lord.

485

O God of grace and glory, we acknowledge before thee our unpayable indebtedness; we are the children of sacrifice; our choicest benedictions have been bought with the price of other blood and tears than our own; thou hast given us the inheritance of them that feared thy name.

O Lord, make us thankful.

For all saints and martyrs, prophets and apostles; for all soldiers of the common good who served thee in scorn of consequence and fell on sleep unashamed, of whom the world was not worthy,

O Lord, make us thankful.

For the cross of Christ and his exceeding bitter sacrifice; for the truths which there were brought to light, the love unbounded which there was freely given, and the costly salvation which there visited thy people,

O Lord, make us thankful.

By his loneliness in the Garden; by his betrayal and his trial; by the humiliation of his people's hate, the mockery of his thorny crown, and the bitterness of scourging; by the anguish of his cross; by his unfailing faith in thee and love for man,

O Lord, make us thankful.

Eternal God, may we, who owe our spiritual blessings to so great a cloud of witnessess, who have suffered before us, and to Christ, whose cross is our peace, walk as become those who are debtors to thy grace. From ingratitude, pride, hardness of heart, and all manner of evil requiting,

Good Lord, deliver us.

From neglect of blessing dearly purchased; from selfish use of opportunities for which good men died; from growing within our hearts the venomous roots of covetousness; from pampering ourselves with vain superfluities; and from all spendthrift wasting of our costly heritage,

Good Lord, deliver us.

Gird us, we beseech thee, with gratitude and fidelity; devote us to the service of mankind with more courageous zeal; free us from the detaining reluctance of our fear, selfishness, and unbelief; and at this altar of remembrance, may we, O Christ, join afresh the honorable company of thy true servants who in sacrificial living share the fellowship of thy cross.

Lord, have mercy upon us and grant us this blessing. Amen.

486

O God, before whose face the empires of the past have risen and fallen away, establish this nation in righteousness; and in personal character and public integrity make her foundations sure.

Lord, hear our prayer and mercifully bless this people.

From the ravages of crime, the disgrace of political corruption, and all malicious designs of lawless men,

Good Lord, deliver us.

From prejudice of race and color, making schism in the common wealth; from all inequity that, causing a few to be rich and many poor, begets ill will and spoils fraternity; from all loss of liberties bequeathed us by our sires and from careless acceptance of our heritage and neglect of its responsibilities,

Good Lord, deliver us.

From the decline of pure religion, from failure of moral fiber in our citizenship, from all accounting of things material above virtues spiritual; from vulgarity of life, loss of social conscience, and collapse of national character,

Good Lord, deliver us.

By the deep faiths on which the foundations of our land were laid and by the sacrifices of its pioneers,

We beseech thee to hear us, O Lord.

By the memory of leaders in the nation, whose wisdom has saved us, whose devotion has chastened us, whose characters have inspired us,

We beseech thee to hear us, O Lord.

By the undeserved wealth of a great continent committed to us and by our trusteeship of power to work weal or woe on the earth,

We beseech thee to hear us, O Lord.

Keep us from pride of mind, and from boasting tongues deliver us; save our national loyalty from narrowness and our flag from selfish shame; by our love for our land may we measure the love of others for their lands, honoring their devotion as we honor our own; and acknowledging thee one God, may we see all mankind one family and so govern our national affairs that the whole world may become one brotherhood of peoples.

Lord, hear our prayer and mercifully bless this people. Amen.

487

Jesus said, "And preach as you go, saying, 'The kingdom of heaven is at hand.' Heal the sick, raise the dead, cleanse lepers, cast out demons. You received without pay, give without pay."

Our Father who art in heaven,
Thy kingdom come,

Thy will be done,
On earth as it is in heaven.

At that time the disciples came to Jesus, saying, "Who is the greatest in the kingdom of heaven?" And calling to him a child, he put him in the midst of them, and said, "Truly, I say to you, unless you turn and become like children, you will never enter the kingdom of heaven."

Our Father who art in heaven,
Thy kingdom come,
Thy will be done,
On earth as it is in heaven.

"Every one then who hears these words of mine and does them will be like a wise man who built his house upon the rock; and the rain fell, and the floods came, and the winds blew and beat upon that house, but it did not fall, because it had been founded on the rock."

Our Father who art in heaven,
Thy kingdom come,
Thy will be done,
On earth as it is in heaven.

"When the Son of man comes in his glory, and all the angels with him, then he will sit on his glorious throne. Before him will be gathered all the nations, and he will separate them one from another as a shepherd separates the sheep from the goats."

Our Father who art in heaven,
Thy kingdom come,
Thy will be done,
On earth as it is in heaven.

Jesus said to them, "The light is with you for a little longer. Walk while you have the light, lest the darkness overtake you; he who walks in the darkness does not know where he goes. While you have the light, believe in the light, that you may become sons of light."

Our Father who art in heaven,
Thy kingdom come,
Thy will be done,
On earth as it is in heaven.

488

For the whole church of Christ, scattered abroad in five continents, and bearing many names, that it may be no longer torn asunder, divided in itself or weak, but may become a glorious church, without spot or blemish, fulfilling the perfect will:

Thy will be done in thy church, we beseech thee, O Lord.

For the churches that are passing through times of suffering and persecution, that their faith and courage may not fail nor their love grow cold:

Save them and us, we beseech thee, O Lord.

For the churches that are strong in faith, that they may abound in grace and in knowledge and love of thee:

Use them and us, we beseech thee, O Lord.

For all weak and struggling churches, that they may persevere and be strong, overcoming those forces which hinder their growth or threaten their existence:

Sustain them and us, we beseech thee, O Lord.

For the younger churches of Asia, Africa, and the islands of the sea, that they may grow into full stature of the completeness of Christ, bringing new treasures into the church of the ages:

Direct their steps and ours, we beseech thee, O Lord.

For the older churches of the east and the west, that they increase in wisdom and humility and find new ways to make the message of the gospel understood in the world of today:

Renew them and us, we beseech thee, O Lord.

For our brotherhood, that we may hold fast to the truth, be delivered from all error, and walk with one another in the way of love and unity:

Teach us and guide us, we beseech thee, O Lord.

For the several councils of the churches that through them Christians may the sooner overcome their reluctance to cooperate with one another, transcend their differences, and be knit more closely together in a fellowship of understanding love.

Draw all churches nearer to one another,
we beseech thee, O Lord.

O sovereign and almighty God, bless all thy people and all thy flock; give thy peace, thy help, thy love to us thy servants, the sheep of thy fold, that we may be united in the bond of peace, one body and one Spirit, in one hope of our calling, in thy divine boundless love, for the sake of Jesus Christ, the great Shepherd of the sheep. *Amen.*

489

All have sinned
and come short of the glory of God.
ST. PAUL'S LETTER TO THE ROMANS

The hatred which divides nation from nation, race from race, class from class,

Father, forgive.

The covetous desires of men and nations to possess what is not their own,

Father, forgive.

The greed which exploits the labors of men, and lays waste the earth,

Father, forgive.

Our envy of the welfare and happiness of others,

Father, forgive.

Our indifference to the plight of the homeless and the refugee,

Father, forgive.

The lust which uses for ignoble ends the bodies of men and women,

Father, forgive.

The pride which leads us to trust in ourselves, and not in God,

Father, forgive.

Be kind one to another, tenderhearted,
forgiving one another,
as God in Christ forgave you.

ST. PAUL'S LETTER TO THE EPHESIANS

Affirmation of Faith

490

We confess that Jesus is the Christ, the Son of the living God, and proclaim him Lord and Savior of the world. In his name and by his grace we accept our mission of witness and service to mankind. We rejoice in God our Father, maker of heaven and earth, and in the covenant of love by which he has bound us to himself. Through baptism into Christ we enter into newness of life and are made one with the whole people of God. In the fellowship and communion of the Holy Spirit we are joined to one another in brotherhood and in obedience to Christ. At the table of the Lord we celebrate with thanksgiving his saving acts and his presence. Within the universal church we receive the gift of ministry and the light of scripture. In the bonds of Christian faith we yield ourselves to God, that we may serve him whose kingdom has no end. Blessing, glory, and honor be to him forever. *Amen.*

491

I believe in God the Father Almighty, Maker of heaven and earth, and in Jesus Christ his only son our Lord, who was conceived by the Holy Ghost, born of the Virgin Mary, suffered under Pontius Pilate, was crucified, dead, and buried. He descended into hell; the third day he rose again from the dead; he ascended into heaven, and sitteth on the right hand of God the Father Almighty. From thence he shall come to judge the quick and the dead.

I believe in the Holy Ghost, the holy Catholic Church, the communion of saints, the forgiveness of sins, the resurrection of the body, and the life everlasting. *Amen.*

492

I believe in one God the Father Almighty, Maker of heaven and earth, and of all things visible and invisible:

And in one Lord Jesus Christ, the only-begotten Son of God; begotten of his Father before all worlds, God of God, Light of Light, Very God of very God; Begotten, not made, Being of one substance with the Father, By whom all things were made: Who for us men and for our salvation came down from heaven; And was incarnate by the Holy Ghost of the Virgin Mary, and was made man; And was crucified also for us under Pontius Pilate. He suffered and was buried: And the third day he rose again according to the Scriptures: And ascended into heaven, And sitteth on the right hand of the Father: And he shall come again, with glory, to judge both the quick and the dead; Whose kingdom shall have no end.

And I believe in the Holy Ghost, the Lord, and Giver of Life, Who proceedeth from the Father and the Son, Who with the Father and the Son together is worshiped and glorified; Who spake by the Prophets: And I believe one Catholic and Apostolic Church; I acknowledge one Baptism for the remission of sins; And I look for the Resurrection of the dead; And the Life of the world to come. *Amen.*

493

We believe that God is Spirit, and they who worship him must worship in spirit and truth.

We believe that God is Light, and if we walk in the light, as he is in the light, we have fellowship with one another.

We believe that God is Love, and he who loves is born of God and knows God.

We believe that Jesus is the Son of God; and as many as are led by the spirit of God, they are sons of God.

We believe that Jesus is the Way, the Truth, and the Life; and that God sent his Son into the world that the world should be saved through him.

We believe that we are children of God, and that God gave us eternal life, and this life is in his Son.

We believe that if we confess our sins, he is faithful and just to forgive us our sins.

We believe that the world passes away, and the lust of it; but he who does the will of God abides forever.

494

We believe in God, the Eternal Spirit, Father of our Lord Jesus Christ and our Father, and to his deeds we testify:

He calls the worlds into being,
creates man in his own image
and sets before him the ways of life and death.

He seeks in holy love to save all people from aimlessness and sin.

He judges men and nations by his righteous will declared through prophets and apostles.

In Jesus Christ, the man of Nazareth, our crucified and risen Lord,
he has come to us
and shared our common lot,
conquering sin and death
and reconciling the world to himself.

He bestows upon us his Holy Spirit,
creating and renewing the Church of Jesus Christ,
binding in covenant faithful people of all ages,
tongues, and races.

He calls us into his church
to accept the cost and joy of discipleship,
to be his servants in the service of men,
to proclaim the gospel to all the world,
and resist the powers of evil,
to share in Christ's baptism and eat at his table,
to join him in his passion and victory.

He promises to all who trust him
forgiveness of sins and fullness of grace,
courage in the struggle for justice and peace,
his presence in trial and rejoicing,
and eternal life in his kingdom which has no end.

Blessing and honor, glory and power be unto him. *Amen.*

Scripture Readings

495

In the beginning God created the heavens and the earth. The earth was without form and void, and darkness was upon the face of the deep; and the Spirit of God was moving over the face of the waters.

And God said, "Let there be light"; and there was light. And God saw that the light was good; and God separated the light from the darkness. God called the light Day, and the darkness he called Night. And there was evening and there was morning, one day.

Genesis 1:1-5

496

And God spoke all these words, saying,

"I am the LORD your God, who brought you out of the land of Egypt, out of the house of bondage.

"You shall have no other gods before me.

"You shall not make for yourself a graven image, or any likeness of anything that is in heaven above, or that is in the earth beneath, or that is in the water under the earth; you shall not bow down to them or serve them; for I the LORD your God am a jealous God, visiting the iniquity of the fathers upon the children to the third and the fourth generation of those who hate me, but showing steadfast love to thousands of those who love me and keep my commandments.

"You shall not take the name of the LORD your God in vain; for the LORD will not hold him guiltless who takes his name in vain.

"Remember the sabbath day, to keep it holy. Six days you shall labor, and do all your work; but the seventh day is a sabbath to the LORD your God; in it you shall not do any work, you, or your son, or your daughter, your manservant, or your maidservant, or your cattle, or the sojourner who is within your gates; for in six days the LORD made heaven and earth, the sea, and all that is in them, and rested the seventh day; therefore the LORD blessed the sabbath day and hallowed it.

"Honor your father and your mother, that your days may be long in the land which the LORD your God gives you.

"You shall not kill.

"You shall not commit adultery.

"You shall not steal.

"You shall not bear false witness against your neighbor.

"You shall not covet your neighbor's house; you shall not covet your neighbor's wife, or his manservant, or his maidservant, or his ox, or his ass, or anything that is your neighbor's."

Exodus 20:1-17

497

"Hear, O Israel: The LORD our God is one LORD; and you shall love the LORD your God with all your heart, and with all your soul, and with all your might. And these words which I command you this day shall be upon your heart; and you shall teach them diligently to your children, and shall talk of them when you sit in your house, and when you walk by the way, and when you lie down, and when you rise. And you shall bind them as a sign upon your hand, and they shall be as frontlets between your eyes. And you shall write them on the doorposts of your house and on your gates."

Deuteronomy 6:4-9

498

"Blessed art thou, O LORD, the God of Israel our father, for ever and ever. Thine, O LORD, is the greatness, and the power, and the glory, and the victory, and the majesty; for all that is in the heavens and in the earth is thine; thine is the kingdom, O LORD, and thou art exalted as head above all. Both riches and honor come from thee, and thou rulest over all. In thy hand are power and might; and in thy hand it is to make great and to give strength to all. And now we thank thee, our God, and praise thy glorious name."

1 Chronicles 29:10b-13

499

Happy is the man who finds wisdom,
  and the man who gets understanding,
for the gain from it is better than gain from silver
  and its profit better than gold.

She is more precious than jewels,
  and nothing you desire can compare with her.
Long life is in her right hand;
  in her left hand are riches and honor.
Her ways are ways of pleasantness,
  and all her paths are peace.
She is a tree of life to those who lay hold of her;
  those who hold her fast are called happy.

The LORD by wisdom founded the earth;
  by understanding he established the heavens;
by his knowledge the deeps broke forth,
  and the clouds drop down the dew.

My son, keep sound wisdom and discretion;
  let them not escape from your sight,
and they will be life for your soul
  and adornment for your neck.
Then you will walk on your way securely
  and your foot will not stumble.
If you sit down, you will not be afraid;
  when you lie down, your sleep will be sweet.
Do not be afraid of sudden panic,
  or of the ruin of the wicked, when it comes;
for the LORD will be your confidence
  and will keep your foot from being caught.
Proverbs 3:13-26

500

In the year that King Uzziah died I saw the Lord sitting upon a throne, high and lifted up; and his train filled the temple. Above him stood the seraphim; each had six wings: with two he covered his face, and with two he covered his feet, and with two he flew. And one called to another and said:

"Holy, holy, holy is the LORD of hosts;
the whole earth is full of his glory."

And the foundations of the thresholds shook at the voice of him who called, and the house was filled with smoke. And I said: "Woe is me! For I am lost;

for I am a man of unclean lips, and I dwell in the midst of a people of unclean lips; for my eyes have seen the King, the LORD of hosts!"

Then flew one of the seraphim to me, having in his hand a burning coal which he had taken with tongs from the altar. And he touched my mouth, and said: "Behold, this has touched your lips; your guilt is taken away, and your sin forgiven." And I heard the voice of the Lord saying, "Whom shall I send, and who will go for us?" Then I said, "Here am I! Send me."

Isaiah 6:1-8

501

The people who walked in darkness
  have seen a great light;
those who dwelt in a land of deep darkness,
  on them has light shined.
Thou hast multiplied the nation,
  thou hast increased its joy;
they rejoice before thee
  as with joy at the harvest,
  as men rejoice when they divide the spoil.
For the yoke of his burden,
  and the staff for his shoulder,
  the rod of his oppressor,
  thou hast broken as on the day of Midian.
For every boot of the tramping warrior in battle tumult
  and every garment rolled in blood
  will be burned as fuel for the fire.
For to us a child is born,
  to us a son is given;
and the government will be upon his shoulder,
  and his name will be called
"Wonderful Counselor, Mighty God,
  Everlasting Father, Prince of Peace."
Of the increase of his government and of peace
  there will be no end,
upon the throne of David, and over his kingdom,
  to establish it, and to uphold it
with justice and with righteousness
  from this time forth and for evermore.

Isaiah 9:2-7

502

There shall come forth a shoot from the stump of Jesse,
and a branch shall grow out of his roots.
And the Spirit of the LORD shall rest upon him,
the spirit of wisdom and understanding,
the spirit of counsel and might,
the spirit of knowledge and the fear of the LORD.
And his delight shall be in the fear of the LORD.

He shall not judge by what his eyes see,
or decide by what his ears hear;
but with righteousness he shall judge the poor,
and decide with equity for the meek of the earth;
and he shall smite the earth with the rod of his mouth,
and with the breath of his lips he shall slay the wicked.
Righteousness shall be the girdle of his waist,
and faithfulness the girdle of his loins.

The wolf shall dwell with the lamb,
and the leopard shall lie down with the kid,
and the calf and the lion and the fatling together,
and a little child shall lead them.
The cow and the bear shall feed;
their young shall lie down together;
and the lion shall eat straw like the ox.
The sucking child shall play over the hole of the asp,
and the weaned child shall put his hand on the adder's den.
They shall not hurt or destroy
in all my holy mountain;
for the earth shall be full of the knowledge of the LORD
as the waters cover the sea.

In that day the root of Jesse shall stand as an ensign to the peoples; him shall the nations seek, and his dwellings shall be glorious.

Isaiah 11:1-10

503

The wilderness and the dry land shall be glad,
the desert shall rejoice and blossom;
like the crocus it shall blossom abundantly,
and rejoice with joy and singing.

The glory of Lebanon shall be given to it,
the majesty of Carmel and Sharon.
They shall see the glory of the LORD,
the majesty of our God.

Strengthen the weak hands,
and make firm the feeble knees.
Say to those who are of a fearful heart,
"Be strong, fear not!
Behold, your God
will come with vengeance,
with the recompense of God.
He will come and save you."

Then the eyes of the blind shall be opened,
and the ears of the deaf unstopped;
then shall the lame man leap like a hart,
and the tongue of the dumb sing for joy.
For waters shall break forth in the wilderness,
and streams in the desert;
the burning sand shall become a pool,
and the thirsty ground springs of water;
the haunt of jackals shall become a swamp,
the grass shall become reeds and rushes.

And a highway shall be there,
and it shall be called the Holy Way;
the unclean shall not pass over it,
and fools shall not err therein.
No lion shall be there,
nor shall any ravenous beast come up on it;
they shall not be found there,
but the redeemed shall walk there.
And the ransomed of the LORD shall return,
and come to Zion with singing;
everlasting joy shall be upon their heads;
they shall obtain joy and gladness,
and sorrow and sighing shall flee away.

Isaiah 35

504

Comfort, comfort my people,
   says your God.
Speak tenderly to Jerusalem,
   and cry to her
that her warfare is ended,
   that her iniquity is pardoned,
that she has received from the LORD's hand
   double for all her sins.

A voice cries:
"In the wilderness prepare the way of the LORD,
   make straight in the desert a highway for our God.
Every valley shall be lifted up,
   and every mountain and hill be made low;
the uneven ground shall become level,
   and the rough places a plain.
And the glory of the LORD shall be revealed,
   and all flesh shall see it together,
   for the mouth of the LORD has spoken."

A voice says, "Cry!"
   And I said, "What shall I cry?"
All flesh is grass,
   and all its beauty is like the flower of the field.
The grass withers, the flower fades,
   when the breath of the LORD blows upon it;
   surely the people is grass.
The grass withers, the flower fades;
   but the word of our God will stand for ever.

Get you up to a high mountain,
   O Zion, herald of good tidings;
lift up your voice with strength,
   O Jerusalem, herald of good tidings,
   lift it up, fear not;
say to the cities of Judah,
   "Behold your God!"
Behold, the Lord GOD comes with might,
   and his arm rules for him;
behold, his reward is with him,
   and his recompense before him.

He will feed his flock like a shepherd,
  he will gather the lambs in his arms,
he will carry them in his bosom,
  and gently lead those that are with young.
Isaiah 40:1-11

505

To whom then will you compare me,
  that I should be like him? says the Holy One.
Lift up your eyes on high and see:
  who created these?
He who brings out their host by number,
  calling them all by name;
by the greatness of his might,
  and because he is strong in power
  not one is missing.

Why do you say, O Jacob,
  and speak, O Israel.
"My way is hid from the LORD,
  and my right is disregarded by my God"?
Have you not known? Have you not heard?
The LORD is the everlasting God,
  the Creator of the ends of the earth.
He does not faint or grow weary,
  his understanding is unsearchable.
He gives power to the faint,
  and to him who has no might he increases strength.
Even youths shall faint and be weary,
  and young men shall fall exhausted;
but they who wait for the LORD shall renew their strength,
  they shall mount up with wings like eagles,
they shall run and not be weary,
  they shall walk and not faint.
Isaiah 40:25-31

506

Behold my servant, whom I uphold,
  my chosen, in whom my soul delights;
I have put my Spirit upon him,

he will bring forth justice to the nations.
He will not cry or lift up his voice,
or make it heard in the street;
a bruised reed he will not break,
and a dimly burning wick he will not quench;
he will faithfully bring forth justice.
He will not fail or be discouraged
till he has established justice in the earth;
and the coastlands wait for his law.

Thus says God, the LORD,
who created the heavens and stretched them out,
who spread forth the earth and what comes from it,
who gives breath to the people upon it
and spirit to those who walk in it:
"I am the LORD, I have called you in righteousness,
I have taken you by the hand and kept you;
I have given you as a covenant to the people,
a light to the nations,
to open the eyes that are blind,
to bring out the prisoners from the dungeon,
from the prison those who sit in darkness.
I am the LORD, that is my name;
my glory I give to no other,
nor my praise to graven images.
Behold, the former things have come to pass,
and new things I now declare;
before they spring forth
I tell you of them."

Sing to the LORD a new song,
his praise from the end of the earth!
Isaiah 42:1-10a

507

Who has believed what we have heard?
And to whom has the arm of the LORD been revealed?
For he grew up before him like a young plant,
and like a root out of dry ground;
he had no form or comeliness that we should look at him,
and no beauty that we should desire him.

He was despised and rejected by men;
a man of sorrows, and acquainted with grief;
and as one from whom men hide their faces
he was despised, and we esteemed him not.

Surely he has borne our griefs
and carried our sorrows;
yet we esteemed him stricken,
smitten by God, and afflicted.
But he was wounded for our transgressions,
he was bruised for our iniquities;
upon him was the chastisement that made us whole,
and with his stripes we are healed.
All we like sheep have gone astray;
we have turned every one to his own way;
and the LORD has laid on him
the iniquity of us all.

He was oppressed, and he was afflicted,
yet he opened not his mouth;
like a lamb that is led to the slaughter,
and like a sheep that before its shearers is dumb,
so he opened not his mouth.
By oppression and judgment he was taken away;
and as for his generation, who considered
that he was cut off out of the land of the living,
stricken for the transgression of my people?
And they made his grave with the wicked
and with a rich man in his death,
although he had done no violence,
and there was no deceit in his mouth.

Yet it was the will of the LORD to bruise him;
he has put him to grief;
when he makes himself an offering for sin,
he shall see his offspring, he shall prolong his days;
the will of the LORD shall prosper in his hand;
he shall see the fruit of the travail of his soul and be satisfied;
by his knowledge shall the righteous one, my servant,
make many to be accounted righteous;
and he shall bear their iniquities.
Therefore I will divide him a portion with the great,
and he shall divide the spoil with the strong;

because he poured out his soul to death,
  and was numbered with the transgressors;
yet he bore the sin of many,
  and made intercession for the transgressors.
Isaiah 53

508

"Ho, every one who thirsts, come to the waters;
and he who has no money,
  come, buy and eat!
Come, buy wine and milk
  without money and without price.
Why do you spend your money for that which is not bread,
  and your labor for that which does not satisfy?
Hearken diligently to me, and eat what is good,
  and delight yourselves in fatness.
Incline your ear, and come to me;
  hear, that your soul may live;
and I will make with you an everlasting covenant,
  my steadfast, sure love for David.
Behold, I made him a witness to the peoples,
  a leader and commander for the peoples.
Behold, you shall call nations that you know not,
  and nations that knew you not shall run to you,
because of the LORD your God, and of the Holy One of Israel,
  for he has glorified you.

"Seek the LORD while he may be found,
  call upon him while he is near;
let the wicked forsake his way,
  and the unrighteous man his thoughts;
let him return to the LORD, that he may have mercy on him,
  and to our God, for he will abundantly pardon.
For my thoughts are not your thoughts,
  neither are your ways my ways, says the LORD.
For as the heavens are higher than the earth,
  so are my ways higher than your ways
  and my thoughts than your thoughts.
"For as the rain and the snow come down from heaven,
  and return not thither but water the earth,
making it bring forth and sprout,

giving seed to the sower and bread to the eater,
so shall my word be that goes forth from my mouth;
it shall not return to me empty,
but it shall accomplish that which I purpose,
and prosper in the thing for which I sent it.

"For you shall go out in joy,
and be led forth in peace;
the mountains and the hills before you
shall break forth into singing,
and all the trees of the field shall clap their hands.
Instead of the thorn shall come up the cypress;
instead of the brier shall come up the myrtle;
and it shall be to the LORD for a memorial,
for an everlasting sign which shall not be cut off."
Isaiah 55

509

"Behold, the days are coming, says the LORD, when I will make a new covenant with the house of Israel and the house of Judah, not like the covenant which I made with their fathers when I took them by the hand to bring them out of the land of Egypt, my covenant which they broke, though I was their husband, says the LORD. But this is the covenant which I will make with the house of Israel after those days, says the LORD: I will put my law within them, and I will write it upon their hearts; and I will be their God, and they shall be my people. And no longer shall each man teach his neighbor and each his brother, saying, 'Know the LORD,' for they shall all know me, from the least of them to the greatest, says the LORD; for I will forgive their iniquity, and I will remember their sin no more."
Jeremiah 31:31-34

510

Seek good, and not evil,
that you may live;
and so the LORD, the God of hosts, will be with you,
as you have said.
Hate evil, and love good,
and establish justice in the gate;
it may be that the LORD, the God of hosts,
will be gracious to the remnant of Joseph.

"I hate, I despise your feasts,
  and I take no delight in your solemn assemblies.
Even though you offer me your burnt offerings and cereal offerings,
  I will not accept them,
and the peace offerings of your fatted beasts
  I will not look upon.
Take away from me the noise of your songs;
  to the melody of your harps I will not listen.
But let justice roll down like waters,
  and righteousness like an ever-flowing stream.

"With what shall I come before the LORD,
  and bow myself before God on high?
Shall I come before him with burnt offerings,
  with calves a year old?
Will the LORD be pleased with thousands of rams,
  with ten thousands of rivers of oil?
Shall I give my first-born for my transgression,
  the fruit of my body for the sin of my soul?"
He has showed you, O man, what is good;
  and what does the LORD require of you
but to do justice, and to love kindness,
  and to walk humbly with your God?

Amos 5:14-15, 21-24; Micah 6:6-8

511

Now when Jesus was born in Bethlehem of Judea in the days of Herod the king, behold, wise men from the East came to Jerusalem, saying, "Where is he who has been born king of the Jews? For we have seen his star in the East, and have come to worship him." When Herod the king heard this, he was troubled, and all Jerusalem with him; and assembling all the chief priests and scribes of the people, he inquired of them where the Christ was to be born. They told him, "In Bethlehem of Judea; for so it is written by the prophet:

'And you, O Bethlehem, in the land of Judah,
are by no means least among the rulers of Judah;
for from you shall come a ruler
who will govern my people Israel.' "

Then Herod summoned the wise men secretly and ascertained from them what time the star appeared; and he sent them to Bethlehem, saying, "Go and search diligently for the child, and when you have found him bring me word, that I too may come and worship him." When they had heard the king they went their way; and lo, the star which they had seen in the East went before them, till it came to rest over the place where the child was. When they saw the star, they rejoiced exceedingly with great joy; and going into the house they saw the child with Mary his mother, and they fell down and worshiped him. Then, opening their treasures, they offered him gifts, gold and frankincense and myrrh. And being warned in a dream not to return to Herod, they departed to their own country by another way.

Now when they had departed, behold, an angel of the Lord appeared to Joseph in a dream and said, "Rise, take the child and his mother, and flee to Egypt, and remain there till I tell you; for Herod is about to search for the child, to destroy him," And he rose and took the child and his mother by night, and departed to Egypt, and remained there until the death of Herod. This was to fulfil what the Lord had spoken by the prophet, "Out of Egypt have I called my son."

Then Herod, when he saw that he had been tricked by the wise men, was in a furious rage, and he sent and killed all the male children in Bethlehem and in all that region who were two years old or under, according to the time which he had ascertained from the wise men.

Matthew 2:1-16

512

Seeing the crowds, he went up on the mountain, and when he sat down his disciples came to him. And he opened his mouth and taught them, saying:

"Blessed are the poor in spirit, for theirs is the kingdom of heaven.

"Blessed are those who mourn, for they shall be comforted.

"Blessed are the meek, for they shall inherit the earth.

"Blessed are those who hunger and thirst for righteousness, for they shall be satisfied.

"Blessed are the merciful, for they shall obtain mercy.

"Blessed are the pure in heart, for they shall see God.

"Blessed are the peacemakers, for they shall be called sons of God.

"Blessed are those who are persecuted for righteousness' sake, for theirs is the kingdom of heaven.

"Blessed are you when men revile you and persecute you and utter all kinds of evil against you falsely on my account. Rejoice and be glad, for your reward is great in heaven, for so men persecuted the prophets who were before you."

Matthew 5:1-12

513

"Beware of practicing your piety before men in order to be seen by them; for then you will have no reward from your Father who is in heaven.

"Thus, when you give alms, sound no trumpet before you, as the hypocrites do in the synagogues and in the streets, that they may be praised by men. Truly, I say to you, they have their reward. But when you give alms, do not let your left hand know what your right hand is doing, so that your alms may be in secret; and your Father who sees in secret will reward you.

"And when you pray, you must not be like the hypocrites; for they love to stand and pray in the synagogues and at the street corners, that they may be seen by men. Truly, I say to you, they have their reward. But when you pray, go into your room and shut the door and pray to your Father who is in secret; and your Father who sees in secret will reward you.

"And in praying do not heap up empty phrases as the Gentiles do; for they think that they will be heard for their many words. Do not be like them, for your Father knows what you need before you ask him. Pray then like this:

Our Father who art in heaven,
Hallowed be thy name.
Thy kingdom come,
Thy will be done,
    On earth as it is in heaven.
Give us this day our daily bread;
And forgive us our debts,
    As we also have forgiven our debtors;
And lead us not into temptation,
    But deliver us from evil.

For if you forgive men their trespasses, your heavenly Father also will forgive you; but if you do not forgive men their trespasses, neither will your Father forgive your trespasses."

Matthew 6:1-15

514

And Jesus went about all the cities and villages, teaching in their synagogues and preaching the gospel of the kingdom, and healing every disease and every infirmity. When he saw the crowds, he had compassion for them, because they were harassed and helpless, like sheep without a shepherd. Then he said to his disciples, "The harvest is plentiful, but the laborers are few; pray therefore the Lord of the harvest to send out laborers into his harvest."

And Jesus came and said to them, "All authority in heaven and on earth has been given to me. Go therefore and make disciples of all nations, baptizing them in the name of the Father and of the Son and of the Holy Spirit, teaching them to observe all that I have commanded you; and lo, I am with you always, to the close of the age."

Matthew 9:35-38; 28:18-20

515

Now when Jesus came into the district of Caesarea Philippi, he asked his disciples, "Who do men say that the Son of man is?" And they said, "Some say John the Baptist, others say Elijah, and others Jeremiah or one of the prophets." He said to them, "But who do you say that I am?" Simon Peter replied, "You are the Christ, the Son of the living God." And Jesus answered him, "Blessed are you, Simon Bar-Jona! For flesh and blood has not revealed this to you, but my Father who is in heaven. And I tell you, you are Peter, and on this rock I will build my church, and the powers of death shall not prevail against it. I will give you the keys of the kingdom of heaven, and whatever you bind on earth shall be bound in heaven, and whatever you loose on earth shall be loosed in heaven." Then he strictly charged the disciples to tell no one that he was the Christ.

Then Jesus told his disciples, "If any man would come after me, let him deny himself and take up his cross and follow me. For whoever would save his life will lose it, and whoever loses his life for my sake will find it. For what will it profit a man, if he gains the whole world and forfeits his life? Or what shall a man give in return for his life? For the Son of man is to come with his angels in the glory of his Father, and then he will repay every man for what he has done. Truly, I say to you, there are some standing here who will not taste death before they see the Son of man coming in his kingdom."

Matthew 16:13-20; 24-28

516

And when they drew near to Jerusalem and came to Bethphage, to the Mount of Olives, then Jesus sent two disciples, saying to them, "Go into the village opposite you, and immediately you will find an ass tied, and a colt with her; untie them and bring them to me. If any one says anything to you, you shall say, 'The Lord has need of them,' and he will send them immediately."

This took place to fulfill what was spoken by the prophet, saying,

"Tell the daughter of Zion,

Behold, your king is coming to you,
humble, and mounted on an ass,
and on a colt, the foal of an ass."

The disciples went and did as Jesus had directed them; they brought the ass and the colt, and put their garments on them, and he sat thereon.
Most of the crowd spread their garments on the road, and others cut branches from the trees and spread them on the road. And the crowds that went before him and that followed him shouted, "Hosanna to the Son of David! Blessed is he who comes in the name of the Lord! Hosanna in the highest!" And when he entered Jerusalem, all the city was stirred, saying, "Who is this?" And the crowds said, "This is the prophet Jesus from Nazareth of Galilee."
Matthew 21:1-11

517

"When the Son of man comes in his glory, and all the angels with him, then he will sit on his glorious throne. Before him will be gathered all the nations, and he will separate them one from another as a shepherd separates the sheep from the goats, and he will place the sheep at his right hand, but the goats at the left. Then the King will say to those at his right hand, 'Come, O blessed of my Father, inherit the kingdom prepared for you from the foundation of the world; for I was hungry and you gave me food, I was thirsty and you gave me drink, I was a stranger and you welcomed me, I was naked and you clothed me, I was sick and you visited me, I was in prison and you came to me.' Then the righteous will answer him. 'Lord, when did we see thee hungry and feed thee, or thirsty and give thee drink? And when did we see thee a stranger and welcome thee, or naked and clothe thee? And when did we see thee sick or in prison and visit thee?' And the King will answer them, 'Truly, I say to you, as you did it to one of the least of these my brethren, you did it to me.' Then he will say to those at his left hand, 'Depart from me, you cursed, into the eternal fire prepared for the devil and his angels; for I was hungry and you gave me no food, I was thirsty and you gave me no drink, I was a stranger and you did not welcome me, naked and you did not clothe me, sick and in prison and you did not visit me.' Then they also will answer, 'Lord, when did we see thee hungry or thirsty or a stranger or naked or sick or in prison, and did not minister to thee?' Then he will answer them, 'Truly, I say to you, as you did it not to one of the least of these, you did it not to me.' And they will go away into eternal punishment, but the righteous into eternal life."
Matthew 25:31-46

518

Now after the sabbath, toward the dawn of the first day of the week, Mary Magdalene and the other Mary went to see the sepulchre. And behold, there was a great earthquake; for an angel of the Lord descended from heaven and came and rolled back the stone, and sat upon it. His appearance was like lightning, and his raiment white as snow. And for fear of him the guards trembled and became like dead men. But the angel said to the women, "Do not be afraid; for I know that you seek Jesus who was crucified. He is not here; for he has risen, as he said. Come, see the place where he lay. Then go quickly and tell his disciples that he has risen from the dead, and behold, he is going before you to Galilee; there you will see him. Lo, I have told you." So they departed quickly from the tomb with fear and great joy, and ran to tell his disciples. And behold, Jesus met them and said, "Hail!" And they came up and took hold of his feet and worshiped him. Then Jesus said to them, "Do not be afraid; go and tell my brethren to go to Galilee, and there they will see me."

Matthew 28:1-10

519

And one of the scribes came up and heard them disputing with one another, and seeing that he answered them well, asked him, "Which commandment is the first of all?" Jesus answered, "The first is, 'Hear, O Israel: The Lord our God, the Lord is one; and you shall love the Lord your God with all your heart, and with all your soul, and with all your mind, and with all your strength.' The second is this, 'You shall love your neighbor as yourself.' There is no other commandment greater than these." And the scribe said to him, "You are right, Teacher; you have truly said that he is one, and there is no other but he; and to love him with all the heart, and with all the understanding, and with all the strength, and to love one's neighbor as oneself, is much more than all whole burnt offerings and sacrifices." And when Jesus saw that he answered wisely, he said to him, "You are not far from the kingdom of God." And after that no one dared to ask him any question.

Mark 12:28-34

520

And Mary said,
"My soul magnifies the Lord,
and my spirit rejoices in God my Savior,
for he has regarded the low estate of his handmaiden.
For behold, henceforth all generations will call me blessed;

for he who is mighty has done great things for me,
and holy is his name.
And his mercy is on those who fear him
from generation to generation.
He has shown strength with his arm,
he has scattered the proud in the imagination of their hearts,
he has put down the mighty from their thrones,
and exalted those of low degree;
he has filled the hungry with good things,
and the rich he has sent empty away.
He has helped his servant Israel,
in remembrance of his mercy,
as he spoke to our fathers,
to Abraham and to his posterity for ever."
Luke 1:46-55

521

"Blessed be the Lord God of Israel,
for he has visited and redeemed his people,
and has raised up a horn of salvation for us
in the house of his servant David,
as he spoke by the mouth of his holy prophets from of old,
that we should be saved from our enemies,
and from the hand of all who hate us;
to perform the mercy promised to our fathers,
and to remember his holy covenant,
the oath which he swore to our father Abraham, to grant us
that we, being delivered from the hand of our enemies,
might serve him without fear,
in holiness and righteousness before him all the days of our life.
And you, child, will be called the prophet of the Most High;
for you will go before the Lord to prepare his ways,
to give knowledge of salvation to his people
in the forgiveness of their sins,
through the tender mercy of our God,
when the day shall dawn upon us from on high
to give light to those who sit in darkness and in the shadow of death,
to guide our feet into the way of peace."
Luke 1:68-79

522

In those days a decree went out from Caesar Augustus that all the world should be enrolled. This was the first enrollment, when Quirinius was governor of Syria. And all went to be enrolled, each to his own city. And Joseph also went up from Galilee, from the city of Nazareth, to Judea, to the city of David, which is called Bethlehem, because he was of the house and lineage of David, to be enrolled with Mary, his betrothed, who was with child. And while they were there, the time came for her to be delivered. And she gave birth to her first-born son and wrapped him in swaddling cloths, and laid him in a manger, because there was no place for them in the inn.

And in that region there were shepherds out in the field, keeping watch over their flock by night. And an angel of the Lord appeared to them, and the glory of the Lord shone around them, and they were filled with fear. And the angel said to them, "Be not afraid; for behold, I bring you good news of a great joy which will come to all the people; for to you is born this day in the city of David a Savior, who is Christ the Lord. And this will be a sign for you: you will find a babe wrapped in swaddling cloths and lying in a manger." And suddenly there was with the angel a multitude of the heavenly host praising God and saying,

"Glory to God in the highest,
and on earth peace among men with whom he is pleased!"

When the angels went away from them into heaven, the shepherds said to one another, "Let us go over to Bethlehem and see this thing that has happened, which the Lord has made known to us." And they went with haste, and found Mary and Joseph, and the babe lying in a manger. And when they saw it they made known the saying which had been told them concerning this child; and all who heard it wondered at what the shepherds told them. But Mary kept all these things, pondering them in her heart. And the shepherds returned, glorifying and praising God for all they had heard and seen, as it had been told them.

Luke 2:1-20

523

And he came to Nazareth, where he had been brought up; and he went to the synagogue, as his custom was, on the sabbath day. And he stood up to read; and there was given to him the book of the prophet Isaiah. He opened the book and found the place where it was written,

"The Spirit of the Lord is upon me,
because he has anointed me to preach good news to the poor.
He has sent me to proclaim release to the captives

and recovering of sight to the blind,
to set at liberty those who are oppressed,
to proclaim the acceptable year of the Lord."

And he closed the book, and gave it back to the attendant, and sat down; and the eyes of all in the synagogue were fixed on him. And he began to say to them, "Today this scripture has been fulfilled in your hearing."
Luke 4:16-21

524

"But I say to you that hear, Love your enemies, do good to those who hate you, bless those who curse you, pray for those who abuse you. To him who strikes you on the cheek, offer the other also; and from him who takes away your cloak do not withold your coat as well. Give to every one who begs from you; and of him who takes away your goods do not ask them again. And as you wish that men would do to you, do so to them.

"If you love those who love you, what credit is that to you? For even sinners love those who love them. And if you do good to those who do good to you, what credit is that to you? For even sinners do the same. And if you lend to those from whom you hope to receive, what credit is that to you? Even sinners lend to sinners, to receive as much again. But love your enemies, and do good, and lend, expecting nothing in return; and your reward will be great, and you will be sons of the Most High; for he is kind to the ungrateful and the selfish. Be merciful, even as your Father is merciful.

"Judge not, and you will not be judged; condemn not, and you will not be condemned; forgive, and you will be forgiven; give, and it will be given to you; good measure, pressed down, shaken together, running over, will be put into your lap. For the measure you give will be the measure you get back."
Luke 6:27-38

525

And behold, a lawyer stood up to put him to the test, saying, "Teacher, what shall I do to inherit eternal life?" He said to him, "What is written in the law? How do you read?" And he answered, "You shall love the Lord your God with all your heart, and with all your soul, and with all your strength, and with all your mind; and your neighbor as yourself." And he said to him, "You have answered right; do this, and you will live."

But he, desiring to justify himself, said to Jesus, "And who is my neighbor?" Jesus replied, "A man was going down from Jerusalem to Jericho, and he fell among robbers, who stripped him and beat him, and departed, leaving him half dead. Now by chance a priest was going down the road; and when

he saw him he passed by on the other side. So likewise a Levite, when he came to the place and saw him, passed by on the other side. But a Samaritan, as he journeyed, came to where he was; and when he saw him, he had compassion, and went to him and bound up his wounds, pouring on oil and wine; then he set him on his own beast and brought him to an inn, and took care of him. And the next day he took out two denarii and gave them to the innkeeper, saying, 'Take care of him; and whatever more you spend, I will repay you when I come back.' Which of these three, do you think, proved neighbor to the man who fell among the robbers?" He said, "The one who showed mercy on him." And Jesus said to him, "Go and do likewise."
Luke 10:25-37

526

And he said, "There was a man who had two sons; and the younger of them said to his father, 'Father, give me the share of property that falls to me.' And he divided his living between them. Not many days later, the younger son gathered all he had and took his journey into a far country, and there he squandered his property in loose living. And when he had spent everything, a great famine arose in that country, and he began to be in want. So he went and joined himself to one of the citizens of that country, who sent him into his fields to feed swine. And he would gladly have fed on the pods that the swine ate; and no one gave him anything. But when he came to himself he said, 'How many of my father's hired servants have bread enough and to spare, but I perish here with hunger! I will arise and go to my father, and I will say to him, "Father, I have sinned against heaven and before you; I am no longer worthy to be called your son; treat me as one of your hired servants."' And he arose and came to his father. But while he was yet at a distance, his father saw him and had compassion, and ran and embraced him and kissed him. And the son said to him, 'Father, I have sinned against heaven and before you; I am no longer worthy to be called your son.' But the father said to his servants, 'Bring quickly the best robe, and put it on him; and put a ring on his hand, and shoes on his feet; and bring the fatted calf and kill it, and let us eat and make merry; for this my son was dead, and is alive again; he was lost, and is found.' And they began to make merry.

"Now his elder son was in the field; and as he came and drew near to the house, he heard music and dancing. And he called one of the servants and asked what this meant. And he said to him, 'Your brother has come, and your father has killed the fatted calf, because he has received him safe and sound.' But he was angry and refused to go in. His father came out and entreated him, but he answered his father, 'Lo, these many years I have served you, and I never disobeyed your command; yet you never gave me a kid, that

I might make merry with my friends. But when this son of yours came, who has devoured your living with harlots, you killed for him the fatted calf!' And he said to him, 'Son, you are always with me, and all that is mine is yours. It was fitting to make merry and be glad, for this your brother was dead, and is alive; he was lost, and is found.' "

Luke 15:11-24, 25-32

527

That very day two of them were going to a village named Emmaus, about seven miles from Jerusalem, and talking with each other about all these things that had happened. While they were talking and discussing together, Jesus himself drew near and went with them. But their eyes were kept from recognizing him. And he said to them, "What is this conversation which you are holding with each other as you walk?" And they stood still, looking sad. Then one of them named Cleopas, answered him, "Are you the only visitor to Jerusalem who does not know the things that have happened there in these days?" And he said to them, "What things?" And they said to him, "Concerning Jesus of Nazareth, who was a prophet mighty in deed and word before God and all the people, and how our chief priests and rulers delivered him up to be condemned to death, and crucified him. But we had hoped that he was the one to redeem Israel. Yes, and besides all this, it is now the third day since this happened. Moreover, some women of our company amazed us. They were at the tomb early in the morning and did not find his body; and they came back saying that they had even seen a vision of angels, who said that he was alive. Some of those who were with us went to the tomb, and found it just as the women had said; but him they did not see." And he said to them, "O foolish men, and slow of heart to believe all that the prophets have spoken! Was it not necessary that the Christ should suffer these things and enter into his glory?" And beginning with Moses and all the prophets, he interpreted to them in all the scriptures the things concerning himself.

So they drew near to the village to which they were going. He appeared to be going further, but they constrained him, saying, "Stay with us, for it is toward evening and the day is now far spent." So he went in to stay with them. When he was at table with them, he took the bread and blessed, and broke it, and gave it to them. And their eyes were opened and they recognized him; and he vanished out of their sight. They said to each other, "Did not our hearts burn within us while he talked to us on the road, while he opened to us the scriptures?" And they rose that same hour and returned to Jerusalem; and they found the eleven gathered together and those who were with them, who said, "The Lord has risen indeed, and has appeared to

Simon!" Then they told what had happened on the road, and how he was known to them in the breaking of the bread.

Luke 24:13-35

528

In the beginning was the Word, and the Word was with God, and the Word was God. He was in the beginning with God; all things were made through him, and without him was not anything made that was made. In him was life, and the life was the light of men. The light shines in the darkness, and the darkness has not overcome it.

There was a man sent from God, whose name was John. He came for testimony, to bear witness to the light, that all might believe through him. He was not the light, but came to bear witness to the light.

The true light that enlightens every man was coming into the world. He was in the world, and the world was made through him, yet the world knew him not. He came to his own home, and his own people received him not. But to all who received him, who believed in his name, he gave power to become children of God; who were born, not of blood nor of the will of the flesh nor of the will of man, but of God.

And the Word became flesh and dwelt among us, full of grace and truth; we have beheld his glory, glory as of the only Son from the Father.

John 1:1-14

529

For God so loved the world that he gave his only Son, that whoever believes in him should not perish but have eternal life. For God sent the Son into the world, not to condemn the world, but that the world might be saved through him. He who believes in him is not condemned; he who does not believe is condemned already, because he has not believed in the name of the only Son of God. And this is the judgment, that the light has come into the world, and men loved darkness rather than light, because their deeds were evil. For every one who does evil hates the light, and does not come to the light, lest his deeds should be exposed. But he who does what is true comes to the light, that it may be clearly seen that his deeds have been wrought in God.

John 3:16-21

530

So Jesus again said to them, "Truly, truly, I say to you, I am the door of the sheep. All who came before me are thieves and robbers; but the sheep did not heed them. I am the door; if any one enters by me, he will be saved, and will go in and out and find pasture. The thief comes only to steal and kill and destroy; I came that they may have life, and have it abundantly. I am the good shepherd. The good shepherd lays down his life for the sheep. He who is a hireling and not a shepherd, whose own the sheep are not, sees the wolf coming and leaves the sheep and flees; and the wolf snatches them and scatters them. He flees because he is a hireling and cares nothing for the sheep. I am the good shepherd; I know my own and my own know me, as the Father knows me and I know the Father; and I lay down my life for the sheep. And I have other sheep, that are not of this fold; I must bring them also, and they will heed my voice. So there shall be one flock, one shepherd. For this reason the Father loves me, because I lay down my life, that I may take it again. No one takes it from me, but I lay it down of my own accord. I have power to lay it down, and I have power to take it again; this charge I have received from my Father."

John 10:7-18

531

"Let not your hearts be troubled; believe in God, believe also in me. In my Father's house are many rooms; if it were not so, would I have told you that I go to prepare a place for you? And when I go and prepare a place for you, I will come again and will take you to myself, that where I am you may be also. And you know the way where I am going." Thomas said to him, "Lord, we do not know where you are going; how can we know the way?" Jesus said to him, "I am the way, and the truth, and the life; no one comes to the Father, but by me. If you had known me, you would have known my Father also; henceforth you know him and have seen him."

Philip said to him, "Lord, show us the Father, and we shall be satisfied." Jesus said to him, "Have I been with you so long, and yet you do not know me, Philip? He who has seen me has seen the Father; how can you say, 'Show us the Father'? Do you not believe that I am in the Father and the Father in me? The words that I say to you I do not speak on my own authority; but the Father who dwells in me does his works. Believe me that I am in the Father and the Father in me; or else believe me for the sake of the works themselves.

"Truly, truly, I say to you, he who believes in me will also do the works that I do; and greater works than these will he do, because I go to the Father. Whatever you ask in my name, I will do it, that the Father may be glorified in the Son; if you ask anything in my name, I will do it."

John 14:1-14

532

"I am the true vine, and my Father is the vinedresser. Every branch of mine that bears no fruit, he takes away, and every branch that does bear fruit he prunes, that it may bear more fruit. You are already made clean by the word which I have spoken to you. Abide in me, and I in you. As the branch cannot bear fruit by itself, unless it abides in the vine, neither can you, unless you abide in me. I am the vine, you are the branches. He who abides in me, and I in him, he it is that bears much fruit, for apart from me you can do nothing. If a man does not abide in me, he is cast forth as a branch and withers; and the branches are gathered, thrown into the fire and burned. If you abide in me, and my words abide in you, ask whatever you will, and it shall be done for you. By this my Father is glorified, that you bear much fruit, and so prove to be my disciples. As the Father has loved me, so have I loved you; abide in my love. If you keep my commandments, you will abide in my love, just as I have kept my Father's commandments and abide in his love. These things I have spoken to you, that my joy may be in you, and that your joy may be full.

"This is my commandment, that you love one another as I have loved you. Greater love has no man than this, that a man lay down his life for his friends. You are my friends if you do what I command you. No longer do I call you servants, for the servant does not know what his master is doing; but I have called you friends, for all that I have heard from my Father I have made known to you. You did not choose me, but I chose you and appointed you that you should go and bear fruit and that your fruit should abide; so that whatever you ask the Father in my name, he may give it to you. This I command you, to love one another."

John 15:1-17

533

When the day of Pentecost had come, they were all together in one place. And suddenly a sound came from heaven like the rush of a mighty wind, and it filled all the house where they were sitting. And there appeared to them tongues as of fire, distributed and resting on each one of them. And they were all filled with the Holy Spirit and began to speak in other tongues, as the Spirit gave them utterance.

But Peter, standing with the eleven, lifted up his voice and addressed them, "Men of Judea and all who dwell in Jerusalem, let this be known to you, and give ear to my words.

"Jesus of Nazareth, a man attested to you by God with mighty works and wonders and signs which God did through him in your midst, as you yourselves know—this Jesus, delivered up according to the definite plan and foreknowledge of God, you crucified and killed by the hands of lawless men. But God raised him up, having loosed the pangs of death, because it was not possible for him to be held by it.

"Let all the house of Israel therefore know assuredly that God has made him both Lord and Christ, this Jesus whom you crucified."

Now when they heard this they were cut to the heart, and said to Peter and the rest of the apostles, "Brethren, what shall we do?" And Peter said to them, "Repent, and be baptized every one of you in the name of Jesus Christ for the forgiveness of your sins; and you shall receive the gift of the Holy Spirit. For the promise is to you and to your children and to all that are far off, every one whom the Lord our God calls to him." And he testified with many other words and exhorted them, saying, "Save yourselves from this crooked generation." So those who received his word were baptized, and there were added that day about three thousand souls. And they devoted themselves to the apostles' teaching and fellowship, to the breaking of bread and the prayers.

Acts 2:1-4; 14; 22b-24; 36-42

534

So Paul, standing in the middle of the Areopagus, said: "Men of Athens, I perceive that in every way you are very religious. For as I passed along and observed the objects of your worship, I found also an altar with this inscription, 'To an unknown god.' What therefore you worship as unknown, this I proclaim to you. The God who made the world and everything in it, being Lord of heaven and earth, does not live in shrines made by man, nor is he served by human hands, as though he needed anything, since he himself gives to all men life and breath and everything. And he made from one every nation of men to live on all the face of the earth, having determined allotted periods and the boundaries of their habitation, that they should seek God, in the hope that they might feel after him and find him. Yet he is not far from each one of us, for

'In him we live and move and have our being';

as even some of your poets have said,

'For we are indeed his offspring.'

Being then God's offspring, we ought not to think that the Deity is like gold, or silver, or stone, a representation by the art and imagination of man. The times of ignorance God overlooked, but now he commands all men everywhere to repent, because he has fixed a day on which he will judge the world in righteousness by a man whom he has appointed, and of this he has given assurance to all men by raising him from the dead."

Acts 17:22-31

535

Therefore, since we are justified by faith, we have peace with God through our Lord Jesus Christ. Through him we have obtained access to this grace in which we stand, and we rejoice in our hope of sharing the glory of God. More than that, we rejoice in our sufferings, knowing that suffering produces endurance, and endurance produces character, and character produces hope, and hope does not disappoint us, because God's love has been poured into our hearts through the Holy Spirit which has been given to us.

While we were yet helpless, at the right time Christ died for the ungodly. Why, one will hardly die for a righteous man—though perhaps for a good man one will dare even to die. But God shows his love for us in that while we were yet sinners Christ died for us.

Romans 5:1-8

536

We know that in everything God works for good with those who love him, who are called according to his purpose.

What then shall we say to this? If God is for us, who is against us? He who did not spare his own Son but gave him up for us all, will he not also give us all things with him? Who shall bring any charge against God's elect? It is God who justifies; who is to condemn? Is it Christ Jesus, who died, yes, who was raised from the dead, who is at the right hand of God, who indeed intercedes for us? Who shall separate us from the love of Christ? Shall tribulation, or distress, or persecution, or famine, or nakedness, or peril, or sword? As it is written,

"For thy sake we are being killed all the day long;
we are regarded as sheep to be slaughtered."

No, in all these things we are more than conquerors through him who loved us. For I am sure that neither death, nor life, nor angels, nor principalities, nor things present, nor things to come, nor powers, nor height, nor depth, nor anything else in all creation, will be able to separate us from the love of God in Christ Jesus our Lord.

Romans 8:28, 31-39

537

The word is near you, on your lips and in your heart (that is, the word of faith which we preach); because, if you confess with your lips that Jesus is Lord and believe in your heart that God raised him from the dead, you will be saved. For man believes with his heart and so is justified, and he confesses with his lips and so is saved. The scripture says, "No one who believes in him will be put to shame." For there is no distinction between Jew and Greek; the same Lord is Lord of all and bestows his riches upon all who call upon him. For, "every one who calls upon the name of the Lord will be saved." But how are men to call upon him in whom they have not believed? And how are they to believe in him of whom they have never heard? And how are they to hear without a preacher? And how can men preach unless they are sent? As it is written, "How beautiful are the feet of those who preach good news!" So faith comes from what is heard, and what is heard comes by the preaching of Christ.

Romans 10:8b-15, 17

538

I appeal to you therefore, brethren, by the mercies of God, to present your bodies as a living sacrifice, holy and acceptable to God, which is your spiritual worship. Do not be conformed to this world but be transformed by the renewal of your mind, that you may prove what is the will of God, what is good and acceptable and perfect.

Let love be genuine; hate what is evil, hold fast to what is good; love one another with brotherly affection; outdo one another in showing honor. Never flag in zeal, be aglow with the Spirit, serve the Lord. Rejoice in your hope, be patient in tribulation, be constant in prayer. Contribute to the needs of the saints, practice hospitality.

Bless those who persecute you; bless and do not curse them. Rejoice with those who rejoice, weep with those who weep. Live in harmony with one another; do not be haughty, but associate with the lowly; never be conceited. Repay no one evil for evil, but take thought for what is noble in the sight of all. If possible, so far as it depends upon you, live peaceably with all. Beloved, never avenge yourselves, but leave it to the wrath of God; for it is written, "Vengeance is mine, I will repay, says the Lord." No, "if your enemy is hungry, feed him; if he is thirsty, give him drink; for by so doing you will heap burning coals upon his head." Do not be overcome by evil, but overcome evil with good.

Romans 12:1-2, 9-21

539

Now there are varieties of gifts, but the same Spirit; and there are varieties of service, but the same Lord; and there are varieties of working, but it is the same God who inspires them all in every one. To each is given the manifestation of the Spirit for the common good. To one is given through the Spirit the utterance of wisdom, and to another the utterance of knowledge according to the same Spirit, to another faith by the same Spirit, to another gifts of healing by the one Spirit, to another the working of miracles, to another prophecy, to another the ability to distinguish between spirits, to another various kinds of tongues, to another the interpretation of tongues. All these are inspired by one and the same Spirit, who apportions to each one individually as he wills.

For just as the body is one and has many members, and all the members of the body, though many, are one body, so it is with Christ. For by one Spirit we were all baptized into one body—Jews or Greeks, slaves or free—and all were made to drink of one Spirit.

1 Corinthians 12:4-13

540

Now you are the body of Christ and individually members of it. And God has appointed in the church first apostles, second prophets, third teachers, then workers of miracles, then healers, helpers, administrators, speakers in various kinds of tongues. Are all apostles? Are all prophets? Are all teachers? Do all work miracles? Do all possess gifts of healing? Do all speak with tongues? Do all interpret? But earnestly desire the higher gifts.

And I will show you a still more excellent way.

If I speak in the tongues of men and of angels, but have not love, I am a noisy gong or a clanging cymbal. And if I have prophetic powers, and understand all mysteries and all knowledge, and if I have all faith, so as to remove mountains, but have not love, I am nothing. If I give away all I have, and if I deliver my body to be burned, but have not love, I gain nothing.

Love is patient and kind; love is not jealous or boastful; it is not arrogant or rude. Love does not insist on its own way; it is not irritable or resentful; it does not rejoice at wrong, but rejoices in the right. Love bears all things, believes all things, hopes all things, endures all things.

Love never ends; as for prophecies, they will pass away; as for tongues, they will cease; as for knowledge, it will pass away. For our knowledge is imperfect and our prophecy is imperfect; but when the perfect comes, the imperfect will pass away. When I was a child, I spoke like a child, I thought like a child, I reasoned like a child; when I became a man, I gave up childish ways. For now we see in a mirror dimly, but then face to face. Now I know in part; then I shall understand fully, even as I have been fully understood. So faith, hope, love abide, these three; but the greatest of these is love.

1 Corinthians 12:27-31; 13

541

Now I would remind you, brethren, in what terms I preached to you the gospel, which you received, in which you stand, by which you are saved, if you hold it fast—unless you believed in vain.

For I delivered to you as of first importance what I also received, that Christ died for our sins in accordance with the scriptures, that he was buried, that he was raised on the third day in accordance with the scriptures, and that he appeared to Cephas, then to the twelve.

Lo! I tell you a mystery. We shall not all sleep, but we shall all be changed, in a moment, in the twinkling of an eye, at the last trumpet. For the trumpet will sound, and the dead will be raised imperishable, and we shall be changed. For this perishable nature must put on the imperishable, and this mortal nature must put on immortality. When the perishable puts on the imperishable, and the mortal puts on immortality, then shall come to pass the saying that is written:

"Death is swallowed up in victory."
"O death, where is thy victory?
O death, where is thy sting?"

The sting of death is sin, and the power of sin is the law. But thanks be to God, who gives us the victory through our Lord Jesus Christ.

Therefore, my beloved brethren, be steadfast, immovable, always abounding in the work of the Lord, knowing that in the Lord your labor is not in vain.

1 Corinthians 15:1-5, 51-58

542

For what we preach is not ourselves, but Jesus Christ as Lord, with ourselves as your servants for Jesus' sake. For it is the God who said, "Let light shine out of darkness," who has shone in our hearts to give the light of the knowledge of the glory of God in the face of Christ.

But we have this treasure in earthen vessels, to show that the transcendent power belongs to God and not to us. We are afflicted in every way, but not crushed; perplexed, but not driven to despair; persecuted, but not forsaken; struck down, but not destroyed; always carrying in the body the death of Jesus, so that the life of Jesus may also be manifested in our bodies. For while we live we are always being given up to death for Jesus' sake, so that the life of Jesus may be manifested in our mortal flesh. So death is at work in us, but life in you.

2 Corinthians 4:5-12

543

For the love of Christ controls us, because we are convinced that one has died for all; therefore all have died. And he died for all, that those who live might live no longer for themselves but for him who for their sake died and was raised.

From now on, therefore, we regard no one from a human point of view; even though we once regarded Christ from a human point of view, we regard him thus no longer. Therefore, if any one is in Christ, he is a new creation; the old has passed away, behold, the new has come. All this is from God, who through Christ reconciled us to himself and gave us the ministry of reconciliation; that is, God was in Christ reconciling the world to himself, not counting their trespasses against them, and entrusting to us the message of reconciliation. So we are ambassadors for Christ, God making his appeal through us. We beseech you on behalf of Christ, be reconciled to God. For our sake he made him to be sin who knew no sin, so that in him we might become the righteousness of God.

2 Corinthians 5:14-21

544

For freedom Christ has set us free; stand fast therefore, and do not submit again to a yoke of slavery.

For you were called to freedom, brethren; only do not use your freedom as an opportunity for the flesh, but through love be servants of one another. For the whole law is fulfilled in one word, "You shall love your neighbor as yourself." But if you bite and devour one another take heed that you are not consumed by one another.

But I say, walk by the Spirit, and do not gratify the desires of the flesh. For the desires of the flesh are against the Spirit, and the desires of the Spirit are against the flesh; for these are opposed to each other, to prevent you from doing what you would. But if you are led by the Spirit you are not under the law. Now the works of the flesh are plain: immorality, impurity, licentiousness, idolatry, sorcery, enmity, strife, jealousy, anger, selfishness, dissension, party spirit, envy, drunkenness, carousing, and the like. I warn you, as I warned you before, that those who do such things shall not inherit the kingdom of God. But the fruit of the Spirit is love, joy, peace, patience, kindness, goodness, faithfulness, gentleness, self-control; against such there is no law. And those who belong to Christ Jesus have crucified the flesh with its passions and desires.

If we live by the Spirit, let us also walk by the Spirit.

Galatians 5:1, 13-25

545

I therefore, a prisoner for the Lord, beg you to lead a life worthy of the calling to which you have been called, with all lowliness and meekness, with patience, forbearing one another in love, eager to maintain the unity of the Spirit in the bond of peace. There is one body and one Spirit, just as you were called to the one hope that belongs to your call, one Lord, one faith, one baptism, one God and Father of us all, who is above all and through all and in all. But grace was given to each of us according to the measure of Christ's gift.

And his gifts were that some should be apostles, some prophets, some evangelists, some pastors and teachers, for the equipment of the saints, for the work of ministry, for building up the body of Christ, until we all attain to the unity of the faith and of the knowledge of the Son of God, to mature manhood, to the measure of the stature of the fulness of Christ; so that we may no longer be children, tossed to and fro and carried about with every wind of doctrine, by the cunning of men, by their craftiness in deceitful wiles. Rather, speaking the truth in love, we are to grow up in every way into him who is the head, into Christ, from whom the whole body, joined and knit together by every joint with which it is supplied, when each part is working properly, makes bodily growth and upbuilds itself in love.

Ephesians 4:1-7, 11-16

546

Have this mind among yourselves, which you have in Christ Jesus, who, though he was in the form of God, did not count equality with God a thing to be grasped, but emptied himself, taking the form of a servant, being born in the likeness of men. And being found in human form he humbled himself and became obedient unto death, even death on a cross. Therefore God has highly exalted him and bestowed on him the name which is above every name, that at the name of Jesus every knee should bow, in heaven and on earth and under the earth, and every tongue confess that Jesus Christ is Lord, to the glory of God the Father.

Philippians 2:5-11

547

May you be strengthened with all power, according to his glorious might, for all endurance and patience with joy, giving thanks to the Father, who has qualified us to share in the inheritance of the saints in light. He has delivered us from the dominion of darkness and transferred us to the kingdom of his beloved Son, in whom we have redemption, the forgiveness of sins.

He is the image of the invisible God, the first-born of all creation; for in him all things were created, in heaven and on earth, visible and invisible, whether thrones or dominions or principalities or authorities—all things were created through him and for him. He is before all things, and in him all things hold together. He is the head of the body, the church; he is the beginning, the first-born from the dead, that in everything he might be pre-eminent. For in him all the fulness of God was pleased to dwell, and through him to reconcile to himself all things, whether on earth or in heaven, making peace by the blood of his cross.

Colossians 1:11-20

548

If then you have been raised with Christ, seek the things that are above, where Christ is, seated at the right hand of God. Set your minds on things that are above, not on things that are on earth. For you have died, and your life is hid with Christ in God. When Christ who is our life appears, then you also will appear with him in glory.

Put on then, as God's chosen ones, holy and beloved, compassion, kindness, lowliness, meekness, and patience, forbearing one another and, if one has a complaint against another, forgiving each other; as the Lord has forgiven you, so you also must forgive. And above all these put on love, which binds everything together in perfect harmony. And let the peace of Christ rule in your hearts, to which indeed you were called in the one body. And be thankful. Let the word of Christ dwell in you richly, as you teach and admonish one another in all wisdom, and as you sing psalms and hymns and spiritual songs with thankfulness in your hearts to God. And whatever you do, in word or deed, do everything in the name of the Lord Jesus, giving thanks to God the Father through him.

Colossians 3:1-4; 12-17

549

Blessed be the God and Father of our Lord Jesus Christ! By his great mercy we have been born anew to a living hope through the resurrection of Jesus Christ from the dead, and to an inheritance which is imperishable, undefiled, and unfading, kept in heaven for you, who by God's power are guarded through faith for a salvation ready to be revealed in the last time.

In this you rejoice, though now for a little while you may have to suffer various trials, so that the genuineness of your faith, more precious than gold which though perishable is tested by fire, may redound to praise and glory and honor at the revelation of Jesus Christ. Without having seen him you love him; though you do not now see him you believe in him and rejoice with unutterable and exalted joy. As the outcome of your faith you obtain the salvation of your souls.

1 Peter 1:3-9

550

That which was from the beginning, which we have heard, which we have seen with our eyes, which we have looked upon and touched with our hands, concerning the word of life—the life was made manifest, and we saw it, and testify to it, and proclaim to you the eternal life which was with the Father and was made manifest to us—that which we have seen and heard we proclaim also to you, so that you may have fellowship with us; and our fellowship is with the Father and with his Son Jesus Christ. And we are writing this that our joy may be complete.

This is the message we have heard from him and proclaim to you, that God is light and in him is no darkness at all. If we say we have fellowship with him while we walk in darkness, we lie and do not live according to the truth; but if we walk in the light, as he is in the light, we have fellowship with one another, and the blood of Jesus his Son cleanses us from all sin. If we say we have no sin, we deceive ourselves, and the truth is not in us. If we confess our sins, he is faithful and just, and will forgive our sins and cleanse us from all unrighteousness. If we say we have not sinned, we make him a liar, and his word is not in us.

1 John 1:1-10

551

See what love the Father has given us, that we should be called children of God; and so we are. The reason why the world does not know us is that it did not know him. Beloved, we are God's children now; it does not yet appear what we shall be, but we know that when he appears we shall be like him, for we shall see him as he is. And every one who thus hopes in him purifies himself as he is pure.

Every one who commits sin is guilty of lawlessness; sin is lawlessness. You know that he appeared to take away sins, and in him there is no sin. No one who abides in him sins; no one who sins has either seen him or known him. Little children, let no one deceive you. He who does right is righteous, as he is righteous. He who commits sin is of the devil; for the devil has sinned from the beginning. The reason the Son of God appeared was to destroy the works of the devil. No one born of God commits sin; for God's nature abides in him, and he cannot sin because he is born of God. By this it may be seen who are the children of God, and who are the children of the devil: whoever does not do right is not of God, nor he who does not love his brother.

1 John 3:1-10

552

Beloved, let us love one another; for love is of God, and he who loves is born of God and knows God. He who does not love does not know God; for God is love. In this the love of God was made manifest among us, that God sent his only Son into the world, so that we might live through him. In this is love, not that we loved God but that he loved us and sent his Son to be the expiation for our sins. Beloved, if God so loved us, we also ought to love one another. No man has ever seen God; if we love one another, God abides in us and his love is perfected in us.

By this we know that we abide in him and he in us, because he has given us of his own Spirit. And we have seen and testify that the Father has sent his Son as the Savior of the world. Whoever confesses that Jesus is the Son of God, God abides in him, and he in God. So we know and believe the love God has for us. God is love, and he who abides in love abides in God, and God abides in him. In this is love perfected with us, that we may have confidence for the day of judgment, because as he is so are we in this world. There is no fear in love, but perfect love casts out fear. For fear has to do with punishment, and he who fears is not perfected in love. We love, because he first loved us. If any one says, "I love God," and hates his brother, he is a liar; for he who does not love his brother whom he has seen, cannot love God whom he has not seen. And this commandment we have from him, that he who loves God should love his brother also.

1 John 4:7-21

553

Then I saw a new heaven and a new earth; for the first heaven and the first earth had passed away, and the sea was no more. And I saw the holy city, new Jerusalem, coming down out of heaven from God, prepared as a bride adorned for her husband; and I heard a great voice from the throne saying, "Behold, the dwelling of God is with men. He will dwell with them, and they shall be his people, and God himself will be with them; he will wipe away every tear from their eyes, and death shall be no more, neither shall there be mourning nor crying nor pain any more, for the former things have passed away."

And he who sat upon the throne said, "Behold, I make all things new." Also he said, "Write this, for these words are trustworthy and true." And he said to me, "It is done! I am the Alpha and the Omega, the beginning and the end. To the thirsty I will give water without price from the fountain of the water of life. He who conquers shall have this heritage, and I will be his God and he shall be my son."

Revelation 21:1-7

Psalms

554

Blessed is the man
who walks not in the counsel of the wicked,
nor stands in the way of sinners,
nor sits in the seat of scoffers;

but his delight is in the law of the Lord,
and on his law he meditates day and night.

He is like a tree
planted by streams of water,
that yields its fruit in its season,
and its leaf does not wither.
In all that he does, he prospers.

The wicked are not so,
but are like chaff which the wind drives away.

Therefore the wicked will not stand in the judgment,
nor sinners in the congregation of the righteous;

for the Lord *knows the way of the righteous,*
but the way of the wicked will perish.

Psalm 1

555

O Lord, rebuke me not in thy anger,
nor chasten me in thy wrath.

Be gracious to me, O Lord, *for I am languishing;*
O Lord, *heal me, for my bones are troubled.*

My soul also is sorely troubled.
But thou, O Lord—how long?
Turn, O Lord, save my life;
deliver me for the sake of thy steadfast love.

For in death there is no remembrance of thee;
in Sheol who can give thee praise?

I am weary with my moaning;
every night I flood my bed with tears;
I drench my couch with my weeping.

My eye wastes away because of grief,
it grows weak because of all my foes.

Depart from me, all you workers of evil;
for the LORD has heard the sound of my weeping.

The Lord *has heard my supplication;*
the Lord *accepts my prayer.*
All my enemies shall be ashamed and sorely troubled;
they shall turn back, and be put to shame in a moment.

Psalm 6

556

O LORD, our Lord,
how majestic is thy name in all the earth!

Thou whose glory above the heavens is chanted
by the mouth of babes and infants,
thou hast founded a bulwark because of thy foes,
to still the enemy and the avenger.

When I look at thy heavens, the work of thy fingers,
the moon and the stars which thou hast established;
what is man that thou art mindful of him,
and the son of man that thou dost care for him?

Yet thou hast made him little less than God,
and dost crown him with glory and honor.

Thou hast given him dominion over the works of thy hands;
thou hast put all things under his feet,
all sheep and oxen,
and also the beasts of the field,
the birds of the air, and the fish of the sea,
whatever passes along the paths of the sea.

O Lord, *our Lord,*
how majestic is thy name in all the earth!

Psalm 8

557

How long, O LORD? Wilt thou forget me for ever?
How long wilt thou hide thy face from me?

How long must I bear pain in my soul,
and have sorrow in my heart all the day?
How long shall my enemy be exalted over me?

Consider and answer me, O LORD my God;
lighten my eyes, lest I sleep the sleep of death;

lest my enemy say, "I have prevailed over him";
lest my foes rejoice because I am shaken.

But I have trusted in thy steadfast love;
my heart shall rejoice in thy salvation.

I will sing to the Lord,
because he has dealt bountifully with me.

Psalm 13

558

Preserve me, O God, for in thee
I take refuge.

I say to the Lord, *"Thou art my Lord,*
I have no good apart from thee."

The Lord is my chosen portion and my cup;
thou holdest my lot.
The lines have fallen for me in pleasant places;
yea, I have a goodly heritage.

I bless the Lord *who gives me counsel;*
in the night also my heart instructs me.

I keep the Lord always before me;
because he is at my right hand,
I shall not be moved.

Therefore my heart is glad, and my soul rejoices;
my body also dwells secure.

For thou dost not give me up to Sheol,
or let thy godly one see the Pit.

Thou dost show me the path of life;
in thy presence there is fulness of joy,
in thy right hand are pleasures for evermore.

Psalm 16:1-2, 5-11

559

I love thee, O Lord, my strength.
The Lord is my rock, and my fortress, and my deliverer,
my God, my rock, in whom I take refuge,
my shield, and the horn of my salvation, my stronghold.

I call upon the Lord, *who is worthy to be praised,*
and I am saved from my enemies.

The cords of death encompassed me,
the torrents of perdition assailed me;
the cords of Sheol entangled me,
the snares of death confronted me.

In my distress I called upon the Lord,
to my God I cried for help.
From his temple he heard my voice,
and my cry to him reached his ears.

He reached from on high, he took me,
he drew me out of many waters.

He delivered me from my strong enemy,
and from those who hated me;
for they were too mighty for me.

They came upon me in the day of my calamity;
but the Lord was my stay.

He brought me forth into a broad place;
he delivered me, because he delighted in me.

Psalm 18:1-6, 16-19

560

The heavens are telling the glory of God;
and the firmament proclaims his handiwork.
Day to day pours forth speech,
and night to night declares knowledge.

There is no speech, nor are there words;
their voice is not heard;

yet their voice goes out through all the earth,
and their words to the end of the world.

In them he has set a tent for the sun,
which comes forth like a bridegroom leaving his chamber,
and like a strong man runs its course with joy.

Its rising is from the end of the heavens,
and its circuit to the end of them;
and there is nothing hid from its heat.

The law of the LORD is perfect,
reviving the soul;
the testimony of the LORD is sure,
making wise the simple;

the precepts of the Lord *are right,*
rejoicing the heart;
the commandment of the Lord *is pure,*
enlightening the eyes;

the fear of the LORD is clean,
enduring for ever;
the ordinances of the LORD are true,
and righteous altogether.

More to be desired are they than gold,
even much fine gold;
sweeter also than honey
and drippings of the honeycomb.

Moreover by them is thy servant warned;
in keeping them there is great reward.

But who can discern his errors?
Clear thou me from hidden faults.

Keep back thy servant also from presumptuous sins;
let them not have dominion over me!
Then I shall be blameless,
and innocent of great transgression.

Let the words of my mouth and the meditation of my heart
be acceptable in thy sight,
O Lord, *my rock and my redeemer.*

Psalm 19

561

The Lord *is my shepherd, I shall not want;*
he makes me lie down in green pastures.
He leads me beside still waters;
he restores my soul.
He leads me in paths of righteousness
for his name's sake.

Even though I walk through the valley of the shadow of death,
I fear no evil;
for thou art with me;
thy rod and thy staff,
they comfort me.
Thou preparest a table before me in the presence of my enemies;
thou anointest my head with oil,
my cup overflows.
Surely goodness and mercy shall follow me
all the days of my life;
and I shall dwell in the house of the Lord
for ever.

Psalm 23

562

The earth is the LORD's and the fulness thereof,
the world and those who dwell therein;

for he has founded it upon the seas,
and established it upon the rivers.

Who shall ascend the hill of the LORD?
And who shall stand in his holy place?

He who has clean hands and a pure heart,
who does not lift up his soul to what is false,
and does not swear deceitfully.

He will receive blessing from the LORD,
and vindication from the God of his salvation.

Such is the generation of those who seek him,
who seek the face of the God of Jacob.

Lift up your heads, O gates!
and be lifted up, O ancient doors!
that the King of glory may come in.

Who is the King of glory?
The Lord, *strong and mighty,*
the Lord, *mighty in battle!*

Lift up your heads, O gates!
and be lifted up, O ancient doors!
that the King of glory may come in!

Who is this King of glory?
The Lord *of hosts,*
he is the King of glory!

Psalm 24

563

To thee, O LORD, I lift up my soul.

O my God, in thee I trust,
let me not be put to shame;
let not my enemies exult over me.

Yea, let none that wait for thee be put to shame;
let them be ashamed who are wantonly treacherous.

Make me to know thy ways, O Lord;
teach me thy paths.

Lead me in thy truth, and teach me,
for thou art the God of my salvation;
for thee I wait all day long.

Be mindful of thy mercy, O Lord,
and of thy steadfast love,
for they have been from of old.

Remember not the sins of my youth,
or my transgressions;
according to thy steadfast love remember me,
for thy goodness' sake, O LORD!

Good and upright is the Lord;
therefore he instructs sinners in the way.

He leads the humble in what is right,
and teaches the humble his way.

All the paths of the Lord *are steadfast love and faithfulness,*
for those who keep his covenant and his testimonies.

Psalm 25:1-10

564

The LORD is my light and my salvation;
whom shall I fear?
The LORD is the stronghold of my life;
of whom shall I be afraid?

When evildoers assail me,
uttering slanders against me.
my adversaries and foes,
they shall stumble and fall.

Though a host encamp against me,
my heart shall not fear;
though war arise against me,
yet I will be confident.

One thing have I asked of the Lord,
that will I seek after;
that I may dwell in the house of the Lord
all the days of my life,
to behold the beauty of the Lord,
and to inquire in his temple.

For he will hide me in his shelter
in the day of trouble;
he will conceal me under the cover of his tent.
he will set me high upon a rock.

And now my head shall be lifted up
above my enemies round about me;
and I will offer in his tent
sacrifices with shouts of joy;
I will sing and make melody to the Lord,

Psalm 27:1-6

565

In thee, O LORD, do I seek refuge;
let me never be put to shame;
in thy righteousness deliver me!

Incline thy ear to me,
rescue me speedily!
Be thou a rock of refuge for me,
a strong fortress to save me!

Yea, thou art my rock and my fortress;
for thy name's sake lead me and guide me,
take me out of the net which is hidden for me,
for thou art my refuge.

Into thy hand I commit my spirit;
thou hast redeemed me, O LORD,
faithful God.

Thou hatest those who pay regard
to vain idols;
but I trust in the Lord.

I will rejoice and be glad for thy
steadfast love,
because thou hast seen my affliction,
thou hast taken heed of my adversities,
and hast not delivered me into the
hand of the enemy;
thou hast set my feet in a broad
place.

Be gracious to me, O Lord, for I
am in distress;
my eye is wasted from grief,
my soul and my body also.

For my life is spent with sorrow,
and my years with sighing;
my strength fails because of my
misery,
and my bones waste away.

But I trust in thee, O Lord,
I say, "Thou art my God."

My times are in thy hand;
deliver me from the hand of my
enemies and persecutors!
Let thy face shine on thy servant;
save me in thy steadfast love!

Psalm 31:1-10, 14-16

566

Blessed is he whose transgression is
forgiven,
whose sin is covered.

Blessed is the man to whom the
Lord *imputes no iniquity,*
and in whose spirit there is no
deceit.

When I declared not my sin, my
body wasted away
through my groaning all day
long.

For day and night thy hand was
heavy upon me;
my strength was dried up as by
the heat of summer.

I acknowledged my sin to thee,
and I did not hide my iniquity;
I said, 'I will confess my transgressions to the Lord";
then thou didst forgive the guilt
of my sin.

Therefore let every one who is
godly
offer prayer to thee;
at a time of distress, in the rush
of great waters,
they shall not reach him.

Thou art a hiding place for me,
thou preservest me from trouble;
thou dost encompass me with
deliverance.

I will instruct you and teach you
the way you should go;
I will counsel you with my eye
upon you.

Be not like a horse or a mule, without understanding,
which must be curbed with bit
and bridle,
else it will not keep with you.

Many are the pangs of the wicked;
but steadfast love surrounds him
who trusts in the Lord.

Be glad in the LORD, and rejoice, O righteous,
and shout for joy, all you upright in heart!

Psalm 32

567

I will bless the LORD at all times;
his praise shall continually be in my mouth.

My soul makes its boast in the Lord;
let the afflicted hear and be glad.

O magnify the LORD with me,
and let us exalt his name together!

I sought the Lord, *and he answered me,*
and delivered me from all my fears.

Look to him, and be radiant;
so your faces shall never be ashamed.

This poor man cried, and the Lord *heard him,*
and saved him out of all his troubles.

The angel of the LORD encamps around those who fear him, and delivers them.

O taste and see that the Lord *is good!*
Happy is the man who takes refuge in him!

O fear the LORD, you his saints,
for those who fear him have no want!

The young lions suffer want and hunger;
but those who seek the Lord *lack no good thing.*

Come, O sons, listen to me,
I will teach you the fear of the LORD.

What man is there who desires life,
and covets many days, that he may enjoy good?

Keep your tongue from evil,
and your lips from speaking deceit.

Depart from evil, and do good;
seek peace, and pursue it.

The eyes of the LORD are toward the righteous,
and his ears toward their cry.

The face of the Lord *is against evildoers,*
to cut off the remembrance of them from the earth.

When the righteous cry for help, the LORD hears,
and delivers them out of all their troubles.

The Lord *is near to the brokenhearted,*
and saves the crushed in spirit.

Many are the afflictions of the righteous;
but the LORD delivers him out of them all.

He keeps all his bones;
not one of them is broken.

Evil shall slay the wicked;
and those who hate the righteous will be condemned.

The Lord *redeems the life of his servants;*
none of those who take refuge in him will be condemned.

Psalm 34

568

O LORD, rebuke me not in thy anger,
nor chasten me in thy wrath!

For thy arrows have sunk into me,
and thy hand has come down on me.

There is no soundness in my flesh
because of thy indignation;
there is no health in my bones
because of my sin.

For my iniquities have gone over my head;
they weigh like a burden too heavy for me.

I am utterly spent and crushed;
I groan because of the tumult of my heart.

Lord, *all my longing is known to thee,*
my sighing is not hidden from thee.

My heart throbs, my strength fails me;
and the light of my eyes—it also has gone from me.
My friends and companions stand aloof from my plague,
and my kinsmen stand afar off.

Those who seek my life lay their snares,
those who seek my hurt speak of ruin,
and meditate treachery all the day long.

But I am like a deaf man, I do not hear,
like a dumb man who does not open his mouth.

Yea, I am like a man who does not hear,
and in whose mouth are no rebukes.

But for thee, O LORD, do I wait;
it is thou, O LORD my God, who wilt answer.

Do not forsake me, O Lord!
O my God, be not far from me!
Make haste to help me,
O Lord, *my salvation!*

Psalm 38:1-4, 8-15, 21-22

569

I waited patiently for the LORD;
he inclined to me and heard my cry.

He drew me up from the desolate pit,
out of the miry bog,
and set my feet upon a rock,
making my steps secure.

He put a new song in my mouth,
a song of praise to our God.
Many will see and fear,
and put their trust in the LORD.

Blessed is the man who makes the Lord *his trust,*
who does not turn to the proud,
to those who go astray after false gods!

Thou hast multiplied, O Lord my God,
thy wondrous deeds and thy thoughts toward us;
none can compare with thee!

Were I to proclaim and tell of them,
they would be more than can be numbered.

Sacrifice and offering thou dost not desire;
but thou hast given me an open ear.
Burnt offering and sin offering thou hast not required.

Then I said, "Lo, I come;
in the roll of the book it is written of me;
I delight to do thy will, O my God;
thy law is within my heart."

I have told the glad news of deliverance
in the great congregation;
lo, I have not restrained my lips,
as thou knowest, O Lord.

I have not hid thy saving help within my heart,
I have spoken of thy faithfulness and thy salvation;
I have not concealed thy steadfast love and thy faithfulness
from the great congregation

Do not thou, O Lord, *withhold thy mercy from me,*
let thy steadfast love and thy faithfulness
ever preserve me!

Psalm 40:1-11

570

As a hart longs
for flowing streams,
so longs my soul
for thee, O God.

My soul thirsts for God,
for the living God.
When shall I come and behold
the face of God?

My tears have been my food
day and night,
while men say to me continually,
"Where is your God?"

These things I remember,
as I pour out my soul:
how I went with the throng,
and led them in procession to the house of God,
with glad shouts and songs of thanksgiving,
a multitude keeping festival.

Why are you cast down, O my soul,
and why are you disquieted within me?
Hope in God; for I shall again praise him,
my help and my God.

By day the Lord *commands his steadfast love;*
and at night his song is with me,
a prayer to the God of my life.

I say to God, my rock:
"Why hast thou forgotten me?

Why go I mourning
because of the oppression of the enemy?"

As with a deadly wound in my body,
my adversaries taunt me,
while they say to me continually,
"Where is your God?"

Why are you cast down, O my soul,
and why are you disquieted within me?
Hope in God; for I shall again praise him,
my help and my God.

Psalm 42:1-5, 8-11

571

Vindicate me, O God, and defend my cause
against an ungodly people;
from deceitful and unjust men deliver me!

For thou art the God in whom I take refuge;
why hast thou cast me off?
Why go I mourning
because of the oppression of the enemy?

Oh send out thy light and thy truth;
let them lead me,
let them bring me to thy holy hill
and to thy dwelling!

Then I will go to the altar of God,
to God my exceeding joy;
and I will praise thee with the lyre,
O God, my God.

Why are you cast down, O my soul,
and why are you disquieted within me?

Hope in God; for I shall again praise him,
my help and my God.

Psalm 43

572

God is our refuge and strength,
a very present help in trouble.

Therefore we will not fear though the earth should change,
though the mountains shake in the heart of the sea;

though its waters roar and foam,
though the mountains tremble with its tumult.

There is a river whose streams make glad the city of God,
the holy habitation of the Most High.

God is in the midst of her, she shall not be moved;
God will help her right early.

The nations rage, the kingdoms totter;
he utters his voice, the earth melts.

The LORD of hosts is with us;
the God of Jacob is our refuge.

Come, behold the works of the Lord;
how he has wrought desolations in the earth.

He makes wars cease to the end of the earth;

he breaks the bow, and shatters the spear,
he burns the chariots with fire!

*"Be still, and know that I am God.
I am exalted among the nations,
I am exalted in the earth!"*

The LORD of hosts is with us;
the God of Jacob is our refuge.

Psalm 46

573

Have mercy on me, O God,
according to thy steadfast love;
according to thy abundant mercy
blot out my transgressions.

*Wash me thoroughly from my iniquity,
and cleanse me from my sin!*

For I know my transgressions,
and my sin is ever before me.

*Against thee, thee only, have I sinned,
and done that which is evil in thy sight,
so that thou are justified in thy sentence
and blameless in thy judgment.*

Behold, I was brought forth in iniquity,
and in sin did my mother conceive me.

*Behold, thou desirest truth in the inward being;
therefore teach me wisdom in my secret heart.*

Purge me with hyssop, and I shall be clean;
wash me, and I shall be whiter than snow.

*Fill me with joy and gladness;
let the bones which thou hast broken rejoice.*

Hide thy face from my sins,
and blot out all my iniquities.

*Create in me a clean heart, O God,
and put a new and right spirit within me.*

Cast me not away from thy presence,
and take not thy holy Spirit from me.

*Restore to me the joy of thy salvation,
and uphold me with a willing spirit.*

Then I will teach transgressors thy ways,
and sinners will return to thee.

*Deliver me from bloodguiltiness, O God,
thou God of my salvation,
and my tongue will sing aloud of thy deliverance.*

O Lord, open thou my lips,
and my mouth shall show forth thy praise.

*For thou hast no delight in sacrifice;
were I to give a burnt offering, thou wouldst not be pleased.*

The sacrifice acceptable to God is a broken spirit;
a broken and contrite heart, O God, thou wilt not despise.

Psalm 51:1-17

574

Hear my cry, O God,
listen to my prayer;
from the end of the earth I call to thee,
when my heart is faint.

Lead thou me
to the rock that is higher than I;
for thou art my refuge,
a strong tower against the enemy.

Let me dwell in thy tent for ever!
Oh to be safe under the shelter of thy wings!

For thou, O God, hast heard my vows,
thou hast given me the heritage of those who fear thy name.
So will I ever sing praises to thy name,
as I pay my vows day after day.

Psalm 61:1-5, 8

575

O God, thou art my God, I seek thee,
my soul thirsts for thee;
my flesh faints for thee,
as in a dry and weary land where no water is.

So I have looked upon thee in the sanctuary,
beholding thy power and glory.

Because thy steadfast love is better than life,
my lips will praise thee.

So I will bless thee as long as I live;
I will lift up my hands and call on thy name.

My soul is feasted as with marrow and fat,
and my mouth praises thee with joyful lips,
when I think of thee upon my bed,
and meditate on thee in the watches of the night;

for thou hast been my help,
and in the shadow of thy wings I sing for joy.
My soul clings to thee;
thy right hand upholds me.

Psalm 63:1-8

576

Praise is due to thee,
O God in Zion;
and to thee shall vows be performed,

O thou who hearest prayer!
To thee shall all flesh come
on account of sins.

When our transgressions prevail over us,
thou dost forgive them.

Blessed is he whom thou dost choose and bring near,
to dwell in thy courts!
We shall be satisfied with the goodness of thy house,
thy holy temple!

By dread deeds thou dost answer us with deliverance,
O God of our salvation,
who art the hope of all the ends of the earth,
and of the farthest seas:

who by thy strength hast established the mountains,
being girded with might;

who dost still the roaring of the seas,
the roaring of their waves,
the tumult of the peoples;

so that those who dwell at earth's farthest bounds
are afraid at thy signs;
thou makest the outgoings of the morning and the evening
to shout for joy.

Thou visitest the earth and waterest it,
thou greatly enrichest it;
the river of God is full of water;
thou providest their grain,
for so thou hast prepared it.

Thou waterest its furrows abundantly,
settling its ridges,
softening it with showers,
and blessing its growth.

Thou crownest the year with thy bounty;
the tracks of thy chariot drip with fatness.

The pastures of the wilderness drip,
the hills gird themselves with joy,
the meadows clothe themselves with flocks,
the valleys deck themselves with grain,
they shout and sing together for joy.

Psalm 65

577

May God be gracious to us and bless us
and make his face to shine upon us,

that thy way may be known upon earth,
thy saving power among all nations.

Let the peoples praise thee, O God;
let all the peoples praise thee!

Let the nations be glad and sing for joy,
for thou dost judge the peoples with equity
and guide the nations upon earth.

Let the peoples praise thee, O God;
let all the peoples praise thee!

The earth has yielded its increase;
God, our God, has blessed us.
God has blessed us;
let all the ends of the earth fear him!

Psalm 67

578

How lovely is thy dwelling place,
O LORD of hosts!

My soul longs, yea, faints
for the courts of the Lord;
my heart and flesh sing for joy
to the living God.

Even the sparrow finds a home,
and the swallow a nest for herself,

where she may lay her young,
at thy altars, O LORD of hosts,
my King and my God.

Blessed are those who dwell in thy house,
ever singing thy praise!

Blessed are the men whose strength is in thee,
in whose heart are the highways to Zion.

O Lord *God of hosts, hear my prayer;*
give ear, O God of Jacob!

Behold our shield, O God;
look upon the face of thine anointed!

For a day in thy courts is better
than a thousand elsewhere.

I would rather be a doorkeeper
in the house of my God
than dwell in the tents of wickedness.

For the Lord *God is a sun and shield;*
he bestows favor and honor.

No good thing does the LORD withhold
from those who walk uprightly.

O Lord *of hosts,*
blessed is the man who trusts in thee!

Psalm 84:1-5, 8-12

579

Incline thy ear, O LORD, and answer me,
for I am poor and needy.

Preserve my life, for I am godly;
save thy servant who trusts in thee.

Thou art my God; be gracious to me, O Lord,
for to thee do I cry all the day.

Gladden the soul of thy servant,
for to thee, O Lord, do I lift up my soul.

For thou, O Lord, art good and forgiving,
abounding in steadfast love to all who call on thee.

Give ear, O Lord, *to my prayer;*
hearken to my cry of supplication.

In the day of my trouble I call on thee,
for thou dost answer me.

There is none like thee among the gods, O Lord,
nor are there any works like thine.

All the nations thou hast made shall come
and bow down before thee, O Lord,
and shall glorify thy name.

For thou art great and doest wondrous things,
thou alone art God.

Teach me thy way, O LORD,
that I may walk in thy truth;
unite my heart to fear thy name.

I give thanks to thee, O Lord my God, with my whole heart,
and I will glorify thy name for ever.

Psalm 86:1-12

580

Lord, thou hast been our dwelling place
in all generations.

Before the mountains were brought forth,
or ever thou hadst formed the earth and the world,
from everlasting to everlasting thou art God.

Thou turnest man back to the dust,
and sayest, "Turn back, O children of men!"

For a thousand years in thy sight
are but as yesterday when it is past,
or as a watch in the night.

Thou dost sweep men away; they are like a dream,
like grass which is renewed in the morning:

in the morning it flourishes and is renewed;
in the evening it fades and withers

For we are consumed by thy anger;
by thy wrath we are overwhelmed.

Thou hast set our iniquities before thee,
our secret sins in the light of thy countenance.

For all our days pass away under thy wrath,
our years come to an end like a sigh.

The years of our life are threescore and ten,
or even by reason of strength fourscore;

yet their span is but toil and trouble;
they are soon gone, and we fly away.

Who considers the power of thy anger,
and thy wrath according to the fear of thee?

So teach us to number our days
that we may get a heart of wisdom.

Return, O Lord! *How long?*
Have pity on thy servants!

Satisfy us in the morning with thy steadfast love,
that we may rejoice and be glad all our days.

Make us glad as many days as thou hast afflicted us,
and as many years as we have seen evil.

Let thy work be manifest to thy servants,
and thy glorious power to their children.

Let the favor of the Lord our God be upon us,
and establish thou the work of our hands upon us,
yea, the work of our hands establish thou it.

Psalm 90

581

He who dwells in the shelter of the Most High,
who abides in the shadow of the Almighty,

will say to the LORD, "My refuge, and my fortress;
my God in whom I trust."

For he will deliver you from the snare of the fowler
and from the deadly pestilence;

he will cover you with his pinions,
and under his wings you will find refuge;
his faithfulness is a shield and buckler.

You will not fear the terror of the night,
nor the arrow that flies by day,
nor the pestilence that stalks in darkness,
nor the destruction that wastes at noonday.

A thousand may fall at your side,
ten thousand at your right hand;
but it will not come near you.

You will only look with your eyes
and see the recompense of the wicked.

Because you have made the LORD your refuge,
the Most High your habitation.
no evil shall befall you,
no scourge come near your tent.

For he will give his angels charge of you
to guard you in all your ways.

On their hands they will bear you up,
lest you dash your foot against a stone.

You will tread on the lion and the adder,
the young lion and the serpent you will trample under foot.

Because he cleaves to me in love,
I will deliver him;
I will protect him, because he knows my name.

When he calls to me, I will answer him;
I will be with him in trouble,
I will rescue him and honor him.
With long life I will satisfy him,
and show him my salvation.

Psalm 91

582

O come, let us sing to the LORD;
let us make a joyful noise to the rock of our salvation!

Let us come into his presence with thanksgiving;
let us make a joyful noise to him with songs of praise!

For the LORD is a great God,
and a great King above all gods.

In his hand are the depths of the earth;
the heights of the mountains are his also.

The sea is his, for he made it;
for his hands formed the dry land.

O come, let us worship and bow down,
let us kneel before the Lord, *our Maker!*

For he is our God,
and we are the people of his pasture,
and the sheep of his hand.

Psalm 95:1-7

583

O sing to the LORD a new song;
sing to the LORD, all the earth

Sing to the LORD, *bless his name;*
tell of his salvation from day to day.

Declare his glory among the nations,
his marvelous works among all the peoples!

For great is the LORD, *and greatly to be praised,*
he is to be feared above all gods.

For all the gods of the peoples are idols;
but the LORD made the heavens.

Honor and majesty are before him;
strength and beauty are in his sanctuary.

Ascribe to the LORD, O families of the peoples,
ascribe to the LORD glory and strength!

Ascribe to the LORD *the glory due his name;*
bring an offering, and come into his courts!

Worship the LORD in holy array;
tremble before him, all the earth!

Say among the nations, "The LORD *reigns!*
Yea the world is established, it shall never be moved;
he will judge the peoples with equity."

Let the heavens be glad, and let the earth rejoice;
let the sea roar, and all that fills it;
let the field exult, and everything in it!

Then shall all the trees of the wood sing for joy
before the LORD, *for he comes,*
for he comes to judge the earth.

He will judge the world with righteousness,
and the peoples with his truth.

Psalm 96

584

O sing to the LORD a new song,
for he has done marvelous things!
His right hand and his holy arm
have gotten him victory.

The LORD *has made known his victory,*
he has revealed his vindication in the sight of the nations.

He has remembered his steadfast love and faithfulness
to the house of Israel.
All the ends of the earth have seen
the victory of our God.

Make a joyful noise to the LORD, *all the earth;*
break forth into joyous song and sing praises!

Sing praises to the LORD with the lyre,
with the lyre and the sound of melody!
With trumpets and the sound of the horn
make a joyful noise before the King, the LORD!
Let the sea roar, and all that fills it;
the world and those who dwell in it!
Let the floods clap their hands;
let the hills sing for joy together
before the LORD, *for he comes*
to judge the earth.
He will judge the world with righteousness,
and the peoples with equity.

Psalm 98

585

Make a joyful noise to the LORD *all the lands!*
Serve the LORD *with gladness!*
Come into his presence with singing!
Know that the LORD *is God!*
It is he that made us, and we are his;
we are his people, and the sheep of his pasture.
Enter his gates with thanksgiving,
and his courts with praise!
Give thanks to him, bless his name!
For the LORD *is good;*
his steadfast love endures for ever,
and his faithfulness to all generations.

Psalm 100

586

Hear my prayer, O LORD;
let my cry come to thee!

Do not hide thy face from me
in the day of my distress!
Incline thy ear to me;
answer me speedily in the day when I call!

For my days pass away like smoke,
and my bones burn like a furnace.

My heart is smitten like grass, and withered;
I forget to eat my bread.

Because of my loud groaning
my bones cleave to my flesh.

I am like a vulture of the wilderness,
like an owl of the waste places;
I lie awake,
I am like a lonely bird on the housetop.

All the day my enemies taunt me,
those who deride me use my name for a curse.

For I eat ashes like bread,
and mingle tears with my drink,
because of thy indignation and anger;
for thou hast taken me up and thrown me away.

My days are like an evening shadow;
I wither away like grass.

But thou, O LORD, *are enthroned for ever;*
thy name endures to all generations.

Thou wilt arise and have pity on Zion;
it is the time to favor her;
the appointed time has come.

For thy servants hold her stones dear,
and have pity on her dust.

The nations will fear the name of the LORD,
and all the kings of the earth thy glory.

For the LORD *will build up Zion,*
he will appear in his glory;

he will regard the prayer of the destitute,
and will not despise their supplication.

Psalm 102:1-17

587

Bless the LORD, O my soul;
and all that is within me,
bless his holy name!

Bless the LORD, *O my soul;*
and forget not all his benefits
who forgives all your iniquity,
who heals all your diseases,

who redeems your life from the Pit,
who crowns you with steadfast love and mercy,

who satisfies you with good as long as you live
so that your youth is renewed like the eagle's.

The LORD works vindication
and justice for all who are oppressed.

He made known his ways to Moses,
his acts to the people of Israel.

The LORD is merciful and gracious,
slow to anger and abounding in steadfast love.

He will not always chide,
nor will he keep his anger for ever.

He does not deal with us according to our sins,
nor requite us according to our iniquities.

For as the heavens are high above the earth,
so great is his steadfast love
toward those who fear him;

as far as the east is from the west,
so far does he remove our transgressions from us.

As a father pities his children,
so the LORD *pities those who fear him.*

For he knows our frame;
he remembers that we are dust.

As for man, his days are like grass;
he flourishes like a flower of the field;
for the wind passes over it, and it is gone,
and its place knows it no more.

But the steadfast love of the LORD is from everlasting to everlasting
upon those who fear him,
and his righteousness to children's children,
to those who keep his covenant
and remember to do his commandments.

The Lord *has established his throne in the heavens,*
and his kingdom rules over all.

Bless the LORD, O you his angels,
you mighty ones who do his word,
hearkening to the voice of his word!

Bless the Lord, *all his hosts,*
his ministers that do his will!
Bless the Lord, *all his works,*
in all places of his dominion.
Bless the Lord, *O my soul!*

Psalm 103

588

I love the LORD, because he has heard
my voice and my supplications.

Because he inclined his ear to me,
therefore I will call on him as long as I live.

The snares of death encompassed me;
the pangs of Sheol laid hold on me;
I suffered distress and anguish.

Then I called on the name of the Lord:
"O Lord, *I beseech thee, save my life!"*

Gracious is the LORD, and righteous;
our God is merciful.

The Lord *preserves the simple;*
when I was brought low, he saved me.

Return, O my soul, to your rest;
for the LORD has dealt bountifully with you.

For thou hast delivered my soul from death,
my eyes from tears,
my feet from stumbling;

I walk before the LORD
in the land of the living.

I kept my faith, even when I said,
"I am greatly afflicted";
I said in my consternation,
"Men are all a vain hope."

What shall I render to the LORD
for all his bounty to me?

I will lift up the cup of salvation
and call on the name of the Lord,
I will pay my vows to the Lord
in the presence of all his people.

Precious in the sight of the LORD
is the death of his saints.

O Lord, *I am thy servant;*
I am thy servant, the son of thy handmaid.
Thou hast loosed my bonds.

I will offer to thee the sacrifice of thanksgiving
and call on the name of the LORD.

I will pay my vows to the Lord
in the presence of all his people,
in the courts of the house of the Lord,
in your midst, O Jerusalem.
Praise the Lord!

Psalm 116

589

I lift up my eyes to the hills.
From whence does my help come?

My help comes from the Lord, *who made heaven and earth.*

He will not let your foot be moved,
he who keeps you will not slumber.

Behold, he who keeps Israel
will neither slumber nor sleep.

The Lord is your keeper;
the Lord is your shade
on your right hand.

The sun shall not smite you by day,
nor the moon by night.

The Lord will keep you from all evil;
he will keep your life.

The Lord *will keep*
your going out and your coming in
from this time forth and for evermore.

Psalm 121

590

To thee I lift up my eyes,
O thou who art enthroned in the heavens!
Behold, as the eyes of servants
look to the hand of their master,
as the eyes of a maid
to the hand of her mistress,
so our eyes look to the Lord *our God,*
till he have mercy upon us.
Have mercy upon us, O Lord, *have mercy upon us,*
for we have had more than enough of contempt.
Too long our soul has been sated
with the scorn of those who are at ease,
the contempt of the proud.

Psalm 123

591

Out of the depths I cry to thee, O Lord!
Lord, hear my voice!
Let thy ears be attentive
to the voice of my supplications!
If thou, O Lord, *shouldst mark iniquities,*
Lord, who could stand?
But there is forgiveness with thee,
that thou mayest be feared.
I wait for the Lord, *my soul waits,*
and in his word I hope;
my soul waits for the Lord
more than watchmen for the morning,
more than watchmen for the morning.
O Israel, hope in the Lord!
For with the Lord *there is steadfast love,*
and with him is plenteous redemption.
And he will redeem Israel
from all his iniquities.

Psalm 130

592

O Lord, *my heart is not lifted up,*
my eyes are not raised too high;

I do not occupy myself with things too great and too marvelous for me.
But I have calmed and quieted my soul,
like a child quieted at its mother's breast;
like a child that is quieted is my soul.
O Israel, hope in the Lord
from this time forth and for evermore.

Psalm 131

593

I give thee thanks, O LORD, with my whole heart;
before the gods I sing thy praise;

I bow down toward the holy temple
and give thanks to thy name for thy steadfast love and thy faithfulness;
for thou hast exalted above everything
thy name and thy word.

On the day I called, thou didst answer me,
my strength of soul thou didst increase.

All the kings of the earth shall praise thee, O Lord,
for they have heard the words of thy mouth;

and they shall sing of the ways of the LORD,
for great is the glory of the LORD.

For though the Lord *is high, he regards the lowly;*
but the haughty he knows from afar.

Though I walk in the midst of trouble,
thou dost preserve my life;
thou dost stretch out thy hand
against the wrath of my enemies,
and thy right hand delivers me.

The Lord *will fulfill his purpose for me;*
thy steadfast love, O Lord, *endures for ever.*
Do not forsake the work of thy hands.

Psalm 138

594

O LORD, thou hast searched me and known me!

Thou knowest when I sit down and when I rise up;
thou discernest my thoughts from afar.

Thou searchest out my path and my lying down,
and art acquainted with all my ways.

Even before a word is on my tongue,
lo, O Lord, *thou knowest it altogether.*

Thou dost beset me behind and before,
and layest thy hand upon me.

Such knowledge is too wonderful for me;
it is high, I cannot attain it.

Whither shall I go from thy Spirit?
Or whither shall I flee from thy presence?

If I ascend to heaven, thou art there!
If I make my bed in Sheol, thou art there!

If I take the wings of the morning
and dwell in the uttermost parts of the sea.
even there thy hand shall lead me,
and thy right hand shall hold me.

If I say, "Let only darkness cover me,
and the light about me be night."
even the darkness is not dark to thee,
the night is bright as the day;
for darkness is as light with thee.

How precious to me are thy thoughts, O God!
How vast is the sum of them!

If I would count them, they are more than the sand.
When I awake, I am still with thee.

Search me, O God, and know my heart!
Try me and know my thoughts!
And see if there be any wicked way in me,
and lead me in the way everlasting!

Psalm 139:1-12, 17-18, 23-24

595

Hear my prayer, O LORD;
give ear to my supplications.
In thy faithfulness answer me, in thy righteousness!

Enter not into judgment with thy servant;
for no man living is righteous before thee.

For the enemy has pursued me;
he has crushed my life to the ground;
he has made me sit in darkness like those long dead.

Therefore my spirit faints within me;
my heart within me is appalled.

I remember the days of old,
I meditate on all that thou hast done;
I muse on what thy hands have wrought.

I stretch out my hands to thee;
my soul thirsts for thee like a parched land.

Make haste to answer me, O LORD!
My spirit fails!
Hide not thy face from me,
lest I be like those who go down to the Pit.

Let me hear in the morning of thy steadfast love,
for in thee I put my trust.
Teach me the way I should go,
for to thee I lift up my soul.

Deliver me, O LORD, from my enemies!
I have fled to thee for refuge!

Teach me to do thy will,
for thou art my God!

Let thy good spirit lead me
on a level path!

For thy name's sake, O LORD, preserve my life!
In thy righteousness bring me out of trouble!

Psalm 143:1-11

596

I will extol thee, my God and King,
and bless thy name for ever and ever.

Every day I will bless thee,
and praise thy name for ever and ever.

Great is the LORD, and greatly to be praised,
and his greatness is unsearchable.

One generation shall laud thy works to another,
and shall declare thy mighty acts.

On the glorious splendor of thy majesty,
and on thy wondrous works, I will meditate.

Men shall proclaim the might of thy terrible acts,
and I will declare thy greatness.

They shall pour forth the fame of thy abundant goodness,
and shall sing aloud of thy righteousness.

The Lord *is gracious and merciful,*
slow to anger and abounding in steadfast love.

The LORD is good to all,
and his compassion is over all that he has made.

All thy works shall give thanks to thee, O Lord,
and all thy saints shall bless thee!

They shall speak of the glory of thy kingdom,
and tell of thy power,
to make known to the sons of men thy mighty deeds,
and the glorious splendor of thy kingdom.

Thy kingdom is an everlasting kingdom,
and thy dominion endures throughout all generations.

The LORD is faithful in all his words,
and gracious in all his deeds.

The Lord *upholds all who are falling,*
and raises up all who are bowed down.

The eyes of all look to thee,
and thou givest them their food in due season.

Thou openest thy hand,
thou satisfiest the desire of every living thing.

The LORD is just in all his ways,
and kind in all his doings.

The Lord *is near to all who call upon him,*
to all who call upon him in truth.

He fulfills the desire of all who fear him,

he also hears their cry, and saves them.

The Lord *preserves all who love him;*
but all the wicked he will destroy.

My mouth will speak the praise of the LORD,
and let all flesh bless his holy name for ever and ever.

Psalm 145

597

Praise the LORD!
Praise the LORD, O my soul!

I will praise the Lord *as long as I live;*
I will sing praises to my God while I have being.

Put not your trust in princes,
in a son of man, in whom there is no help.

When his breath departs he returns to his earth;
on that very day his plans perish.

Happy is he whose help is the God of Jacob,
whose hope is in the LORD his God,

who made heaven and earth,
the sea, and all that is in them;
who keeps faith for ever;

who executes justice for the oppressed;
who gives food to the hungry.

The Lord *sets the prisoners free;*
the Lord *opens the eyes of the blind.*
The Lord *lifts up those who are bowed down;*
the Lord *loves the righteous.*

The LORD watches over the sojourners,
he upholds the widow and the fatherless;
but the way of the wicked he brings to ruin.

The Lord *will reign for ever,*
thy God, O Zion, to all generations.
Praise the Lord!

Psalm 146

598

Praise the LORD!
For it is good to sing praises to our God;
for he is gracious, and a song of praise is seemly.

The Lord *builds up Jerusalem;*
he gathers the outcasts of Israel.

He heals the brokenhearted,
and binds up their wounds.

He determines the number of the stars,
he gives to all of them their names.

Great is our LORD, and abundant in power;
his understanding is beyond measure.

The Lord *lifts up the downtrodden,*
he casts the wicked to the ground.

Sing to the LORD with thanksgiving;
make melody to our God upon the lyre!

He covers the heavens with clouds,
he prepares rain for the earth,
he makes grass grow upon the hills.

He gives to the beasts their food,
and to the young ravens which cry.

His delight is not in the strength of the horse,
nor his pleasure in the legs of a man;

but the LORD takes pleasure in those who fear him,
in those who hope in his steadfast love.

Praise the Lord, *O Jerusalem!*
Praise your God, O Zion!

For he strengthens the bars of your gates;
he blesses your sons within you.

He makes peace in your borders;
he fills you with the finest of the wheat.

He sends forth his command to the earth;
his word runs swiftly.

He gives snow like wool;
he scatters hoarfrost like ashes.

He casts forth his ice like morsels;
who can stand before his cold?

He sends forth his word, and melts them;
he makes his wind blow, and the waters flow.

He declares his word to Jacob,
his statutes and ordinances to Israel.

He has not dealt thus with any other nation;
they do not know his ordinances.
Praise the Lord!

Psalm 147

599

Praise the LORD!
Praise the LORD from the heavens,
praise him in the heights!

Praise him, all his angels,
praise him, all his host!

Praise him, sun and moon,
praise him, all you shining stars!

Praise him, you highest heavens,
and you waters above the heavens!

Let them praise the name of the LORD!
For he commanded and they were created.

And he established them for ever and ever;
he fixed their bounds which cannot be passed.

Praise the LORD from the earth,
you sea monsters and all deeps,
fire and hail, snow and frost,
stormy wind fulfilling his command!

Mountains and all hills,
fruit trees and all cedars!
Beasts and all cattle,
creeping things and flying birds!

Kings of the earth and all peoples,
princes and all rulers of the earth!

Young men and maidens together,
old men and children!

Let them praise the name of the LORD,
for his name alone is exalted;
his glory is above earth and heaven.

He has raised up a horn for his people,
praise for all his saints,
for the people of Israel who are near to him.
Praise the Lord!

Psalm 148

600

Praise the LORD!
Praise God in his sanctuary;
praise him in his mighty firmament!

Praise him for his mighty deeds;
praise him according to his exceeding greatness!

Praise him with trumpet sound;
praise him with lute and harp!

Praise him with timbrel and dance;
praise him with strings and pipe!

Praise him with sounding cymbals;
praise him with loud clashing cymbals!

Let everything that breathes praise the Lord!
Praise the Lord!

Psalm 150

Prayers of Worship

601

O God, thou source of all pure desires and holy affections, give me now a quiet mind and a reverent heart, that I may worthily worship thee at this time. *Amen.*

602

Our Father, who art in heaven,
Hallowed be thy name.
Thy kingdom come,
Thy will be done,
    On earth as it is in heaven.
Give us this day our daily bread;
And forgive us our debts,
    As we also have forgiven our debtors;
And lead us not into temptation,
    But deliver us from evil.
For thine is the kingdom and the power
and the glory, forever. *Amen.*

603

Almighty God, unto whom all hearts are open, all desires known, and from whom no secrets are hid; Cleanse the thoughts of our hearts by the inspiration of thy Holy Spirit, that we may perfectly love thee, and worthily magnify thy holy Name; through Christ our Lord. *Amen.*

604

Almighty God, who pourest out upon all who desire it the spirit of grace and supplication: Deliver us, when we draw nigh unto thee, from coldness of heart and wanderings of mind; that with steadfast thoughts and kindled affections we may worship thee in spirit and in truth; through Jesus Christ our Lord. *Amen.*

605

O thou Eternal God, speak to each of us the word that we need, and let thy word abide with us until it has wrought in us thy holy will. Cleanse, quicken, and refresh our hearts; direct and increase our faith; and grant that we, by our worship at this time, may be enabled to see thee more clearly, to love thee more fully, and to serve thee more perfectly. *Amen.*

606

Almighty and everlasting God, in whom we live and move and have our being, who hast made us for thyself, so that our hearts are restless till they rest in thee: Grant us purity of heart and strength of purpose, that no selfish passion may hinder us from knowing thy will, no weakness from doing it; that in thy light we may see light clearly, and in thy service find perfect freedom. *Amen.*

607

Almighty God, who art beyond the reach of our highest thought, and yet within the heart of the lowliest; we pray thee to come to us in all the beauty of light, in all the tenderness of love, in all the liberty of truth, and make thyself known unto us. Mercifully help us in the struggle to be pure and good; encourage us in every effort to be true, loyal and loving; to do justly, to love mercy and to walk humbly with thee. Sanctify all our desires and purposes, and unto each of us let thy blessing rest. *Amen.*

608

Almighty God, whose glory the heavens are telling, the earth thy power, and sea thy might, and whose greatness all feeling and thinking creatures everywhere proclaim; to thee belongeth glory, honor, might, greatness, and magnificence, now and forever, and unto ages of ages, through Jesus Christ our Lord. *Amen.*

609

O Lord our God, grant us grace to desire thee with our whole heart; that so desiring we may seek and find thee; and so finding thee may love thee; and loving thee, may hate those sins from which thou has redeemed us. *Amen.*

610

Most holy and merciful Father, we confess in thy presence the sinfulness of our nature, and our shortcomings and offenses against thee. Thou alone knowest how often we have sinned, in wandering from thy ways, in wasting thy gifts, in forgetting thy love. Have mercy, O Lord, upon us, who are ashamed and sorry for all we have done to displease thee; and forgive our sins, through Jesus Christ thy Son, our Savior. *Amen.*

611

Almighty and most merciful Father; We have erred and strayed from thy ways like lost sheep. We have followed too much the devices and desires of our own hearts. We have offended against thy holy laws. We have left undone those things which we ought to have done; And we have done those things which we ought not to have done. . . . But thou, O Lord, have mercy upon us. . . . Spare thou those, O God, who confess their faults. Restore thou those who are penitent; According to thy promises declared unto mankind in Christ Jesus our Lord. And grant, O most merciful Father, for his sake; That we may hereafter live a godly, righteous, and sober life, To the glory of thy holy Name. *Amen.*

612

Almighty and most merciful Father, we humbly confess our manifold sins and shortcomings. We acknowledge our transgressions as a nation and people: our pride and vainglory, our self-sufficiency and forgetfulness of thee. We have been unthankful for thy great goodness to us. We have been slow to obey thy command to make disciples of all nations. We have broken the unity of thy church, and by our divisions have weakened thy cause and hindered the gospel of Christ. Blot out our transgressions, O Lord, we beseech thee. Revive thy work in the midst of the years, and cause thy power and glory to be seen in the sanctuary, as in the days of old, through Jesus Christ our Lord. Amen.

613

Heavenly Father, we confess that we have sinned against thee and our neighbor. We have walked in darkness rather than in light; we have named the name of Christ, but have not departed from iniquity. Have mercy upon us, we beseech thee; for the sake of Jesus Christ forgive us all our sins; cleanse us by thy Holy Spirit; quicken our consciences; and enable us to forgive others; that we may henceforth serve thee.in newness of life, to the glory of thy holy name. Amen.

614

O Thou who art the Light of the minds that know thee, the Life of the souls that love thee, and the strength of the wills that serve thee; help us so to know thee that we may truly love thee, so to love thee that we may fully serve thee, whom to serve is perfect freedom; through Jesus Christ our Lord. *Amen.*

615

Almighty God, who hast given us grace at this time with one accord to make our common supplications unto thee; and dost promise that when two or three are gathered together in thy name thou will grant their requests; Fulfill now, O Lord, the desires and petitions of thy servants, as may be most expedient for them; granting us in this world knowledge of thy truth, and in the world to come life everlasting. *Amen.*

616

Almighty and everlasting God, who art always more ready to hear than we to pray, and art wont to give more than either we desire or deserve; Pour down upon us the abundance of thy mercy; forgiving us those things whereof our conscience is afraid, and giving us those good things which we are not worthy to ask, but through the merits and mediation of Jesus Christ, thy Son, our Lord. *Amen.*

617

O Lord, support us all the day long, until the shadows lengthen and the evening comes, and the busy world is hushed, and the fever of life is over, and our work is done. Then in thy mercy grant us a safe lodging, and a holy rest, and peace at the last. *Amen.*

618

Almighty God, who in Jesus Christ taught us to pray, and promised that what we ask in his name will be given us, so guide us by thy Holy Spirit that our prayers for others may serve thy will and show thy steadfast love; through the same Jesus Christ our Lord. *Amen.*

619

Almighty God, Father of all mercies, we thine unworthy servants, do give thee most humble and hearty thanks for all thy goodness and loving-kindness to us, and to all men. We bless thee for our creation, preservation, and all the blessings of this life; but above all, for thine inestimable love in the redemption of the world by our Lord Jesus Christ; for the means of grace, and for the hope of glory. And, we beseech thee, give us that due sense of all thy mercies, that our hearts may be unfeignedly thankful; and that we show forth thy praise, not only with our lips, but in our lives, by giving up ourselves to thy service, and by walking before thee in holiness and righteousness all our days; through Jesus Christ our Lord, to whom, with thee and the Holy Spirit, be all honour and glory, world without end. *Amen.*

620

O Lord, who hast set before us the great hope that thy kingdom shall come on earth, and hast taught us to pray for its coming, make us ever ready to thank thee for the signs of its dawning, and to pray and work for that perfect day when thy will shall be done on earth as it is in heaven. *Amen.*

621

Almighty God, who dwellest in light unapproachable, whom no man hath seen or can see; grant that we may know thee in him whom thou hast given to be the light of the world, our Savior Jesus Christ, and in the joy of his gospel may worship thee in spirit and in truth. *Amen.*

622

O God, our Father, help us remember the birth of Jesus, that we may share in the song of the angels, the gladness of the shepherds, and the worship of the wisemen.

Close the door of hate, and open the door of love over the world. Let kindness come with every gift, and good desires with every greeting. Deliver us from evil by the blessing that Christ brings and teach us to be merry with clear hearts.

May the Christmas morning make us happy to be thy children, and the Christmas evening bring us to our beds with grateful thoughts, forgiving and forgiven, for Jesus' sake. *Amen.*

623

O God our Father, who hast brought us again to the glad season when we commemorate the birth of thy Son Jesus Christ our Lord: Grant that his Spirit may be born anew in our hearts this day and that we may joyfully welcome him to reign over us. Open our ears that we may hear again the angelic chorus of old. Open our lips that we too may sing with uplifted hearts, Glory to God in the highest, and on earth peace, good will toward men. *Amen.*

624

O Lord God, whose chosen dwelling is the heart of the lowly: We give thanks that thou didst reveal thyself in the Holy Child Jesus, thereby sanctifying all childhood in him. We beeseech thee to make us humble in faith and love, that we may know the joy of the gospel that is hidden from the wise and prudent and revealed unto babes. This we ask in his name, who, wearing our mortal flesh, grew in wisdom and in favor with God and man. *Amen.*

625

O God of grace, who at this time didst give Jesus Christ to be our Savior: We beseech thee to overcome our darkness with his light, our selfishness with his love, our indolence and cowardice with his steadfast devotion, that we may live ever as in thy presence, and perform faithfully our appointed tasks, and finally come to everlasting life; through the same Jesus Christ our Lord. *Amen.*

626

Almighty and everlasting God, who hatest nothing that thou hast made, and dost forgive the sins of all those who are penitent; Create and make in us new and contrite hearts, that we, worthily lamenting our sins . . . , may obtain of thee, the God of all mercy, perfect remission and forgiveness; though Jesus Christ our Lord. *Amen.*

627

O God, who knowest us to be set in the midst of so many and great dangers, that by reason of the frailty of our nature we cannot always stand upright; Grant to us such strength and protection, as may support us in all dangers, and carry us through all temptations; through Jesus Christ our Lord. *Amen.*

628

Almighty God, who hast shown us in the life and teaching of thy Son the true way of blessedness, thou hast also showed us in his suffering and death that the path of love may lead to the cross, and the reward of faithfulness may be a crown of thorns. Give us grace to learn these hard lessons. May we take up our cross and follow Christ, in the strength of patience and the constancy of faith; and may we have such fellowship with him in his sorrow, that we may know the secret of his strength and peace, and see, even in our darkest hour . . . the shining of the eternal light. *Amen.*

629

Almighty God, whose most dear Son went not up to joy but first he suffered pain, and entered not into glory before he was crucified; Mercifully grant that we, walking in the way of the cross, may find it none other than the way of life and peace; through the same thy Son Jesus Christ our Lord. *Amen.*

630

O Lord most holy, God most mighty, who hast found us wanting and yet hast not forsaken us, deliver us in these days of Lenten devotion from all the luxuries and comforts of a smug private righteousness, and impel us by thy love for our fellowmen to set our faces steadfastly toward that great city of the world where power and pride corrupt and waste the life of man, turning the hope of God to no account. Lift up our hearts as we recall the labor of our Lord and grant us his grace to take upon ourselves the burden of that sin which darkens our time and will not be lightened except by the cross of suffering. *Amen.*

631

O Thou Eternal God, whose dearly beloved Son was, for our sakes, content to bear sorrow and want and death, and who looked upon the great city and was touched with pity: Grant unto us such a measure of thy Spirit that we may follow him in courage and self-denial, and help us by thy great love to comfort the afflicted, to relieve the needy and destitute, to share the burdens of the heavy laden, and to see thee in all who are poor and desolate; through Jesus Christ our Lord. *Amen.*

632

Almighty God, whose mercies are everlasting, and whose grace is infinite: remember us with the favor thou bearest unto thy people. As on this day we call to mind our Lord's triumphal entry into the city that was to reject him, we beseech thee to give us such grace that we may welcome and crown him, our Lord and King forevermore; through the same Jesus Christ our Lord. *Amen.*

633

Father Everlasting, who hast set us in the fellowship of thy Son Jesus Christ, be near to us in this hour of solemn meditation. May our hearts be open to every holy affection, and ready to receive and cherish every sacred memory and serious impression. Give us to know the power of that death which this day commemorates.

Let a portion of the spirit which led our Savior to the cross descend upon us and fill our hearts with the love of thee and man. Here and now may every selfish passion and desire be quieted, and may that peace which passeth all understanding keep our hearts and minds in Christ Jesus. *Amen.*

634

O God, as we remember on this day the suffering and death of our Lord Jesus Christ, grant that we may confess our share in the sins which crucified him, that we may also be partakers in that reconciliation which is assured to those who belong to thee, through the merit and mediation of the same Jesus Christ our Lord. *Amen.*

635

Lord of heaven and of earth, we pray thee for all thy servants who have entered into the victory of eternal life, whose living was light to our darkness, and whose death, revealing their immortal stature, bound us with powerful and tender ties to heaven and to thee, our God. *Amen.*

636

Grant, we beseech thee, merciful God, that thy church, being gathered together in unity by thy Holy Spirit, may manifest thy power among all peoples, to the glory of thy name; through Jesus Christ our Lord, who liveth and reigneth with thee and the same Spirit, one God, world without end. *Amen.*

637

O God, who in the exaltation of thy Son Jesus Christ dost sanctify thy universal church; shed abroad in every race and nation the gift of his Spirit; that the work wrought by his power at the first preaching of the gospel may be extended throughout the whole world; through the same our Lord Jesus Christ. *Amen.*

638

O God, the Father Almighty, who has promised to give the Holy Spirit to them that ask thee; look graciously upon us assembled with one accord in one place to make our prayer unto thee, and to wait for thy promise; and of thy abundant mercy renew in our longing hearts thy Holy Gift; through Jesus Christ our Lord. *Amen.*

639

Send, we beseech thee, Almighty God, thy Holy Spirit into our hearts, that he may direct and rule us according to thy will, comfort us in all our afflictions, defend us from all error, and lead us into all truth; through Jesus Christ, our Lord. *Amen.*

640

Almighty God, who makest all things new, and abidest forever the same, encourage us to reach forward and to set our hope upon thy promises; so that, going on into the new year with trustful hearts, we may be able in all that we do to please thy loving eyes, through Jesus Christ our Lord. *Amen.*

641

O Thou whom we cannot love unless we love our brother, remove from us and all men both hate and prejudice, that thy children may be reconciled with those whom they fear, resent, or threaten; and thereafter live in peace; through Jesus Christ our Lord. *Amen.*

642

O God our Father, good beyond all that is good, fair beyond all that is fair, in whom is calmness, peace, and concord; reconcile we pray thee thy servants separated one from another by dissension, and lead us back into a unity of love which may bear some likeness to thy sublime nature. And as thou art above all things, grant that we may be united in generosity of spirit; that by the bonds of love and ties of affection we may become spiritually one, as well within ourselves as with each other, through that peace of thine which maketh all things peaceful in the grace, mercy, and pity of thy beloved Son. *Amen.*

643

O God, we thank thee for this universe, our great home; for its vastness and its riches, and for the manifoldness of the life which teems upon it and of which we are part. We praise thee for the arching sky and the blessed winds, for the driving clouds and the constellations on high. We praise thee for the salt sea and the running water, for the everlasting hills, for the trees, and for the grass under our feet. We thank thee for our senses by which we can see the splendor of the morning, and hear the jubilant songs of love, and smell the breath of the springtime. Grant us, we pray thee, a heart wide open to all this joy and beauty, and save our souls from being so steeped in care or so darkened by passion that we pass heedless and unseeing when even the thornbush by the wayside is aflame with the glory of God.

Enlarge within us the sense of fellowship with all the living things, our little brothers, to whom thou hast given this earth as their home in common with us. We remember with shame that in the past we have exercised the high dominion of man with ruthless cruelty, so that the voice of the earth, which should have gone up to thee in song, has been a groan of travail. May we realize that they live, not for us alone, but for themselves and for thee, and that they love the sweetness of life even as we, and serve thee in their place better than we in ours.

When our use of this world is over and we make room for others, may we not leave anything ravished by our greed or spoiled by our ignorance, but may we hand on our common heritage fairer and sweeter through our use of it, undiminished in fertility and joy, that so our bodies may return in peace to the great mother who nourished them and our spirits may round the circle of a perfect life in thee. *Amen.*

644

O God, who hast made of one blood all nations to dwell on the face of the earth, and who hast revealed thy will for men by thy Son, the Prince of Peace: Give us charity, we pray thee, to regard all men as our brethren, and to share with them the heritage we have received from thee. Deliver us from pride, prejudice, and arrogance. Put far from us all selfishness and malice, suspicion, envy, and anger, and the unrighteous passions which make men to be enemies one of another. Turn all peoples unto thee, that following thy holy example and united in thy service, they may become one brotherhood in thee, and that thy peace may possess every heart and rule in all the nations of the world; through Jesus Christ thy Son our Lord. *Amen.*

645

Endue thy church, O God, with the spirit of wisdom and power in Christ, that where others question, thy church may affirm; where others flee, thy church may advance; and where others fall, thy church may stand, through the same Jesus Christ our Lord. *Amen.*

646

Gracious Father, we humbly beseech thee for thy universal church. Fill it with all truth, and in all truth with all peace. Where it is corrupt, purge it; and where it is in error, direct it; where it is superstitious, rectify it; where anything is amiss, reform it; where it is right, strengthen and confirm it; where it is in want, furnish it; where it is divided and rent asunder, make up the breaches thereof, O thou holy One of Israel; for the sake of Jesus Christ our Lord and Savior. *Amen.*

647

O God, we pray for thy church, which is set today amid the perplexities of a changing order, and face to face with a great new task. We remember with love the nurture she gave to our spiritual life in its infancy, the tasks she set for our growing strength, the influence of the devoted hearts she gathers, the steadfast power for good she has exerted. When we compare her with all other human institutions, we rejoice, for there is none like her.

But when we judge her by the mind of her Master, we bow in pity and contrition. Oh, baptize her afresh in the life-giving spirit of Jesus! . . . Put upon her lips the ancient gospel of her Lord. . . . Fill her with the prophet's scorn of tyranny, and with a Christlike tenderness for the heavy-laden and downtrodden. . . . Bid her cease from seeking her own life, lest she lose it. Make her valiant to give up her life to humanity, that like her crucified Lord she may mount by the path of the cross to a higher glory. *Amen.*

648

Eternal God, send peace on earth, and by thy grace put down the pride, greed, and anger that turn man against man, and nation against nation. Speed the day when wars are ended and all men call thee Father; through Jesus Christ our Lord. *Amen.*

649

O Lord Jesus Christ, who hath established thy church as the bulwark of true freedom, and hath committed to all believers the ministry of reconciliation, continue thy work of reforming and cleansing within the church and within our own heart, that being renewed by thy spirit thy church may bear faithful witness to the gospel, and we live out our days in thy service. We pray in thine own strong Name. *Amen.*

Offering

650

Every man shall give as he is able, according to the blessing of the LORD your God which he has given you.

Deuteronomy 16:17

651

Honor the LORD with your substance,
and with the first fruits of all your produce.

Proverbs 3:9

652

"Do not lay up for yourselves treasures on earth, where moth and rust consume and where thieves break in and steal, but lay up for yourselves treasures in heaven, where neither moth nor rust consumes and where thieves do not break in and steal. For where your treasure is, there will your heart be also."

Matthew 6:19-21

653

"Give, and it will be given to you; good measure, pressed down, shaken together, running over, will be put into your lap. For the measure you give will be the measure you get back."

Luke 6:38

654

"In all things I have shown you that by so toiling one must help the weak, remembering the words of the Lord Jesus, how he said, 'It is more blessed to give than to receive.' "

Acts 20:35

655

Having gifts that differ according to the grace given to us, let us use them: if prophecy, in proportion to our faith; if service, in our serving; he who teaches, in his teaching; he who exhorts, in his exhortation; he who contributes, in liberality; he who gives aid, with zeal; he who does acts of mercy, with cheerfulness.

Romans 12:6-8

656

For you know the grace of our Lord Jesus Christ, that though he was rich, yet for your sake he became poor, so that by his poverty you might become rich.

2 Corinthians 8:9

657

The point is this: he who sows sparingly will also reap sparingly, and he who sows bountifully will also reap bountifully. Each one must do as he has made up his mind, not reluctantly or under compulsion, for God loves a cheerful giver. And God is able to provide you with every blessing in abundance, so that you may always have enough of everything and may provide in abundance for every good work.

2 Corinthians 9:6-8

658

You will be enriched in every way for great generosity, which through us will produce thanksgiving to God; for the rendering of this service not only supplies the wants of the saints but also overflows in many thanksgivings to God.

2 Corinthians 9:11-12

659

But if any one has the world's goods and sees his brother in need, yet closes his heart against him, how does God's love abide in him? Little children, let us not love in word or speech but in deed and in truth.

1 John 3:17-18

660

Loving Father, we remember in our offering today the needs of our fellow men in every part of the world, and the command of Christ that we share with them the good news of thy love. Bless the work of those servants of Christ who are supported by our gifts and our prayers. Enable them by thy power to kindle lights in the midst of darkness to the end that all people may know him who is the Light of the world. *Amen.*

661

Almighty God, Giver of every good and perfect gift, teach us to render unto thee all that we have and all that we are, that we may praise thee not with our lips only but with our whole lives, turning the duties, the sorrows, and the joys of each successive day into a living sacrifice to thee. *Amen.*

662

O God, the God of all goodness and grace, who art worthy of a greater love than we can either give or understand; Fill our hearts, we beseech thee, with such love toward thee that nothing may seem too hard for us to do or to suffer in obedience to thee; and grant that by thus loving, we may become daily more like unto thee and finally obtain the crown of life which thou hast promised to those who unfeignedly love thee; through Jesus Christ our Lord. *Amen.*

The Lord's Supper

SCRIPTURES

663

Now as they were eating, Jesus took bread, and blessed, and broke it, and gave it to the disciples and said, "Take, eat; this is my body." And he took a cup, and when he had given thanks he gave it to them, saying, "Drink of it, all of you; for this is my blood of the covenant, which is poured out for many for the forgiveness of sins. I tell you I shall not drink again of this fruit of the vine until that day when I drink it new with you in my Father's kingdom."

Matthew 26:26-29

664

"Do not labor for the food which perishes, but for the food which endures to eternal life, which the Son of man will give to you; for on him has God the Father set his seal." "For the bread of God is that which comes down from heaven, and gives life to the world."

John 6:27, 33

665

Jesus said to them, "I am the bread of life; he who comes to me shall not hunger, and he who believes in me shall never thirst. For this is the will of my Father, that every one who sees the Son and believes in him should have eternal life; and I will raise him up at the last day."

John 6:35, 40

666

"Truly, truly, I say to you, he who believes has eternal life. I am the bread of life. I am the living bread which came down from heaven; if any one eats of this bread, he will live for ever; and the bread which I shall give for the life of the world is my flesh."

John 6:47-48, 51

667

"A new commandment I give to you, that you love one another; even as I have loved you, that you also love one another. By this all men will know that you are my disciples, if you have love for one another."

John 13:34-35

668

The cup of blessing which we bless, is it not a participation in the blood of Christ? The bread which we break, is it not a participation in the body of Christ? Because there is one bread, we who are many are one body, for we all partake of the one bread.

1 Corinthians 10:16-17

669

For I received from the Lord what I also delivered to you, that the Lord Jesus on the night when he was betrayed took bread, and when he had given thanks, he broke it, and said, "This is my body which is for you. Do this in remembrance of me." In the same way also the cup, after supper, saying, "This cup is the new covenant in my blood. Do this, as often as you drink it, in remembrance of me." For as often as you eat this bread and drink the cup, you proclaim the Lord's death until he comes.

1 Corinthians 11:23-26

670

Whoever, therefore, eats the bread or drinks the cup of the Lord in an unworthy manner will be guilty of profaning the body and blood of the Lord. Let a man examine himself, and so eat of the bread and drink of the cup. For any one who eats and drinks without discerning the body eats and drinks judgment upon himself.

1 Corinthians 11:27-29

INVITATION

671

Ye who do truly and earnestly repent you of your sins, and are in love and charity with your neighbors, and intend to lead a new life, following the commandments of God, and walking from henceforth in his holy ways; Draw near with faith, and take this holy Sacrament to your comfort; and make your humble confession to Almighty God.

672

Come to this sacred table, not because you must but because you may; come to testify, not that you are righteous, but that you sincerely love our Lord Jesus Christ, and desire to be his true disciples: come, not because you are strong, but because you are weak; not because you have any claim on heaven's rewards, but because in your frailty and sin you stand in constant need of heaven's mercy and help: come, not to express an opinion, but to seek a Presence and to pray for a Spirit.

And now that the Supper of the Lord is spread before you, lift up your minds and hearts above all selfish fears and cares; let this bread and this wine be to you the witnesses and signs of the grace of our Lord Jesus Christ, the love of God, and the communion of the Holy Spirit. Before the throne of the heavenly Father and the cross of the Redeemer consecrate your lives to the Christian obedience and service, and pray for strength to do and to bear the holy and blessed will of God.

PRAYERS

673

O heavenly Father, who dost govern the thoughts of men: bring to our minds the upper room where the Lord Jesus broke the bread with his disciples in the night before he was crucified; grant to us that, being of that company, we may look into the face of him who gave himself for the world. While we eat of his bread and drink of his cup, fill our lives with his life and send us forth to think his thoughts, to say his words, to do his deeds; and so, O Father, grant that, though we may know it not, the light of his face may shine in our faces, and all men may take note that we have been with Jesus, who liveth and reigneth with thee and the Holy Spirit, the God of everlasting love, world without end. *Amen.*

674

O Master of life, who didst gather thy disciples round thee in the upper room to give them there the sacrament of thy body and thy blood; take us also, unworthy as we are, into the fellowship of those who would follow thee. We acknowledge our shortcomings and our sins, our inconstant minds and hearts, and our slackness in devotion. But thou dost not forsake us even when we fail thee. Accept us not for what we are, but for what thou canst create in us, O Savior who by thy sacrifice hast sealed us for thine own. *Amen.*

675

O Thou who art the God and Father of all who dwell upon the face of the earth, make us one family this day at the table of our Lord, that remembering the gift of his life laid down, we may take up our pilgrimage again renewed by the bread of life, and made glad by our common salvation, through Jesus Christ our Lord. *Amen.*

676

Holy Father, thy glory makes the earth a temple and all life a sacrament; in the house of thy presence we lift up our hearts in adoration. O thou whose love is our life, reveal thyself to us as we gather at the table of the Lord, to break the loaf broken for us by a broken hand. Lead us beyond the symbol into the mystery of his grace and truth: may it be a festival of his living presence, as when he broke the bread in the gloaming of the day.

God of the living, we praise thee for the company of those gone before, who by their love and loyalty have left us a legacy of faith and hope. We give thee thanks for the fellowship of those who gather here, our comrades and fellow workers, with whom we share thy mercy and adore thy name. Make us members one of another, unite us in one heart with all who seek thee, in one communion with all who love thee, in one steadfast purpose with all who serve thy holy will in faithfulness and joy.

Bless the lonely of soul with thy nearness, and the wounded of heart with thy healing. Give to the hungry of spirit thyself, his bread, even the hidden manna whereof if he eat he shall hunger no more. O thou who hearest what our words cannot tell, lift our spirits to a loftier melody, that our song on earth may blend with the song of the redeemed. *Amen.*

677

We do not presume to come to this thy table, O merciful Lord, trusting in our own righteousness, but in thy manifold and great mercies. We are not worthy so much as to gather up the crumbs under thy table. But thou art the same Lord, whose property is always to have mercy: Grant us therefore, gracious Lord, so to eat the flesh of thy dear Son Jesus Christ, and to drink his blood, that our sinful bodies may be made clean by his body, and our souls washed through his most precious blood, and that we may evermore dwell in him, and he in us. *Amen.*

678

Most merciful heavenly Father, in whose likeness we have been created, and by whose grace we have been redeemed, with grateful hearts we approach this thy table to commemorate the sufferings of our dear Lord. . . . We thank thee for the great love which caused thee to give us thy only-begotten Son to redeem us from sin through his own death for us. And we thank thee for the great privilege of being numbered among his disciples and counted worthy of a place at thy table. Assist us, we pray thee, our heavenly Father, to partake of this bread and wine worthily, discerning the Lord's body and blood; and as we partake of these material emblems, grant that we also may be partakers of Christ's spirit and life, so that, as he gave himself for us, we also may give ourselves freely to thy service and to one another in acts of brotherly love. Give us, we beseech thee, a realizing sense of thy spiritual presence that we may each be strengthened thereby; and thus go forward in life's duties, stronger and purer for thy service. And grant us at last the unspeakable joy of sitting down together, with the innumerable company of the redeemed, at the Marriage Supper of the Lamb in thy everlasting kingdom; through Jesus Christ our Lord. *Amen.*

679

Lift up your hearts.

We lift them up to the Lord.

Let us glorify God.

For all his goodness to us.

All glory is yours, Eternal God, who made the universe. We praise you for this earth, for life and breath, for beauty we have seen and wonders still to come. From the beginning, your living Word has guided and corrected us. Your prophets have called us from disobedience, and prepared us for the coming of your Son.

We praise you for the Christ, who chose to come as one of us, and lived among us full of grace and truth. For us he became poor, and knew the sadness in our days; and for us he died on the cross and was buried. In him we know forgiveness and the lifting of burdens. He brings light to our darkness and opens our eyes to your great glory.

For you raised him from the dead and set him over all creation. Through your Holy Spirit we are members of his body, the church, and heirs of the promise of eternal life. Therefore with grateful hearts we join the faithful who, in all times and places, praise your name, saying

Holy, holy, holy,
God of power and majesty,
Heaven and earth are full of your glory,
O God Most High!

Holy Father, we thank you that the Lord Jesus, on the night when he was arrested, took bread, and when he had given thanks, he broke it, and said, "This is my body which is for you. Do this in remembering me." In the same way, he took the cup, after supper, saying, "This cup is the new covenant in my blood. Do this, as often as you drink it, in remembering me."

We remember you, Lord Jesus, as you commanded, confident we shall know you in the breaking of bread. We remember you, O Christ, confident you will seal the new covenant in our hearts as we drink this cup.

O Holy Spirit, who brought us here to proclaim the risen Lord, unite us in one body with him who loved us and gave himself for us.

O God, who called us from death to life: we give ourselves to you; and with the church through all ages, we thank you for your saving love in Jesus Christ our Lord. Amen.

Our Father in heaven, may your name be honored. May your kingdom come and your will be done on earth as it is in heaven. Give us today the food we need; and forgive us our sins as we forgive those who have wronged us. Keep us clear of temptation, and save us from evil. For the kingdom and power and glory are yours forever. Amen.

680

Lift up your hearts.

We lift them to the Lord.

Let us give thanks to the Lord God.

It is good that we do.

We give you thanks, Lord God, Creator and Father, for bringing the worlds into being, for forming man in your likeness, for recalling us when we rebel against you, and for keeping the world in your steadfast love. We praise you especially for Jesus Christ; who was born of Mary and lived as one of us; who knew exactly the life we know, and yet was obedient to your purposes, even to his death on a cross. We thank you that you stamped his death with victory by raising him in power and by making him head over all things. We rejoice in the continuing presence of the Holy Spirit; in the church you have gathered; in its task of obedience; and in the promise of eternal life. With the faithful in every place and time, we praise with joy your holy name.

Holy, holy, holy,
God of love and majesty;
The whole universe speaks of your glory,
O God, Most High.

Therefore bless now, by your Word and Spirit, both us and these gifts of bread and wine, that in receiving them at this table, and in offering here our faith and praise, we may be united with Christ and one another, and remain faithful to the tasks he sets before us.

In the strength Christ gives we offer ourselves to you, giving thanks that you have called us to serve you. Amen.

681

Almighty God, we praise thee as the giver of all things that are good and true—life and health, material comforts, and the beauties of nature, and this fellowship together with those we love. More than all we thank thee for the gift of thy Son who offered up his life for the remission of our sins. Father, we know that we are not worthy to sit at the table where his first disciples sat, just as they were not worthy. Yet we approach this table with confidence, knowing that if we come with sincere repentance, thy pardoning grace will be given freely. So we ask thee to cleanse our hearts of all that is impure, or petty, or selfish. As we receive these emblems of the love of our Lord, make us receptive to the incoming of his spirit. Inspire us by thy presence to go from here to live lives of greater service so that others will see in us the image of the Master and be led to give their lives to him. In his name we pray. *Amen.*

682

The Lord be with you.

And with you also.

Lift up your hearts.

We lift them to the Lord.

Let us give thanks to the Lord our God.

It is right indeed that we should do so.

It is most right and proper, holy Lord, almighty Father, everlasting God, that we should at all times, and in all places, give thanks to you through Jesus Christ, your only Son, our Lord; through whom you have created all things from the beginning and made man in your own image; through whom in the fullness of time you redeemed us, when we had fallen into sin, giving him to be born as man; to die on the cross and to rise again for us; setting him in glory at your right hand; through whom you have made us a holy people by sending forth your holy and lifegiving Spirit; through him therefore with the faithful who rest in him and all the glorious company of heaven, joyfully we praise you and say:

Holy, Holy, Holy, Lord God of Hosts, heaven and earth are full of your glory. Glory to you, Lord most high. Blessed is he who comes in the name of the Lord, Hosanna in the highest.

All glory to you, heavenly Father, who in your tender mercy gave your only Son Jesus Christ that all who believe in him might have eternal life. Hear us, merciful Father, and grant that receiving this bread and this wine in remembrance of the death and passion of your Son and Savior Jesus Christ, we may be partakers of his most blessed body and blood; who the night before he gave himself to death, took bread, and when he had given thanks he broke it and gave it to his disciples and said, Take, eat, this is my body which is given for you: do this in remembrance of me. In the same way after supper he took the cup, and when he had given thanks he gave it to them, and said, Drink this, all of you, for this is my blood of the new covenant which is shed for you and for many, for the forgiveness of sins; do this, as often as you drink it, in remembrance of me.

His death, Father, we show forth, his resurrection we proclaim, his coming we await. Glory to you, Lord most high.

Therefore, Father, we do this as your Son commanded, offering to you our praise and thanksgiving for his one perfect sacrifice made on the cross for the sin of the world, for his mighty resurrection and glorious ascension, which we recall before you in this sacrament of the bread of life and the cup of salvation. Accept us, in him, we pray, with this our sacrifice of praise and thanksgiving, and grant that all we who are partakers of this holy communion may be filled with the Holy Spirit and made one in your holy church, the body of your Son, Jesus Christ our Lord, through whom and in whom, in the unity of the Holy Spirit, all honor and glory be to you, almighty Father, for ever and ever. *Amen.*

683

(FOR THE BREAD) All glory and praise be unto thee, O God, our Father, who of thy tender mercy, gave thine only Son, Jesus Christ our Lord, to suffer death upon the cross for us all. Mercifully grant that thy Holy Spirit and Word may sanctify us and this bread, which thou hast given to be the symbol of the body of our Lord, that it may be for us spiritual food, that by faith we may feed in our hearts on him who is our only Savior and Lord. For his name's sake. *Amen.*

(FOR THE CUP) We give thanks, O God, for this cup, symbol of the most precious blood of our Lord. We commemorate his Last Supper with his disciples, his death upon the cross, His glorious resurrection and exaltation, and his coming again to receive us to share in his heavenly banquet. We pray thee to grant that thy Holy Spirit and Word may so sanctify us and this cup that we may feed in our hearts by faith upon the blood of our Lord, and that this cup may be for us the cup of fellowship and salvation. Let thy grace be upon us now and bless us beyond our asking. Through Jesus Christ our Lord. *Amen.*

Baptism

684

And when Jesus was baptized, he went up immediately from the water, and behold, the heavens were opened and he saw the Spirit of God descending like a dove, and alighting on him; and lo, a voice from heaven, saying, "This is my beloved Son, with whom I am well pleased."

Matthew 3:16-17

685

And Jesus came and said to them, "All authority in heaven and on earth has been given to me. Go therefore and make disciples of all nations, baptizing them in the name of the Father and of the Son and of the Holy Spirit, teaching them to observe all that I have commanded you; and lo, I am with you always, to the close of the age."

Matthew 28:18-20

686

And Peter said to them, "Repent, and be baptized every one of you in the name of Jesus Christ for the forgiveness of your sins; and you shall receive the gift of the Holy Spirit."

Acts 2:38

687

Do you not know that all of us who have been baptized into Christ Jesus were baptized into his death? We were buried therefore with him by baptism into death, so that as Christ was raised from the dead by the glory of the Father, we too might walk in newness of life.

Romans 6:3-4

688

For just as the body is one and has many members, and all the members of the body, though many, are one body, so it is with Christ. For by one Spirit we were all baptized into one body—Jews or Greeks, slaves or free—and all were made to drink of one Spirit.

1 Corinthians 12:12-13

689

In Christ Jesus you are all sons of God, through faith. For as many of you as were baptized into Christ have put on Christ. There is neither Jew nor Greek, there is neither slave nor free, there is neither male nor female; for you are all one in Christ Jesus.

Galatians 3:26-28

690

There is one body and one Spirit, just as you were called to the one hope that belongs to your call, one Lord, one faith, one baptism, one God and Father of us all, who is above all and through all and in all.

Ephesians 4:4-6

691

For Christ also died for sins once for all, the righteous for the unrighteous, that he might bring us to God, being put to death in the flesh but made alive in the spirit. Baptism, which corresponds to this, now saves you, not as a removal of dirt from the body but as an appeal to God for a clear conscience, through the resurrection of Jesus Christ.

1 Peter 3:18, 21

Benedictions

692

The LORD bless you and keep you:
The LORD make his face to shine upon you, and be gracious to you:
The LORD lift up his countenance upon you, and give you peace.

Numbers 6:24-26

693

May God be gracious to us and bless us
  and make his face to shine upon us,
that thy way may be known upon earth,
  thy saving power among all nations.

Psalm 67:1-2

694

"Lord, now lettest thou thy servant depart in peace,
according to thy word;
for mine eyes have seen thy salvation
which thou hast prepared in the presence of all peoples,
a light for revelation to the Gentiles,
and for glory to thy people Israel."

Luke 2:29-32

695

Grace to you and peace from God our Father and the Lord Jesus Christ.
Romans 1:7b

696

May the God of steadfastness and encouragement grant you to live in such harmony with one another, in accord with Christ Jesus, that together you may with one voice glorify the God and Father of our Lord Jesus Christ.
Romans 15:5-6

697

May the God of hope fill you with all joy and peace in believing, so that by the power of the Holy Spirit you may abound in hope.
Romans 15:13

698

The grace of the Lord Jesus Christ, and the love of God and the fellowship of the Holy Spirit be with you all.
2 Corinthians 13:14

699

Now may the Lord of peace himself give you peace at all times in all ways. The Lord be with you all.
2 Thessalonians 3:16

700

May grace and peace be multiplied to you in the knowledge of God and of Jesus our Lord.
2 Peter 1:2

Acknowledgments

Acknowledgments

Grateful appreciation is extended to those publishers and individuals who have so kindly permitted us to use their copyrighted materials. Every effort has been made to trace ownership of the materials used and to make proper acknowledgment. If omissions are discovered, they will be included in future editions.

Scripture quotations are from The Revised Standard Version of the Bible, copyrighted 1946 and 1952 by the Division of Christian Education, National Council of Churches, and are used by permission.

456 From *The New Church Hymnal* edited by H. Augustine Smith, © 1937 by Fleming H. Revell Company.

457 From *The New Church Hymnal* edited by H. Augustine Smith, © 1937 by Fleming H. Revell Company.

481 By Thomas B. McDormand.

482 By James G. Clague.

483 From *The Lutheran Service Book and Hymnal,* by permission of the Commission on the Liturgy and Hymnal. Used by permission.

484 From *A Book of Worship for Free Churches.* Used by permission.

485 "A Litany of the Cross" from *A Book of Public Prayers* by Harry Emerson Fosdick. Copyright © 1959 by Harry Emerson Fosdick.

486 "A Litany of the Nation" from *A Book of Public Prayers* by Harry Emerson Fosdick. Copyright © 1959 by Harry Emerson Fosdick.

487 Arranged by Kenneth L. Potee and used by permission.

488 Source unknown.

489 This litany is recited on the ruins of Coventry Cathedral every Friday at noon. It is reprinted with the permission of the Provost of Coventry Cathedral.

490 From the Preamble to "A Provisional Design for the Christian Church (Disciples of Christ)."

491 The Apostles' Creed.

492 The Nicene Creed.

493 Adapted by Dr. Major and reprinted by permission of his son, H. M. A. Major, and the executors of the Estate of Dr. Major.

494 This statement of faith is used in the United Church of Christ.

603 From *The Book of Common Prayer.*

604 Adapted from *Christian Worship and Praise,* edited by Henry Hallam Tweedy (Harper & Row, 1939). Reprinted by permission of Harper & Row, Publishers.

605 From the book *Devotional Services* by John Hunter, D.D. Published by E. P. Dutton & Co., Inc. and reprinted with the permission of E. P. Dutton & Co., Inc. and of J. M. Dent & Sons Ltd.

606 From *The Book of Common Worship,* Revised, 1932, the Board of Christian Education, Presbyterian Church, U.S.A. Copyright renewed, 1960. Used by permission.

607 From the *Service Book and Ordinal of the Presbyterian Church of South Africa.*

608 Adapted from *A Book of Public Worship* by permission of Oxford University Press.

609 By Saint Anselm, 1033-1109.

611 Adapted from *The Book of Common Prayer.*

612 From *Prayers for the Christian Year* by permission of the Committee on Public Worship and Aids to Devotion of the Church of Scotland.

613 From *The Book of Common Worship of the Church of South India* by permission of the Synod of the Church of South India.

614 From the Gelasian Sacramentary, 5th century.

615 From *The Book of Common Prayer.*

616 From *The Book of Common Prayer.*

618 From *The Book of Common Worship,* Provisional Services. The Westminster Press. Copyright © 1966, W. L. Jenkins. Used by permission.

619 From *The Book of Common Prayer.*

620 From *The Kingdom, the Power, and the Glory,* American Edition. Copyright 1933. Used by permission of Oxford University Press.

621 By Hugh Cameron from *Service Book for Ministers* by Joseph E. McCabe. Copyright © 1961 by Joseph E. McCabe. Used by permission of McGraw-Hill Book Company.

623 From *The Book of Worship,* Abingdon Press.

625 From *A Book of Pastoral Prayer* by Ernest Fremont Tittle. Copyright 1951 by Pierce and Smith (Abingdon Press).

626 Adapted from *The Book of Common Prayer.*

627 From *The Book of Common Prayer.*

628 From *The Kingdom, the Power, and the Glory,* American Edition. Copyright 1933. Used by permission of Oxford University Press.

629 From *The Book of Common Prayer.*

630 From *Prayers for Daily Use* by Samuel H. Miller. Copyright © 1957 by Samuel H. Miller.

631 From *The Kingdom, the Power, and the Glory,* American Edition. Copyright 1933. Used by permission of Oxford University Press.

632 From *Prayers for the Christian Year* by permission of the

Committee on Public Worship and Aids to Devotion of the Church of Scotland.

633 From the book *Devotional Services* by John Hunter, D.D. Published by E. P. Dutton & Co., Inc. and reprinted by permission of E. P. Dutton & Co., Inc. and of J. M. Dent & Sons Ltd.

634 From *Service Book for Ministers* by Joseph E. McCabe. Copyright © 1961 by Joseph E. McCabe. Used by permission of McGraw-Hill Book Company.

635 From *Prayers for Daily Use* by Samuel H. Miller. Copyright © 1951 by Samuel H. Miller.

636 From *The Book of Common Prayer.*

637 From *The Kingdom, the Power, and the Glory,* American Edition. Copyright 1933. Used by permission of Oxford University Press.

638 From *Service Book for Ministers* by Joseph E. McCabe. Copyright © 1961 by Joseph E. McCabe. Used by permission of McGraw-Hill Book Company.

639 From *The Book of Common Prayer.*

640 From the Mozarabic Sacramentary.

641 From *The Book of Common Worship,* Provisional Services. The Westminster Press. Copyright © 1966, W. L. Jenkins. Used by permission.

642 Jacobite Liturgy of Saint Dionysius.

643 From *Prayers of the Social Awakening* by Walter Rauschenbusch. The Pilgrim Press.

644 From *The Book of Common Worship,* Revised, 1932, the Board of Christian Education, Presbyterian Church, USA. Copyright renewed, 1960. Used by permission.

645 From *Prayers of the Christian Life* by John Underwood Stephens. Copyright © 1952 and reprinted by permission of Oxford University Press.

646 From *A Chain of Prayers Across the Ages* by Selina Fox. Copyright 1913. John Murray (Publishers) Ltd. Used by permission.

647 From *Prayers of the Social Awakening* by Walter Rauschenbusch. The Pilgrim Press.

648 From *The Book of Common Worship,* Provisional Services. The Westminster Press. Copyright © 1966, W. L. Jenkins. Used by permission.

649 From *Service Book for Ministers* by Joseph E. McCabe. Copyright © 1961 by Joseph E. McCabe. Used by permission of McGraw-Hill Book Company.

660 By Lloyd V. Channels.

661 From *Services of Religion.* Used by permission of Beacon Press.

672 From the book *Devotional Services* by John Hunter, D.D. Published by E. P. Dutton & Co., Inc. and reprinted with the permission of E. P. Dutton & Co., Inc. and of J. M. Dent & Sons Ltd.

673 By Charles Lewis Slattery from *The Table of the Lord* edited by Charles L. Wallis. Reprinted by permission of Harper & Row, Publishers.

674 From *Lift Up Your Hearts* by Walter Russell Bowie. Copyright 1956 by Pierce and Washabaugh (Abingdon Press).

675 From *Service Book for Ministers* by Joseph E. McCabe. Copyright © 1961 by Joseph E. McCabe. Used by permission of McGraw-Hill Book Company.

676 From *Altar Stairs* by Joseph Fort Newton. Copyright 1928. Used by permission of The Macmillan Company.

677 From *The Book of Common Prayer.*

678 Adapted from *Alone with God* by J. H. Garrison. Copyright 1918 by The Christian Board of Publication. Used by permission.

679 From *The Book of Common Worship,* Provisional Services. The Westminster Press. Copyright © 1966, W. L. Jenkins. Used by permission.

680 From *Services of Word and Sacrament.* United Church Press. Used by permission.

681 By Winworth Williams from *Elder at the Lord's Table,* edited by Thomas W. Toler. Copyright 1954 by The Bethany Press. Used by permission.

682 From "The Liturgy on Eucharist" by permission of The New Zealand Provincial Commission for Prayer Book Review.

683 Adapted from *The Administration of the Lord's Supper* by William Robinson. Used by permission of the Publishing Committee of Churches of Christ and Mrs. William Robinson.

Indexes

Index of Authors, Composers, and Sources

Index of Topics

Index of Meters

Index of Tunes

Index of Children's Hymns

Index of First Lines

Index of Authors, Composers, and Sources

Index of Topics

CONFLICT AND CHALLENGE

CONSECRATION

CONSTANCY

COURAGE

CREATION

CROSS

DEDICATION

DISCIPLESHIP

DOXOLOGIES

LENT

LIGHT

LOVE

LOYALTY

MARRIAGE

MINISTRY AND MISSION

MUSIC

NATIVITY

NATURE

NEW YEAR AND CHANGING SEASONS

OBEDIENCE

See CONFESSION AND COMMITMENT; GOSPEL CALL AND RESPONSE

PALM SUNDAY

See JESUS CHRIST: TRIUMPHAL ENTRY

PATRIOTISM

See THE NATION

PEACE

PENITENCE

See GOD: HIS FORGIVENESS; FORGIVENESS

PENTECOST

PRAISE

See ADORATION AND PRAISE

PRAYER

PROCESSIONAL HYMNS

Index of Meters

Short Meter
S.M. 6.6.8.6.

Short Meter
with Refrain

Short Meter Double
S.M.D. 6.6.8.6.D.

Common Meter
C.M. 8.6.8.6.

Common Meter Double
C.M.D. 8.6.8.6.D.

Long Meter
L.M. 8.8.8.8.

Index of Tunes

Index of Children's Hymns

GOD AND CREATION

JESUS CHRIST

Birth

Life and Ministry

Triumphal entry

Resurrection

Passion

Praise to Christ

Index of First Lines